VIEWS
~ Solo around the World ~

Fabienne Wolf

Fabienne Wolf grew up in landlocked Switzerland, which put paid to her childhood dreams of going to sea. She studied visual design instead and worked as a graphic designer in the Swiss advertising industry. Then she retrained as a Waldorf educator and relocated to England, where she taught art, language and a range of other subjects. Ten years later, a spontaneous decision to take time out, travel and see the world put her in touch with her love of writing, and she realized her dream of crossing the great oceans at last.

Copyright © 2012 Fabienne Wolf

The right of Fabienne Wolf to be identified as the Author of the Work, including cover design, illustrations and photographs, has been asserted by her in accordance with the Copyright, Designs and Patents Act 1988.

All rights reserved. No part of this publication may be reproduced, stored in a retrieval system, or transmitted in any form or by any means without prior written permission of the author (fabwolf@hotmail.com), excepting the fair use of quotations, provided that book title and author are cited.
This book may not be circulated in any form of binding or cover other than that in which it is published, and without a similar condition being imposed on the subsequent purchaser.
All names of persons aboard have been changed.

First edition published October 2013
Second, revised edition October 2016
Third, revised edition August 2020

ISBN-13 978-1493729555
ISBN-10 1493729551

Also by Fabienne Wolf:
REPORTS FROM THE ROAD ~ Solo around Britain

VIEWS FROM A CRUISE
~ Solo around the World ~

~ SOLO TRAVEL REPORTS, Book 2 ~

CONTENTS ~ *First Leg*

Introduction	11
Embarkation	19
Beaufort 10	26
At Sea	28
Life on Board	35
Madeira	39
Norovirus	46
Sea Days	49
Leisure	51
Sea Sunrise	52
Being Noticed	54
St Lucia	59
Things to Do	64
Curacao	66
Sleepless	72
Panama Canal	76
The Pacific	81
Hot Bamboo	83
No Acapulco	85
Ocean Thoughts	89
Chinese New Year	92
Sea Legs	93
San Francisco	95
Monterey & Carmel	100

CONTENTS ~ *Second Leg*

Rough Seas	107
New Captain	108
Cold Misery	109
Tropic of Cancer	110
Honolulu	112
Hilo	116
Cruise Fitness	121
Past & Present	123
Equator	124
The Dress	127
Apia	129
Pago Pago	134
Date Line	140
Port Denarau	142
Cyclone Detour	146
Well of Sadness	147
Auckland	149
Bay of Islands	152
Tasman Sea	156
Keeping Busy	157
Sydney	159

CONTENTS ~ *Third Leg*

Limitless Spaces	169
Brisbane	171
Great Barrier Reef	173
Bad News	174
Low Point	176
Passenger Arrested	179
Darwin	181
Problems to Solve	190
A Little Kindness	192
Bali	195
Changing Tables	201
Waste Management	202
Finding a Friend	206
Vietnam	207
Mekong River	210
A Favourite Place	215
Cambodia	216
Thailand	221
Ko Samui	224
Exchange of Views	229
Singapore	231

CONTENTS ~ *Fourth Leg*

Malaysia	241
Penang	245
Age & Health	249
Captain's Life	253
Sri Lanka	255
Pirate Watch	260
Mumbai	265
Piracy Facts	271
Oman	275
Gulf of Dismay	281
Abu Dhabi	283
Dubai	290
More of Dubai	294

CONTENTS ~ *Last Leg*

Litter Indicator Scale	303
No Man in My Life	304
Proving Wilde Wrong	308
Red Sea	310
Process of Revolution	313
Egypt	314
Meeting the Pyramids	318
Cyprus	328
Israel	333
Flooded Cabin Floor	337
Turkey	338
Istanbul	340
Trouble in Istanbul	350
Athens	353
Talking About Tuna	356
Nice Surprises	357
Before & After	360
Lisbon	362
Seasick Again	365
The End of the Journey	369
Southampton	373
Conclusions	377
Before we say Goodbye	381

INTRODUCTION

Have you ever thought of taking a road trip or a cruise? Dreamed of unfettered freedom, of being at liberty to roam and explore as fancy dictates; imagined turning your back on all that you have known, leaving for the sake of leaving to ride solo into the sunset?

This idea took hold of me quite unexpectedly in the year after my son left home and I found myself with what has been termed so cutely an 'empty nest'.

Why wait until retirement and old age to see the world, I asked myself. Why not right now? Why not have a midlife adventure rather than a midlife crisis?

At this point, a colleague died tragically on her way home and her message seemed to be: Don't assume that you have all the time in the world. If something means a lot to you, do it *now!* ... And then I watched Jack Nicholson and Morgan Freeman do just that in the marvellously inspiring film *The Bucket List*.

Another impulse came from teaching World Geography, a subject I had always loved. But as my pupils learnt about oceans and continents and became familiar with the names and locations of far-off places, I experienced pangs of regret that there was so much of the world I had not yet seen.

I was talking about the Pacific Ocean and Hawaii, for example, but my knowledge was gleaned from books and documentaries, not from experience. Dissatisfied, I decided to change that. Go and see what Hawaii is like, I told myself, traverse the Pacific Ocean – and while you're at it, take in as much of the globe as you possibly can!

The academic year was drawing to a close when I saw a full-page ad in the Sunday newspaper and, on impulse, used my savings to book this tempting P&O cruise around the world. I handed in my notice, quit the flat that came with the job, said goodbye to my pupils and the school, put my things in storage and a couple of bags in my car, shook off the role of teacher and the tight corset of the timetable and took to the open road.

Setting out solo on an improvised road trip, I explored parts of Great Britain for two months to bridge the time gap until the beginning of January, when my ocean liner would leave the port of Southampton for a slow circumnavigation of the planet.

In this way I cut loose from the moorings, burnt the bridges and embraced an uncertain future, trusting that everything would turn out right. Would I come to regret an adventure that others saw as sheer foolhardiness? I hoped not.

Having arrived in my late forties, I felt it was time to make space for chance encounters with unknown places and people. Tired of the routine that had been my life for years, I wanted to leave my comfort zone, shake things up and reconnect with my early dream of being a solitary wanderer. This timeout also seemed a well-earned sabbatical after over a decade of tireless teaching, and a reward for two decades of dedicated single parenting.

As I prepared for my journeys, it struck me how intrigued people were with my travel plans; how these touched their imagination, their own dreams and fantasies. The postman, for example, urged me to check out his favourite place in

Scotland when I told him of my imminent departure. And when I informed my bank of an intended change of habits (to ensure that card payments made far from home would not be blocked), the helpful lady at the counter grew wide-eyed and wistful while writing down the list of countries I would visit. Summer sales assistants exclaimed with longing as I equipped myself with necessary gear for both road trip and cruise, and the phone service provider found it all but impossible to understand that I did *not* request to cancel my contract because I was planning to defect to the competition, but simply because it would not be needed in the foreseeable future. (Special offers to tempt me back into the fold arrived weekly thereafter.)

Soon after setting out I began to write some travel updates and emailed them to friends, ex-pupils and acquaintances whenever access to the internet was available. The growing enjoyment of recording my daily experiences in writing was unforeseen, but it soon became an undeniable need to trace the course of my journey in words.

In *Riding the Iron Rooster,* Paul Theroux observes that "travel writing is a minor form of autobiography."

Indeed it is; for, as we study the world around us with heightened awareness, we also perceive ourselves more clearly. Travel writing enables readers to see foreign places and people through the eyes of another, and to follow the author's thoughts – which may or may not echo their own.

"It's always wonderful to find out that there is a view of the world: a pattern to experience, not just experience – and whether you agree with the view offered, or like the pattern, is neither here nor there. Views are possible, patterns discernible – it is exciting and exhilarating and enriching to know it," states Fay Weldon in *Letters to Alice*.

The following pages describe glimpses of our incredibly diverse and magnificent world as they impressed their beauty, their joy, and occasionally their sorrow upon me. Looking back on these solo journeys by car and by ship, I can truly say that I have no regrets. Because, as you will see for yourself, I had a wonderful time.

And you can, too … Don't be afraid to go solo!

~ A World Cruise Begins ~

~ The First Leg ~

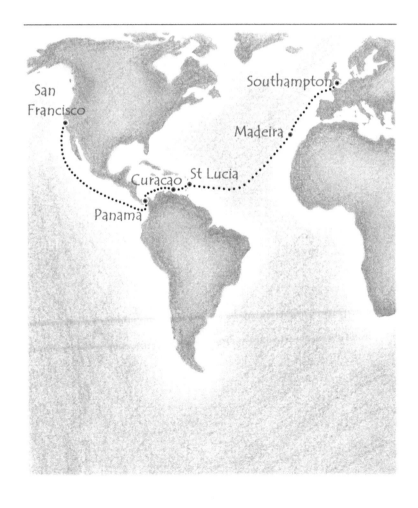

Day 1 ~ Wednesday, 4*th* January 2012 ~ *wind: westerly force 5, fresh breeze ~ weather: overcast ~ temperature: 9°C*

Embarkation

I arrive in Southampton at noon on this grey and chilly winter's day and see the P&O cruise liner Aurora gleaming white in the distance. She looks beautiful among the large dock cranes and piled-up shipping containers, and the sight makes my stomach lurch with sudden excitement.

My friend is driving me to the port with my luggage: three travel bags and two suitcases. She navigates her way towards the Mayflower Dock, where long lines of cars are being unloaded. People mill about, directing porters and embracing family, while Indian crew members are marching in single file along the pavement with purposeful strides and small wheelie-bags in tow.

We open the boot and summon a porter. He whisks away the luggage I had tagged earlier with the tough colour-coded labels sent to our home address by the cruise line. My name and cabin number are printed on them and give me the reassuring feeling that they will not be mislaid. Check-in is in progress and long lines of luggage disappear into the terminal on conveyor belts. My friend hides her envy well. A long hug – and now it is time to part.

My Swiss passport is 'non-EU', so I am directed to a separate desk where there is no queue as yet. There, my e-ticket is scanned, the Indian visa thoroughly inspected and the passport retained for further immigration formalities. A friendly member of staff sets up my onboard account and then hands me my cruise card with the mind-tickling words, "Have a pleasant journey around the world!"

This personal cruise card will serve as identification, cabin key and credit card on the ship.

(*Cruiser's tip: These cabin key ID cards allow the cruise line to operate a safe, cashless system that makes for great convenience and accurate accounting. All of your daily onboard spending and expenses, including any shore excursions, will be charged to your account, and the same goes for refunds, credits and compensations. You will receive a detailed account statement at the end of each cruise segment. This is settled either by credit card or with a cash deposit. The current balance of your account can be viewed, and queried, at any time.)

By now, an extensive queue snakes back and forth across the terminal and advances very slowly. Glad to have beaten the crowds, I go straight to Security where x-ray machines and metal detectors take a close look at all those now boarding. We must even remove our shoes if they have metal buckles.

Oh, the excitement! ... The eagerly awaited moment is here at last and it is a thrill to look up from the gangway and see the ship's side towering overhead. I savour the moment and take in the unfamiliar sight of a ship at berth.

The excitement increases as I enter the ship and am welcomed and directed to my cabin by smiling personnel. Three of my five luggage items have already arrived and the rest is delivered presently. Time to unpack! Now a couple of hours are spent filling cupboards and drawers in a leisurely way, making the space my own. My cabin steward Leandro introduces himself and takes the empty suitcases to a storage room. The travel bags fit easily under the bed.

(*World cruiser's tips: The coat hangers provided are usually the wooden kind, without hook and fixed to a loop so they can't be used anywhere else. On a three-month cruise, those approximately 16 hangers will hardly be enough for one, never mind two people. The cabin steward might be able to provide a few extra wire hangers but everyone else will be wanting some too, so bring a few cheap hangers that can be left behind. A couple of plastic ones are also handy for drying things in the bathroom overnight.

A tension rod takes up hardly any room in your luggage and will provide extra hanging space, and those shoe organizers that hang from a closet or bathroom door will hold many small items and keep your limited space tidy.)

I am particularly pleased with the neat little bathroom and the fact that I won't have to share it with anyone. There is just enough room for all the things I think I shall need for a journey around the planet. How do couples manage? True, the supplement for single passengers is steep, but the extra comfort and space really make up for it. Imagine! You get *all* the cupboard space and *all* the drawers. You can lay out your evening wear on the spare bed and assemble items for your next excursion on the sofa. Have an early night or read as late as you like, spend hours in the bathroom or at your laptop, parked permanently on the dressing table, and enjoy restful nights undisturbed by someone else's snoring (unless it comes from the next cabin).

(*Solo traveller's tip: Increasing numbers of cruise ships are now catering to the solo traveller. Their single cabins come at no extra charge but will hardly be as spacious. Yes, the unpopular single supplement on a cabin for two compensates the cruise company in part for the revenue which that missing passenger would generate,

but the greatest cost factor is the ship's fuel. So, if you are going to enjoy a two-bed cabin alone, be prepared to pay a second per capita share of the million-dollar fuel bill of a trip around the world.)

At five o'clock all passengers are called to a safety drill via the ship's public address system and instructed to bring a lifejacket from their cabin along. There are several assembly points, indicated by a notice on the inside of the cabin door. Mine is the Curzon theatre.

Once we are assembled, the general alarm is sounded. Seven short blasts from the ship's whistle are followed by one long hoot, and then the emergency procedures are duly explained. The correct use of the lifejacket is demonstrated, we are required to put on our own and remain seated while listening to further information. The sight of a large theatre full of people wearing orange-covered Styrofoam blocks is bizarre and slightly surreal.

(*Cruiser's tip: This muster drill is absolutely mandatory for all, including experienced cruisers, under the International Maritime Organization regulations. Should you be unwell or have mobility problems, contact the staff at once so they can help out with special arrangements.

In the wake of the dreadful Costa Concordia disaster, cruise lines have become even stricter about safety drill attendance and allow no exceptions. Occasionally, failing to attend this drill has seen the passengers in question escorted off the ship before their cruise had even begun.

So do follow the announcements and head to your assembly point without delay. If everyone were to do this straight away, the exercise would be over much more quickly.)

At six o'clock Aurora is ready to depart. I take a turn around the empty top deck and enjoy the cold breeze, the twinkling lights in the dusk and the tingling sense of a new adventure unfolding. A smart brass band begins to play lighthearted tunes on the pier, seemingly a remnant of that bygone age when cruising was less common and the departure of such great ships more of a festive occasion. I miss the waving crowds, but they are no longer allowed on the pier for security reasons.

A shower of white confetti is suddenly released and comes dancing upward along the ship's side like a flurry of snow, fluttering along the pier and disappearing overhead into the misty darkness – a perfect visual equivalent to those butterfly-feelings of anticipation that had made sleeping so very difficult those past few nights.

Other passengers gradually join me on the open deck, sipping glasses of complimentary champagne. But because it is dark and cold, most people prefer to stay below, watching from cabin windows or balconies. For seasoned cruisers this sail-away is nothing new, but a novice like myself would not miss it despite the chill.

The music ends and I notice that the ship has moved quietly away from the quayside. Now three powerful blasts from the ship's horn initiate a fireworks display to celebrate the start of our journey: May it be a happy one!

I admire the colourful, sparkling lights as they shoot into the night sky and are reflected on the wavelets below like little comets of pink, green and gold. The acrid tang of black-powder smoke adds its special flavour to the moment.

And now it is time to dress for dinner. A card in my cabin indicates my table number, the name of the restaurant and the time. Unsure of where to go, I just follow a crowd of people who obviously know their way to the Medina – this being not only the city where The Prophet rests in peace, but also one of the ship's main restaurants.

(*Cruiser's tip: Be punctual for your scheduled sitting in the dining room. Late arrivals make well-timed service harder for all involved, though they will naturally do their best. Imagine the complex operation that enables the ship's galleys to serve hundreds or even thousands of guests at each sitting, and don't throw a spanner in their smoothly-running works with your tardiness.)

I am shown to my place at a table for eight and learn the first names of my dinner companions. Smartly uniformed Indian waiters hand us the menu with a friendly smile and take our orders. At this opportunity I notice that all members of the restaurant staff are Indian, from the manager and his headwaiters down to the wine waiters, the table waiters and the assistant waiters.

Am I the only one to find this remnant of a colonial past at all strange or noteworthy? Someone once observed that the British class system and the Indian caste system deserved each other – but, not being used to either, my Swiss upbringing with its emphasis on equality makes me experience the situation as vaguely uncomfortable at first. Then I am struck by how attentive, friendly and courteous these Indians are and, observing the dedicated, professional manner in which they carry out their duties, I realize that it might be difficult to find such agreeable employees among European nationals, or indeed anywhere.

From our dinner table I see the lights along the coast receding, and during the meal I become better acquainted with my dinner companions. I am seated between Tony, an amusing Londoner with a pronounced cockney twang, and Martha, an elderly lady from Holland. Gilbert, in his eighties and formerly of the Royal Navy, has travelled widely and seems to have been to all our destinations before. The same goes for his friend Amanda, an elegant widow of quick wit and stylish clothes. Then there is Beryl, a very forceful and statuesque widow from 'up north'; Nigel – tubby, short and quiet; Simon – gangly, tall and quiet. All of them are mature single travellers and experienced members (Beryl excepted) of the cruising community.

In this group I am the only novice and also by far the youngest. Nearly all are of my parents' generation, and the same goes for the majority of passengers on this ship. It does not bother me that I don't blend in, for I have not booked this cruise for social reasons. My purpose is to experience the size of the globe and to see its oceans, seas and far-flung countries in safety, comfort and style. I would like to embrace the glory of the world, and my existence within it.

(*Cruiser's tip: These days, no one is too young to go on a cruise. Over the past years, the average age of the cruise passenger has dropped significantly since cruise lines began to cater for young adults on party cruises, for honeymooners, for families with small children, and even for teenagers.)

Returning to my cabin after a delicious meal, I notice that the ship is beginning to heave and dip unpleasantly. The motion gets progressively worse and forces me to go to bed at once, for a horizontal position alone seems bearable until one of the recommended tablets, packed as a precaution against such bouts of seasickness, disconnects my stomach from the lurching and rolling of the ship.

Day 2 ~ Thursday, 5th January 2012 ~ sea state: very rough ~ wind: north-west 10, storm ~ weather: rain ~ temperature: 12°C

Beaufort 10

Aurora makes her way into the Bay of Biscay, troubled by a force 10 storm that continues all through the night. It is like trying to sleep on a rollercoaster in slow-motion with eerie sound effects. I witness each and every movement, listen to the noises emanating from the straining vessel and become closely acquainted with the repeating patterns of movement and sound. There is not a wink of sleep to be had – only emergency trips to the bathroom.

This morning the relentless motion continues unabated. The ship is lifted high by each successive wave, and as it sinks slowly to crash into a trough, a dull thud shakes its sturdy frame and reverberates upwards through the decks. At some point in the course of the morning, the captain's competent voice is heard in each cabin as he gives an update on the severe weather conditions. He also strives to assure us that Aurora is coping with the challenge marvellously, as always. His announcement makes me realize that I never had any doubt about the resilience of the ship, and no fear for our safety. The captain concludes his message with the weather forecast: Today's heavy seas and forceful gales are expected to continue well into the night.

Great! I resolve to stay in my supremely comfortable bed and ride out the storm in this fashion, glad that nobody expects me to get up and do anything. With eyes firmly shut I imagine those mariners of old who were tossed about in flimsy wooden vessels that strained their seams in storms like this. After shifts of backbreaking labour in the rigging, they retired to hammocks that were swinging in time with the movements of the ship. How did they cope? It is possible to get used to the ceaseless swaying, apparently, though that seems quite improbable to me right now.

Around nine o'clock my stomach indicates that food replacement is needed, so I attempt to order breakfast by (mistakenly) calling Reception. I am told that Room Service will call me back, but this does not happen and I feel far too unwell to make another effort.

By mid-afternoon, pangs of hunger compel me to try again. A shaky male voice at the other end of the line does not find communicating in English at all easy, and though my cabin number is requested twice, no food arrives.

One hour later, Room Service is no longer answering the phone, so I call Reception once more to find out what the problem might be. If the staff are feeling even half as sick as I do, they have my sympathy. I hate to trouble them under the circumstances, but I really ought to eat a little before taking more tablets. At first I did not *want* food, and now I can't *get* any ... Who would have thought that a cruise might be a most effective diet?

My next call reaches a very competent individual. He informs me that though there is no order registered from my cabin, he will see to a prompt delivery. Only minutes later, he brings the requested fruit and plain rolls to my bedside. Still feeling too ill to eat, I force down some grapes and a few bites of bread, followed by another tablet.

The ship continues to pitch heavily, and a sudden lurching sends a pile of books and pencils over the edge of the side table. The glasses and crockery of the tea tray would like to follow suit, but a dainty brass rail prevents them from crashing to the floor.

This is the reality of the sea! This is what we signed up for ... I picture rows of wind-whipped waves rushing in from the horizon and bobbing Aurora's 76,000 tons like a ping-pong ball. Regrettably, I can't get a glimpse of them, for my cabin is on the inside and does not have a window, and I am unable to contemplate a trip to the deck. And yet other passengers can be heard, stumbling along the corridor, and there is even laughter in the next cabin.

Perfectly resigned to the situation, I hope that there will not be many days like this one in the months to come. Another announcement from the captain informs us that he expects no significant improvements, weatherwise, until at least tomorrow morning.

Day 3 ~ Friday, 6th January 2012 ~ sunrise: 8.17am ~ sunset: 5.30pm ~ sea state: slight ~ wind: NE 4, moderate breeze ~ weather: overcast ~ temperature: 12°C

At Sea

Awaking at seven o'clock, I realize that I slept soundly all night and the ship is no longer heaving. Feeling much better, I go to the Medina and have a lovely breakfast at a little table by the windowfront, overlooking a calm, grey sea that gives no indication of its previous wildness.

The Indian waiters are intrigued (or worried?) by the fact that I appear to be travelling all by myself, and now they approach in turn to make discreet enquiries.

(*Solo traveller's tip: Never allow settings or events which people usually attend as couples or groups to spoil your fun. Yes, you will get inquisitive looks and curious questions, but there is nothing wrong with being a solitary wanderer. Just think of Aragorn! And certainly any number of people, bored with each other's company, will secretly envy you.)

A news leaflet with the lovely name 'Horizon' is delivered to the cabin daily and I read today's programme with a revived interest in life. First I take a turn around the Sun Deck and enjoy a much-longed-for breath of fresh air, and then I visit the Oasis spa to check out today's special offer of treatments. Minutes later I have a first, free consultation with the ship's acupuncturist. Rodrigo is from Brazil and his English not easy to follow, but his calm disposition and insight inspire trust. He diagnoses spleen deficiency and a strong liver that puts too much 'fire' on the heart, leading to mild insomnia. My blood type makes me a natural vegetarian, he adds.

It is an interesting diagnosis and, having always been curious about acupuncture, this opportunity seems too good to miss – but vegetarian am I not.

Now I can see for myself that the needles' insertion is absolutely painless: a tiny tap – and they're in. Soon I am floating as a pin cushion between ocean and sky, wishing I had a better understanding of what is being done, and why. The needles are placed along the body's energy meridians at points corresponding to certain organs to release blocked energy – this much I know from a shiatsu course many years ago, and Rodrigo explains that the skin around each needle shows a subtle reaction by growing red through increased circulation. At the end he applies tiny plasters with mustard seed centres to the inside of my right ear. These should help against bouts of seasickness, referred to by the more elegant term 'motion discomfort'.

At noon I join a large choir of enthusiastic amateurs, the 'Aurora Vocalists'. These undaunted passengers made a start yesterday, despite the storm. It is impressive that there are not only great numbers of ladies, but also numerous male voices singing (and bantering) with gusto. The choir is led by a lovely young woman from the ship's entertainment team, and though the songs she has chosen are not my cup of tea, this choir session is such an enjoyable experience that I decide to attend regularly.

(*World cruiser's tip: If there is a choir, give it a try even if you have never sung before. The music and the good-humoured companionship are uplifting, you may learn new songs or timeless lyrics, and no one expects you to sing really well.)

Now it is time for lunch. A large crowd is queueing outside the Medina, waiting to be seated, but being single gets me a place early when I am called forward by the headwaiter to complete the numbers at a large table. It is an enjoyable meal with a new set of people. Names are exchanged and basic personal information follows. Lucy and Tom, for example, are on their third world cruise already and speak highly of Aurora – as does anyone I have met so far.

After lunch I settle on a deckchair on the sunny side of the Promenade Deck, open a large black notebook and begin to write about my first cruise impressions. Once in a while I look up to enjoy the view across the sea towards the wide horizon. The sea continues to be calm and mild-mannered – Neptune be praised!

This evening with Black Tie dress code also brings the first formal event. Ladies dress up in glamorous gowns, men are elegantly suited, and all are invited to a World Cruisers' Party in the Crow's Nest where the captain welcomes us.

(*Cruiser's tip: To help with your packing, check your cruise line's dress code guide online. Detailed specifications are given for smart casual, semiformal, and formal or Black Tie dinner dress. Onboard, the daily newsletter will inform you of each day's prescribed dress standard which also applies in any of the specialty restaurants. Should you wish to escape these expectations, you may visit the self-service buffet in your leisurewear.)

It is not at all easy to walk alone into such a festive crowd! I choose a table and sit by myself, enduring the questioning glances. A waiter stops by with complimentary drinks and asks if anyone will be joining me. *Hmmm ... who knows?*

Now a very nice elderly couple approaches my table: Would it be all right if they joined me? Why, of course! They introduce themselves as Erin and Paul and we fall easily into conversation about various aspects of cruising and the ship. They are seasoned cruisers, on intimate terms with the entire P&O fleet, and Erin describes Aurora as their favourite ship, being "elegant without being ostentatious".

Paul, formerly engineer with the Royal Navy, is able to answer my questions concerning the provenance, storage and use of the vast amounts of water that are needed on a ship of this size. He explains that it is pumped from the open sea, desalinated and purified by flash evaporators, and then distributed to great storage tanks. It is quite all right to drink the ship's water, he assures me, for it is superior in quality to most of our tap water in the UK.

(*Cruiser's tip: The water on cruise ships is freshly made from sea water each day, both by reverse osmosis and by flash evaporation, but because this pure, distilled water tastes unpleasant, it is also enriched with a special formula of trace elements. Constantly tested and monitored, it is perfectly safe to drink. If you don't trust it, bring a water testing kit and be amazed by the result. Onboard, bottled water is sold at a hefty price, so buy just one bottle and refill it at a self-service station or your own tap – it's all the same water. Store it in your fridge, take it on excursions, and replace the bottle once it is no longer hygienic.)

Soon it is time to go to dinner. My dinner companions greet me with friendly enquiries after my wellbeing. None of them had been seasick! Francis, our table waiter, and Marcus, the assistant waiter, also seem pleased to welcome me back after the storm. The menu appeals and there is enough choice to please a variety of tastes, including vegetarians. Tonight – not ready to join the vegetarian tribe, whatever my blood group – I settle for asparagus and poached quail's egg, wild mushroom soup, and then my very first lobster with a side-dish of creamed potatoes and spinach. (Cruising and lobster go together like Adam and Eve, and the cruise industry's consumption levels of these crustaceans must be enormous.) The delightful meal is rounded off by a delicious sorbet of pink grapefruit.

(*Cruiser's tip: For people with special dietary requirements, a cruise may well be the easiest, most hassle-free holiday available. Be sure to alert the cruise line via your travel agent when you book, so that everything you require can be stocked in good time. Contact the restaurant manager on the first day to confirm that your needs are known. He will then make sure that the kitchen is

informed. Each day, a member of your serving team will show you tomorrow's menu, discuss alternatives or possible adaptations and take note of your wishes. But although special diets and allergies are taken very seriously, not every food outlet on a ship catering for thousands will be aware of your particular situation, and so it is advisable to check carefully before ordering outside your usual restaurant.)

The food is delicious, the portions neither too large nor too small, and second helpings are readily available. Dishes are prepared in a health-conscious way and their presentation is appealing. But best of all is the fact that each course appears as if by magic and, after the meal, all crockery and cutlery vanishes into the galley to be cleaned by other hands than mine – or, more likely, by big machines. No more grocery-shopping or cooking, or indeed any kind of housework for three whole months and a week! *Hallelujah!* I am swept by feelings of appreciation and gratitude.

After dinner, people disperse to sit in bars or attend various entertainments. A different film is shown at the Playhouse cinema every night, and live entertainment acts present their shows at the Curzon theatre. Tonight there is a performance based on famous scenes from American films and musicals. The P&O house company 'The Headliners' are a talented bunch and perform with energy and enthusiasm, but the volume of sound is so powerful that it hurts my ears and compels me to plug them with my fingers.

(**Cruiser's tip: If you are sensitive to overamplified sound, bring ear plugs. On cruise ships, as elsewhere, it is generally assumed that a high volume of sound equals fun, or that the clientele is deaf.*

Unprotected, those traumatized hair cells in your ears will signal an unnecessary acceleration of hearing loss by ringing persistently after each show.)

At the end of the day I return to my cabin and open the door, expecting total darkness inside. But the soft light of the bedside lamp shows that my bed has been made ready for sleep, with one corner of the cover flipped back and a little chocolate nesting on it. The overall effect is very welcoming and is the work of Leandro, my amiable and diligent cabin steward from Mumbai.

(*World cruiser's tip: Greeting cabin stewards with a smile and addressing them by name, stopping to chat about their native country and family, or telling them about impressions of a port comes easily to most passengers and makes for a good relationship.
    Your cabin steward will play an important part on your long journey, for he (or she) tidies and cleans your cabin and bathroom twice a day, every day. Make their job easier by keeping your space tidy and let them know any preferences that could lighten their load. Because cabin doors are left wide open while they clean, they recommend storing your valuables in your cabin's safe.
    Since they serve many cabins, stewards are grateful if you don't confuse their role with that of personal butler, but they will supply additional towels, shampoo, tissues, special pillows, coat hangers, ice and advice, and be there for you as your first point of call in any arising issue.
    These honest, amiable and hardworking individuals really deserve an ample tip at the end of the journey, as well as a personal thank you. And however much you would like to – you can't take your cabin steward home to continue the great service you have become so used to.)

Day 4 ~ Saturday, 7th January 2012 ~ sunrise: 8.12am ~ sunset: 6.01pm ~ sea state: calm ~ wind: NE 4, moderate breeze ~ weather: overcast ~ temperature: 16°C

Life on Board

I awake at six o'clock, feeling well rested and completely recovered from motion discomfort. Up on deck, I take in the early morning mood on the Atlantic Ocean. It is still dark, but small breaks in the cloud cover indicate the coming of dawn. The sea is very calm and Aurora sweeps along at a brisk pace, her engines humming quietly. After a while I go inside to enjoy a breakfast of fresh fruit, plain yoghurt and heavenly croissants. My favourite table is by the window-front, because I like to look out across the sea. The Medina is almost empty at this early hour. Smartly uniformed waiters hover attentively, ready to carry out every wish, and I sense their puzzlement at the fact that I, a woman travelling alone, am so obviously content and enjoying myself. Francis comes to my table to exchange a few words. He asks if I am indeed travelling around the world by myself. (Such independence is probably not as yet conceivable in Indian society.) Then he tells me that he liked the way I had worn my hair last night, pinned back with two combs.

Does he think I am in need of male attention? If so, he could not be more mistaken; but anyhow – it is thoughtful, kindly meant and rather pleasing.

I watch the sky grow light and the sea being churned into foam, swirling alongside the ship in lace-like patterns of ice-blue and white. Sipping hot tea contentedly, I picture myself as I worked every Saturday in the life so recently left behind, marking stacks of weekly maths sheets and essays.

Contemplating this sharp contrast produces a glowing smile that fans out from deep inside until it reaches my lips. It is so exquisitely liberating, not having to live by other people's dictates and be free from demands and constraints of everyday life for a while ... I am hugely pleased with this worldviewing adventure I made happen for myself and can see why cruising appeals to so many!

At half past eight I go to join a group in the Weights & Measures gym for a session of guided stretching exercises that are clearly necessary and likely beneficial. On impulse, I decide to continue with the yoga class at nine o'clock. Yoga is another thing I always wanted to try but never found time for, but on a cruise ship the day's programme is designed to provide such opportunities.

(*Cruiser's tip: Try anything that appeals to you. Discover hidden talents with untapped benefits in onboard watercolour lessons or digital photography seminars, in yoga, Zumba or Pilates sessions, in language, cooking, computer or dance classes, in ping-pong and quoits matches, on tennis and basketball courts. Not to mention more adventurous activities available on larger ships, such as ziplining, skydiving, ice skating, bungee jumping, trampolining, or even a spin on a Formula 1 simulator.

This is a unique chance to broaden your experience with no organizational efforts and negligible additional costs.)

After a shower and some cabin time I head to the lovely and quiet library for more work on my journal, until it is time for choir practice with the Aurora Vocalists again. I begin to see how my preferences are shaping the day and am pleased to find my way around the decks more easily now. If in doubt, there is always a helpful diagram close by with a large red dot proclaiming 'You are here'; and in the three stairwells, carpets of different colours indicate whether one happens to be fore, amidships or aft.

*(*Cruiser's tip: Begin by memorizing the location of your cabin, the restaurant and other important places, for this will make you feel confidently at home on your ship. Then, day by day, explore the decks at leisure to discover all your favourite places.)*

Because there is already a very long queue for lunch at the Medina, we are directed to the Alexandria restaurant at the stern. This place is equally appealing in its light-filled space, soft colour scheme and large windowfront. Now there is a new set of passengers to meet, a new menu of delicacies to choose from, a new view of the sea ... It's a tough life!

In the afternoon I take a walk around the Sun Deck at the top of the ship. Reciting Oliver W. Holmes' beautiful poem 'The Chambered Nautilus' to myself, I look out at what he calls the unbounded main: the sea with no land in sight. This poem is the piece of poetry I had chosen for my class to learn at the beginning of our last year, and my cruise is in effect the result of its topic: A voyage across life's unresting sea, a search for more stately mansions of the soul, and "a dome more vast" between myself and heaven ...

Waiting for the restaurant to open its doors for dinner, I look around the Piccadilly boutique and am surprised to find the prices so reasonable. Turns out that everything we buy on board is free of tax!
    But now it is time for another lovely meal, and tonight our table erupts frequently in shouts of laughter. There is a

convivial mood and much friendly banter, now that we are getting to know each other better.

Afterwards I head back to the shop, conveniently open until ten o'clock, and buy a small Aurora rucksack that will come in handy on future excursions. Also an elegant black-and-white lace wrap to go with my black velvet dress, a camel-coloured pashmina to accessorize the cocktail dress, a box of fudge and a postcard of the ship. All this comes to a mere fifty-five pounds, and a discount of 10% applies today.

(*Cruiser's tip: Onboard shops are open whenever a ship is at sea, and then liquor, perfumes, cosmetics, jewellery and watches can be bought at appealing prices, for the ship's at-sea status makes them duty-free. Ships' boutiques also offer casual clothes and evening wear of distinguished labels, and once in a while hold clearance sales at knockout prices.

Bottled liquor bought onboard is delivered to your cabin on the final day of your cruise. If your purchases should add up to more than the exempt amount, they will be subject to duty upon your return home.

Be sure to check the origins of any expensive item that comes with a certificate. If it was produced in your own country, it may be exempt from duty.)

Day 5 ~ Sunday, 8*th* January 2012 ~ sunrise: 8.17am ~ sunset: 6.17pm ~ wind: 2, light breeze ~ weather: partly cloudy ~ temperature: 19°C ~ distance travelled: 1,324 nautical miles

Madeira

Aurora is already lying alongside the pier when I awake this morning. The island rests in a quiet Sunday dawn, strings of street lights twinkling fairy-like in the hazy morning.

At the appointed time I go to the gangway and check out at a security desk. My cruise card is swiped by a stern-looking female officer and the computer system registers that I am leaving the ship temporarily. A barcode scanner calls up my details on the screen, including a photograph that was snapped as we were boarding the ship. Down the gangway and through the terminal I go to the place where members of the ship's excursions team are stationed. They hand out numbered stickers for different tours and direct us to the right coach.

(*Cruiser's tip: Research tour options early and sign up online for your favourites straight away. Popular excursions sell out quickly, some even before the cruise begins.)

My group will be going for a 'Levada Walk', following the irrigation channels that distribute water among the fields on the slopes, but first we are driven on steep and twisted roads into the hills and learn that *Madeira* means timber and the capital's name *Funchal* means fennel.

(*Solo traveller's tip: Cruise lines will offer a variety of all-day and half-day tours at every port. These are more costly than trips you

negotiate yourself locally, but they offer an unparalleled level of security and convenience. A meal that gives you a taste of the local cuisine is usually included in longer tours.

You can relax and enjoy the excursion in the knowledge that exploring sights far from shore won't prevent you from returning to the ship on time, and you are not going to be tricked, robbed, or held to ransom by entrepreneurial taxi drivers – which is, sadly, a not uncommon occurrence in certain countries.)

From the moment I set foot on firm ground, I notice that it seems to be moving in the manner of the sea. It is an odd sensation and my first experience of this phenomenon.

Now our guide takes us into the woods on a well-maintained path. The irrigation channels, lined with shrubs, weeds and flowers, are overshadowed by pines, blue gum eucalyptus, chestnuts, rhododendron and mimosa trees. Even in this month of January, flowers are already in bloom: clover, violets, camellias, agapanthus, banana-passionfruit, bougainvilleas and canna lilies – to name but a few of the more common varieties.

An affectionate free-roaming dog accompanies our group for a while, clearly hoping for a snack, and I fall in with Gwen, a lady from Cornwall. We talk easily, and she knows Waldorf aka Steiner education from her time as a young co-worker in a Camphill community.

Gwen also tells me about the recently flooded cabins on E Deck of which I had heard some rumours. It seems that a pipe leaked and passengers had to be moved out of their cabins while crew members took up the sodden carpet and dismantled wall panelling in their search for the source of the dripping water. Imagine having your enjoyment of a beginning cruise dampened in this manner. How unpleasant it must have been for the people concerned!

Returning to the ship after this enjoyable half-day excursion, each cruise card is swiped once more to register our return, all bags are x-rayed and we have to pass through the metal-detecting frame once more. This procedure is supervised matter-of-factly by the ship's unsmiling security team and nobody makes a fuss.

(*Cruiser's tip: Don't try to smuggle anything! Learn from the unfortunate attempts of others and accept that any cunning plans will get you into seriously hot water.)

After a delicious lunch I stretch my legs on the Promenade Deck and happen to cross the path of Gilbert. We stop for a little chat, leaning against the railing just as people do in those cruise ads. The gleaming white ship, the sunshine, the dark-blue ocean, those gusts of wind twirling my hair – it is all here, right here and now!

Gilbert, being an experienced traveller, readily shares interesting information about the places we shall be visiting. It is so nice to meet new acquaintances as one moves around the ship, and every day there are more identifiable faces, some already with names attached.

(*Solo traveller's tip: You will soon have an ever-growing circle of acquaintances, and maybe even friends, and it is entirely up to you to determine your daily dose of solitude.)

The afternoon is spent at a quiet table on the Lido Deck, updating my journal. A drinks waiter stops by to ask politely if he could get me anything. I never liked alcohol in any form and won't be keeping these waiters busy, but they do not mind serving a glass of plain water either. It is of course also possible to buy non-alcoholic drinks, some of which go by the funny name of mocktail.

(*Cruiser's tip: Glasses of water are free, and so are coffee and tea, iced tea and lemonade. Soft drinks are not. You also have to pay for fresh fruit juices, specialty drinks and coffees, beer and wine, cocktails and champagne, and their prices come with an additional surcharge or service fee.)

Now it is time to do some ironing, for my cruise clothes have been packed in suitcases, awaiting their moment since July, and now they need to be made presentable. But this is not as easy as it sounds, for the self-service launderette on my deck is situated at the other end of the ship. Arms full of clothes have to be carried back and forth along a seemingly endless corridor, and sometimes all of the complimentary machines and irons are taken. But I am in luck – right now one of the ironing boards is available.

(*Cruiser's tip: To minimize the risk of fire, you are NOT allowed to bring your own iron, hairdryer, kettle or hotplate. You will find a kettle and a hairdryer in your cabin.)

(*Cruiser's tip: How laundry is dealt with varies widely and depends on the length of the cruise, the ship and the cruise line. Check it out online before packing. Self-service laundromats with ironing facilities are free on some ships but come at an extra charge on others. On certain cruises, your laundry bag is collected in the morning and returned the next day, at a fee. Some cruise lines offer

complimentary dry-cleaning and laundry service for passengers in their elite category, others require everyone to purchase a 'laundry package' before sailing.

Silk and other delicate fabrics cost more to treat, and men's clothes are generally cleaned and pressed at a lower price than those of ladies.)

(*Cruiser's tip: Experienced cruisers, just like backpackers, swear by a simple method, of which there are plenty of YouTube videos to study. To wash garments quickly and cheaply, put them in a large, sturdy zip-lock bag, half-filled with water of a suitable temperature and some laundry liquid. Let the items soak for a while, then squeeze and move them about gently inside the bag. Squeeze out the dirt and rinse them well, either in the bag or the sink.

Wring out the water and speed up the drying process by rolling each damp garment in a bath towel. Squeeze this roll to let the towel soak up the excess moisture. Finally, use plastic hangers and pegs, brought along for this purpose, to suspend your washing on a clothes line across the shower, where it can drip and dry overnight.)

Like the car park at school, a ship's launderettes are readily assumed to be the source of all rumours and exaggerations flying around the decks at any time, such as the whispered claims that our ship's morgue is already harbouring several bodies of quietly expired passengers by now.

(*Cruiser's tip: There is a morgue on every cruise ship. Depending on its size, three to ten bodies can be stored in this refrigerated space for up to a week, by which time the ship will have reached a major port. Because cruises are so popular with the most senior age group, deaths from age-related illnesses are a common occurrence.

They are referred to as 'Operation Rising Star' and are handled very discreetly. The Guest Care team is specially trained to assist grieving family members and help with the paperwork, and until a representative from the insurance company takes over, they will contact consular offices and help with the travel arrangements, including the deceased passenger's repatriation.

Travel insurance will cover most of these costs, provided that no medical condition remained undeclared. If this were the case, all costs become the responsibility of the deceased's family. Taking out comprehensive travel insurance is therefore highly recommended.)

I never overhear anyone gossiping in the launderette, which suits me. Whenever I am there, everyone is ironing silently, or waiting for washers and dryers to finish their cycles while reading or doing Sudoku.

(*Cruiser's tip: Listen to the ship's gossip if you like, but don't pass it on. Most of it will turn out to be incorrect.)

At half past five, Aurora gets ready to leave Madeira while a big AIDA cruise liner arrives and docks next to her. This has German and British passengers (many of whom experienced and remember the suffering of the war) waving amicably to each other in passing. Then a sail-away party is held on the aft deck and a sing-along with party dances is led by the energetic entertainment team as Aurora sets out across the Atlantic and follows the sinking sun towards the Caribbean.

Sipping a glass of ginger beer and lime on the top deck, I turn away from the jolly crowd and look towards the ocean where the flame-red sun goes down behind a bank of clouds. A pale full moon, large and luminous, is rising from the purple hills opposite; and I am smiling to myself again, utterly content and happy ... No obligations, no stress, no worries, no fears: Pure bliss!

(*Solo traveller's tip: Feel free to do your own thing, whatever that may be. After all, it's what solo travelling is about. You could do Tai Chi at sunrise on the deserted top deck, or bring a telescope to scan the starry night sky. There is no need to join group activities unless you really want to.)

It is an unaccustomed pleasure to dress for dinner. I enjoy choosing from various outfits, put together last summer, and adding my beautiful string of pearls. It was a present from my father many years ago, purchased as a souvenir on our trip to Japan. These pearls have never yet been worn, due to the distinct lack of opportunity in a Waldorf teacher's life, but now their moment has come at last.

(*Cruiser's tip: In addition to the vault at the purser's desk, where larger amounts of passengers' cash can be kept, there is also a little safe in every cabin, tucked discreetly inside a cupboard, so don't hesitate to bring precious things along. You will be programming the access code yourself, but take care to remember it. Should you forget your PIN, a supervisor has to be called to reset the safe, and this service usually comes at a charge.)

Day 6 ~ Monday, 9th January 2012 ~ sunrise: 7.24am ~ sunset: 6.59pm ~ sea state: slight ~ wind: NE 2, light breeze ~ weather: partly cloudy ~ temperature: 22°C ~ time zone: GMT-1

Norovirus

We have crossed the first time zone and the clocks have been set back by an hour. I begin the day with a turn around the Sun Deck and breakfast in the newly reopened Orangery. This popular self-service restaurant had been closed since the start of our journey because of an outbreak of norovirus, inherited from the previous cruise and now invisibly on the rampage. The crew are battling the spread of this highly contagious nuisance almost around the clock, using buckets of disinfectant to wipe rails, door handles and anything else we might possibly touch.

The captain has requested passengers not to shake hands and to observe the strictest personal hygiene. Hand-sanitizing stations are everywhere. The obligatory squirt of disinfectant, followed by a vigorous rubbing of hands, has become a common ritual at the entrance of every restaurant.

Passengers have to report any symptoms at once and are quarantined in their cabins until fully recovered. I wish that similarly effective measures could have been put in place at our school, but no: This virus was known as the 'January bug' and just had to be borne until it disappeared by itself. But not so on this ship!

(*Cruiser's tip: Do try your best not to bring the norovirus aboard when going on a cruise. Obviously, the cruise line can do nothing to prevent people from causing such a big problem for everyone; they can only deal with the consequences and raise awareness.

Should you feel ill, don't leave your cabin. Report it at once over the phone, as well as any resulting 'accidents'. These will be dealt with promptly by specialists. Medical staff will come to your cabin for treatment, and you may not even have to pay for their services if you caught the virus, already prevalent on the ship, through no fault of your own.

Be aware that, according to the law of any country's port, sick passengers are not allowed to go ashore; but if the illness is deemed the ship's responsibility, a refund for missed excursions can be expected.)

Yesterday, the captain announced that the measures are now showing the desired effect and the situation is so much improved that the self-service restaurant can be opened again. This message prompted delighted applause from so many passengers, it made me curious about this popular facility.

I find the Orangery still very quiet at seven o'clock in the morning. Enjoying a healthy breakfast while looking out at the ocean, I wait for the sun to rise from its waters. I can't recall the last time I saw a sunrise ... It was certainly many years ago! And when was the last time I took a dip?

Soon I am swimming lengths in the Crystal pool and then enjoy my first experience of a Jacuzzi. To be floating in a whirlpool above the Atlantic – what a feeling!

I attend the morning's gym class and then try out one of the treadmills. Britta, the lovely young physiotherapist and fitness trainer from Iceland, shows me how to program the machine because I never used fitness equipment before. In fact, I have never even been to a gym, but now I seize the opportunity and begin to walk briskly to nowhere.

Fifteen minutes later, the computer announces that I burnt all of fifty-five calories ... Well – it's a start, I suppose!

(*Cruiser's tip: Don't pass up the opportunity to use the ship's gym on a daily basis. There is no registering involved, no hefty membership fee, no hassle and no expectation. Pleased to notice how quickly your condition is improving, you will also feel much easier about enjoying all that wonderful food.

Just pack a suitable outfit you feel comfortable in, as well as good sports shoes. They will come in handy for running gentle laps on the designated deck – alone or in company.)

The Oasis spa is offering more treatments at reduced prices today, and I decide to book a follow-up acupuncture session. This cruise is the perfect opportunity to take care of my long neglected fitness and health, and I intend to make the most of it.

(*Cruiser's tip: All spa treatments have to be paid extra and don't come cheap, but as seriously luxurious pampering they are usually worth every penny. If your goal is to relax on your cruise, the spa will become one of your favourite places. Take advantage of special offers, and of discounts on port days.)

The sun breaks through the clouds at last and it is getting pleasantly warm. On the decks, sunbathers are beginning to drag sunloungers to preferred spots and lather themselves in protective lotion. Meanwhile, crew members with small rollers and large buckets of white paint are working their way around the decks, making sure that Aurora's gleaming coat remains immaculate.

Choir practice has us grappling with a rendition of 'Sentimental Journey' (singing "Why did I decide to roam?") and then I want to find out what it is like to have lunch in the Orangery upstairs. A considerable portion of passengers is hugely delighted that their favourite eatery is back on the menu, though self-service is still banned because of possible contagion with the horrid virus. We are served by the staff of the restaurant instead, all of whom are wearing sanitized gloves.

During dinner, my new acquaintance Gwen and I realise that we are seated at neighbouring tables, and after the meal she comes over to introduce her travelling companion. We visit Anderson's bar together, sit in a cosy corner and chat for a while. Then I retire to my lovely cabin, of which I grow fonder each day.

Day 7 ~ Tuesday, 10th January 2012 ~ sunrise: 7.59am ~ sunset: 6.40pm ~ sea state: slight ~ wind: SE 3, gentle breeze ~ weather: mostly sunny ~ temperature: 22°C

Sea Days

After this first week, my days are assuming a more definite pattern. Meals and activities and times of rest are repeating themselves according to my choices. I am glad of the row of sea days which our Atlantic crossing brings, for they allow me to become familiar with life on board. It is enjoyable to meet acquaintances as one moves around the ship, stopping for a few friendly words as paths intersect. To me, the cruise experience is still new enough to be thrilling, and every day fresh opportunities are waiting to be seized.

(*Cruiser's tip: The ship's daily news magazine outlines each day's events in a helpful way. Use it to plan a framework of favourite, recurring activities, and then mix in a few experimental things that pique your interest.)

The enjoyable morning exercise class and a session on the treadmill are followed by a few turns around the sunny top deck. Unfortunately, today's port presentation talk on the Panama Canal coincides with my next acupuncture session, but I am looking forward to having more needles stuck into my blocked energy points and imagine acupuncture to be a little bit like unblocking clogged drains.

(*Cruiser's tip: If any port presentation should clash with other appointments, you can easily watch it later on your TV screen.)

Out of curiosity I begin to write a list of things I have never done before, such as: living on a ship, eating lobster, going to the gym, having acupuncture, wearing a string of pearls to dinner, relaxing in a Jacuzzi, doing yoga ...
    A second list records things I have not done for at least a decade: feeling seasick, wearing high-heeled shoes and nail varnish, watching the sunrise, going out on a Saturday night, sitting in a bar, swimming in a pool, doing no work on a Sunday, practising ballroom dancing ...
    And there will be more to add in time, no doubt.

Day 8 ~ Wednesday, 11th January 2012 ~ sunrise: 7.25am ~ sunset: 6.21pm ~ sea state: calm ~ wind: S-E 3, gentle breeze ~ weather: sunny ~ temperature: 22°C ~ time zone: GMT-2

Leisure

The clocks were set back by another hour at two o'clock this morning, and so I am up on the Sun Deck well before dawn, admiring the calm sea with its 360-degree horizon.

What courage those seafarers of old must have had to set out with insufficient provisions and no clear idea of where they were going! Their inaccurate sea charts depicted a world distorted by superstitious rumour and fearsome myth, and they had no means of establishing their longitude accurately until the late 18th century.

By contrast, our ship is steaming towards her unseen destination as if drawn by a hidden string, connected to the global reference grid by imperceptible satellite signals that pinpoint her exact location on a highly accurate map. And as for provisions – oh, they are plentiful indeed!

Aurora's broad and self-assured wake is doubled by the bright moon's shimmering light, reflected on the ocean's smooth surface and forming a rival pathway to the horizon.

One week has passed since the beginning of this cruise and I find myself getting into its rhythm. For the first time in years I lie on a sunlounger with exposed skin and let the glorious sunshine deal with my undoubted Vitamin D deficiency. And as I soak up the sun's warm rays, I can't help picturing a rainy schoolday at home, with colleagues and pupils hard at work, and this thought makes me appreciate my present situation even more.

In this morning's exercise class, Jovan (the charming fitness coach) had informed me with Serbian directness that I ought to push myself more. I had a lot of potential, he said, "but I think you are a bit lazy!"

There is no arguing with his observation. After years of working sixty-hour weeks, surely the point of this cruise is that I can, at last, be just as lazy as I like.

Day 9 ~ Thursday, 12th January 2012 ~ sunrise: 7.50am ~ sunset: 7.00pm ~ sea state: calm ~ wind: SE 4 ~ weather: cloudy ~ temperature: 23°C

Sea Sunrise

Up on the top deck at six o'clock, I prepare to watch the sun rise again, for it is a sight of which I have grown very fond. And as I watch the fiery ball's ascent from the sea, like a Viking I recite a few favourite lines from the Norse epic 'The Edda' to the glowing sky and the waves:

"Turn eastward, and behold the light that shines on every man! For there is nothing dark it doth not lighten; for there is nothing hard it cannot melt; for there is nothing lost it will not save ..."

How satisfying it is to know meaningful poems, for their word-pictures reflect and enhance every experience the world presents us with.

(*Cruiser's tip: Why not take the opportunity to learn some good poetry by heart as you wander the decks? The mind wants exercising too, and even humorous poetry is seriously enriching.)

After a leisurely breakfast at the Medina I head for Britta's 'Stretch and Relax' class. One has to arrive early to find a spot for one's exercise mat, for these sessions are extremely popular. This may be due in part to the high professional quality of Jovan's and Britta's coaching, and in part to their friendly and humorous approach. They *know* how to make it fun to get all sweaty and short of breath!

I continue to exercise by myself on a fitness machine that works on the thighs and is therefore almost constantly occupied. Afterwards, the scales show that weight has been shed during the last six days. How delightful! I didn't make a conscious effort to slim, but eating healthy food, regularly and at sensible times, may have helped just as much as the unaccustomed exercise.

At ten o'clock I attend the port presentation of San Francisco in the Curzon theatre and then return to my cabin-home for a shower and a change of clothes.

Choir practice is next, and we go through the songs learnt so far. The singing is invigorating, but some of these tunes (particularly 'Delilah') stay in my mind much longer than I would like, tenacious as limpets and impossible to dislodge. That is why I am so delighted to get the new MP3 player (a gift from my son) running at last. Now I can listen to my beloved piano trios, quartets and quintets while doing a bit of sewing on a dress that needs altering. Life is so much better with Mozart!

In the afternoon I attend a most enjoyable dance class. Our dance instructors, a British couple, have a wonderful sense of humour that makes their lessons fun. Today's 'Latin Jam' requires no partner. The steps are easy to pick up, I love the music, enjoy the hip-wiggling moves and am having a great time. As usual, the majority are ladies without a partner, but that doesn't stop us from enjoying our love of dancing.

(*Solo traveller's tip: It is not necessary to bring a partner to any of the dance lessons. If you are solo and female, you will most likely get to dance with one of the instructors at times. Some cruise lines offer 'Dance Hosts' or 'Ambassador Hosts' – "carefully screened, cultured and well-travelled gentlemen who are accomplished ballroom dancers" – but if you are solo and male and willing to dance, you can take your pick.)

Day 10 ~ Friday, 13th January 2012 ~ sunrise: 7.14am ~ sunset: 6.36pm ~ sea state: slight ~ wind: E 3, gentle breeze ~ weather: sunny ~ temperature: 23°C ~ time zone: GMT-3

Being Noticed

Once again the clocks have been set back by an hour, which means that getting up early is pleasantly easy. It also makes me really glad that I did not book a cruise going around the world in an easterly direction! Would one end up sleeping through the day?

As the sun rises from its watery bed, I am approached by a tall, elderly gentleman. He tells me that he observed my enjoyment of yesterday's dance lesson with pleasure and asks if I, like him, am travelling alone … At breakfast, a short, elderly gentleman joins me at my table and proceeds to enumerate the advantages of living on the Isle of Man.

And, as I am getting ready for choir, another elderly gentleman (vaguely familiar-looking) stops by to enquire if our exercise class is making my muscles ache as well.
 What's this? Did I lose my invisibility cloak? It seems that I can no longer go unnoticed, invisible as middle-aged women tend to be. Among these passengers, more advanced in years, I find myself returned to the category of the young. What a surprising and – one has to admit it – pleasant experience! A great pity then that I feel no need for an elderly gentleman by my side, however charming he may be. In love with independence, a move to the 'Isle of Man' is just not going to happen.

(*Solo traveller's tip: If you are not truly solitary by nature, a cruise may provide opportunities to change your single status. There will be others looking for company or love, and events such as the regular coffee mornings for solo travellers support this.)

Unexpectedly, it is the Indian staff who succeed in making me feel as special as a princess. Every day, their kind and respectful ways inspire me to make an effort to look my best. It is a pleasure to see their friendly smiles, and to be treated with such attentive courtesy. God bless them all!

(*Cruiser's tip: Don't forget that these men and women live in cramped quarters far below and work long shifts for very little pay to make your life of ease, pleasure and luxury possible. They are to be treated with respect, kindness and courtesy in return.)

After a couple of hours of swimming and sunbathing on the increasingly busy Lido Deck, the unaccustomed sunshine is fizzing around under my skin. Now it is time to retire to my peaceful cabin for a long siesta. This is such a healthy habit that I intend to make it part of my day whenever possible. My hankering for a spell of rest in the afternoon, impossible to indulge in until now, is easily fulfilled in the context of this cruise.

To mark today's date of Friday, the 13th, I somehow manage to lose my most important accessory: the cruise card. And although I search in all likely and some not-so-likely places, it remains lost. How very strange – I never lose anything! Leandro, my ever-helpful cabin steward, advises to obtain a new card from Reception. This turns out to be easy enough. I am told to destroy one of my cards if the other one should resurface – but, inexplicably and mysteriously, it never will.

(*Cruiser's tip: Get yourself one of those plastic card covers that clip to a lanyard and can be worn around the neck. Of course these handy items can be bought onboard. Keep this ID card with you at all times, especially when going ashore, for you need it to get back on the ship.)

I enjoy watching the Reception team at work, for these well-educated young people (all of them Indian, of course) seem to me like a host of friendly angels, heaven-sent to sort out problem after problem from dawn till dusk and well into the night. Dealing with a never-ending stream of complaints, they remain smiling, courteous and patient at all times. But how do they do it? While queueing at their desk, some of the quibbles I overhear would fray the nerves of a saint.

The sea is livelier today, stippled with white-crested waves, but Aurora continues to sail along smoothly and steadily.

I notice that I am indeed getting used to the motion, and – *hurray* – my inner ears and stomach remain unaffected.

In the afternoon, the cruise director hosts a chat show with our captain. He tells us about his formative years and shares a few glimpses of his childhood. One snapshot shows him as a baby on his first voyage at sea, asleep in a drawer of his father's sea chest, and another as a cute toddler filling his little bucket from a tap on deck.

Born into a naval family, one might say that seawater was in his blood from the start, and now he gives us a brief summary of his rise through the ranks. Asked by a member of the audience which vessel of the P&O fleet would be his dream ship to command, the captain replies without missing a beat, "The one I am on right now."

He too is among those who have nothing but praise for Aurora. But the following session of Questions-and-Answers reminds me of unpleasant Parents' Evenings experienced at school, because a couple of malcontents now puncture the amiable mood with petty issues and complaints. Everyone else, disagreeing with what is being said but unsure how to voice this, becomes the silent majority that is overruled.

Unlike a teacher, the captain has absolute authority on his ship and does not have to enter into any discussion if he deems it unnecessary, but this does not save him from being heckled. From past experience I can't help but feel for him, and to meet this familiar situation here is quite unexpected.

The captain stands his ground, but the general feeling that a bucket of cold water has been thrown over the event is upsetting … How ill-mannered some people are! Surely the captain does not deserve such treatment in return for giving up his time to entertain us?

Tonight is a formal dinner. I choose a cocktail dress of black-and-gold lace. Lacking a necklace to complete the outfit, I stop by the Mayfair boutique *en route* to the restaurant, since they carry tasteful costume jewellery as well as the real stuff. At once I find the right accessory at the attractive price of nine pounds and, fully attired, make my way to dinner.

(*World cruiser's tip: It is not necessary to begin your cruise fully equipped. You will find so many nice things to buy on your way around the world that it is better to leave room in your luggage.)

Our table is on great form tonight. Conversation flows and loud laughter erupts frequently. We even get inquisitive and envious looks from other tables, where people seem to have little to talk and nothing to laugh about.

My choice of dishes begins with a starter of plum tomatoes with mozzarella and basil, followed by a tasty pumpkin-and-coconut soup, a tender partridge with mixed vegetables, rounded off by a delicious cherry tart with white chocolate ice cream. Savouring each course, I wonder briefly about the positive verdict of the gym scales earlier.

After dinner I accompany Martha to the theatre and a cabaret performance by a dynamic lady singer, but we both like the music of the Kool Blue trio better. They are playing in the Crow's Nest bar where we go to enjoy a nightcap and a companionable chat. Towards midnight, pleasantly tired from another long and peaceful day at sea, we return to our cabins which Martha, searching in vain for the English term, charmingly calls "our huts".

And none of us are yet aware that an unlucky cruise ship, the Costa Concordia, capsized this evening – though it will be the number one topic in the days to come.

Day 11 ~ Saturday, 14th January 2012 ~ sunrise: 6.33am ~ sunset: 5.54pm ~ wind: E 3, gentle breeze ~ weather: sunny ~ temperature: 29°C ~ time zone: GMT-4 ~ distance travelled since Madeira: 2,651 nautical miles ~ in total: 3,975 nautical miles

St Lucia

I am looking forward to seeing St Lucia again after nearly thirty years. It was the setting of my first holiday romance, my island in the sun, a first impression of the Caribbean and the place where I first set eyes on an ocean liner. Right here in Castries Harbour where we are berthed now! I recall how impressed I was by the huge ship with its aura of luxury and world travel ... and of course I had no inkling then that I would one day return to this same place on just such a ship. It feels like having come full circle.

We board our coach for the 'St Lucia by Land and Sea' tour and set off down the west coast with a lively young tour guide. Our first stop is a small fishing village where we are invited to look around by ourselves. Pretty, colourful little houses cannot disguise the essential poverty that is shown more bluntly by ramshackle huts, squeezed into the narrow spaces between them. A few skinny dogs roam the unpaved streets while chickens scratch in the seaweeds on the beach. Behind a line of makeshift souvenir stalls, a lone fisherman is gutting fish by the pier.

As I wander along, I am approached by an unhealthy-looking Rastaman wearing a steel drum on a fraying strap around his neck. With a broken-toothed smile he asks for my favourite tune and indicates that he will play it for me.

To please him, I choose *Jammin'* by Bob Marley and refrain from mentioning Mozart's piano trios. My choice meets with nods of approval from a group of curious, idle men gathered nearby, but it proves far too difficult for the musician. He switches to 'No Woman No Cry' with hardly more success and it becomes clear that the instrument just serves as a prop to get talking to tourists. Abandoning his feeble attempts at music, he comments volubly on my "so friendly face, lovely smile and gorgeous figure ..."

What woman would not be pleased to hear it? After having proclaimed his admiration of my person, he goes on to enquire, "You married?"

"I was."

"Maybe you want Caribbean husband for full St Lucia experience?"

"No, thank you," I say. "I'm done with marriage."

My response draws a laugh from the onlooking men, but the Rastaman expresses his regret with a sorrowful shake of his dreadlocks. I give him a dollar bill for his music. Out of a teacher's habit I almost add, "Well done, keep practising!" But I desist, and more verbal lovemaking follows me all the way back to the coach.

This is how I remember the men of St Lucia! In this respect, nothing seems to have changed in thirty years and even now every foreign woman is seen as a potential ticket to a better life. What is considerably different, however, is the effect such an approach has on me today. I well recall the feelings of embarrassment and acute discomfort which keen black men had caused with their relentless and intrusive interest in my young-girl person. Feeling vulnerable, threatened and overwhelmed, the only thing I could think of was to respond with a spiky harshness, hoping in vain that it would protect me and send them away; but now I find that I can meet this kind of banter with a relaxed cheerfulness that arises from a self-confidence I would have given much to possess at the time ... Certainly, in *this* respect a lot has changed in thirty years!

One of the male souvenir stallholders now remarks that I am "definitely not British". This is surprising, given the fact that I just arrived with a coachload of Brits, and I ask how he can tell. He struggles to find the right words, but it seems to come down to basic human knowledge. Of course people who live by tourism get much practice in assessing foreign visitors, but I suspect a tell-tale sign might be the fact that I am the only woman wearing a dress and a light shawl, not shorts and a T-shirt. (I happen to believe that such sporty garments should only be worn by the young and the fit, and the sad proof of this theory can be seen all around.)

We drive into the mountains, past the volcanic twin cones of the Pitons, St Lucia's famous landmark. The road is narrow, steep and winding, but our driver has excellent control of his vehicle and manoeuvres with great skill.

    A stroll around the beautiful botanical gardens by the Diamond Waterfall shows us St Lucia's lush rainforest vegetation. Colourful tropical flowers thrive along a stream of health-giving water rising from the volcanic substrata of the island, and a series of small concrete pools tells of former days when bathing in these waters was more popular.

    Our lunch, a wonderful buffet with a selection of local dishes, is set out at the idyllic Morne Coubaril estate where graceful girls in national dress serve the food with beaming smiles as we settle down at long tables under a shading roof. This roof covers a terrace that is open to the lovely grounds on all sides.

Over the meal I get talking to a new set of people and learn their names, and so the circle of familiar faces among the passenger community expands daily. Topic number one is yesterday's accident of the cruise ship Costa Concordia, of which few details are known yet.

After lunch there is time for shopping on the premises and, recalling its excellent skincare properties, I buy a bottle of homemade coconut oil and the first postcards for friends and family. A little bird is perching on the revolving stand of cards and inclines its head to eye my selection.

Onwards we go and see "the world's only drive-in volcano" above Soufrière, where boiling mud and fumaroles spring from the ground and spread their sulphurous smell. This is the last stop on our land tour, and now we switch to a large catamaran for the return journey along the coast. Our swim stop in the bay of Anse Cochon attracts shell vendors' boats and another exchange along the lines of "Where you from? You not British ... You married?"

James is a big, intense fellow and obviously the boss of the shell-selling venture. One would struggle to imagine a more alpha-type male. He is eager to talk to me and returns repeatedly after having been called away on business. Once I succeed in steering him away from the date-and-mate angle, we have an interesting chat about various aspects of life in St Lucia. I am pleased to discover that I am able to navigate the undercurrent of 'me keen man, you desirable woman' with skill – and without any relevant practice in the past decades.

This unexpected feeling of easy self-assurance when faced with a situation I used to find so unmanageable is a surprise that makes my day.

Now James informs me that it is not often he meets "a good person" and delves into his boat for two fists full of shells. They are a gift, he says, something to remember him by, and regrets that we won't be meeting "in a hotel, to talk some more ..."

Of course all of his mates and half of my boat have been following our conversation with interest. As the catamaran pulls away, a fellow passenger remarks, "He would have come aboard to dance with you in another minute!"

A turn around Marigot Bay reveals the great change that took place here over the years. It is no longer as I remember it – a beautiful, unspoilt inlet with a simple but wonderful little restaurant that was only accessible by a rickety ferry. Here, with family and friends, I had spent the most magical evening of my young life as the sunset coloured the sky and the stars came out one by one in the falling darkness ... but now buildings are dotted all over the hillsides, yachts are anchored throughout the bay in dense rows and the magic is gone. In fact, but for the familiar name I would not have recognized the place.

On the final section of our boat trip, the rum punch kicks in and people begin to dance to modern reggae music, imitating our enthusiastic tour guide. Cinnamon-flavoured coconut sweets are passed around as we bounce over waves and are showered with sea spray. Sunlight scintillates on the water, the scenic coast glides past, and far ahead gleams our destination: the gleaming bulk of Aurora that is always such a heartlifting sight.

By the time I am back on board, it is already late and I have to speed-write my postcards if they are to be ready in time. I run down to Reception and slap on some stamps, assisted by a clerk who is waiting to seal the mailbag.

Then I relax on the top deck, watching as our ship turns around almost on the spot and leaves the darkening harbour with its twinkling, colourful lights. As Aurora sets course for Curacao, I say farewell to dear old St Lucia and wonder if I shall ever see her shores again.

Day 12 ~ Sunday, 15th January 2012 ~ sunrise: 6.42am ~ sunset: 6.16pm ~ sea state: slight ~ wind: N 5, fresh breeze ~ weather: sunny ~ temperature: 27°C

Things To Do

Still rather tired from yesterday's long excursion, I decide to indulge in a day of nothing but rest, relaxation and leisure. Instead of exercising, swimming and singing, I pass the time in the library, writing down my impressions of yesterday's tour and drawing a few sketches with Mozart's piano trios plugged into my ears.

Later I nip to the Medina for lunch and then lie down in my 'hut' for a siesta. By now, the sun is strong on deck. I would not want to join the rows of bronzing flesh up there, laid out on their loungers as if on a grill and headed for a mahogany tan, or possibly skin cancer.

(*Cruiser's tip: Pack enough sunscreen or sunblock. The prices on board or abroad will not compare favourably to those at home. Do

enjoy the sunshine, but remember that sunburn is the number one cause of a spoilt cruise experience.)

At dinner, Martha tells me of a Dutch gentleman whom she had befriended earlier: in his seventies, distinguished, tall, slim and handsome. Apparently he had observed me as I was drawing in the library and expressed a wish to meet me. And indeed, after dinner he comes to our table to introduce himself. We chat for a while, but he manages the rare feat of irritating me within the short space of the first two minutes of our acquaintance with his boastful manner. As a result I have absolutely no wish to spend more time with him, as he so clearly hopes.

I excuse myself as soon as possible and hasten to my cabin-hut, longing to be with my notebook and looking forward to more writing. Isn't it satisfying to have some kind of meaningful task, even on a cruise? It seems that, despite my best intentions, I cannot be completely idle after all.

(*World cruiser's tip: If you have a hobby that fits a long cruise, all the better. Bring your knitting, your embroidery or your paint box along and enjoy hours of uninterrupted delight. And you may find plenty of time to indulge your passion for bridge, poker or chess, for scrapbooking or line dancing in the company of likeminded fellows.)

Day 13 ~ Monday, 16th January 2012 ~ sunrise: 7.02am ~ sunset: 6.30pm ~ wind: SE 4, moderate breeze ~ weather: partly cloudy, rain showers ~ temperature: 26°C ~ distance travelled since St Lucia: 486 nautical miles ~ in total: 4,461 nautical miles

Curaçao

All through the night I awake at hourly intervals, feeling restless. By five o'clock I conclude that there is no point in trying to capture sleep while it flees me, so I get up to haunt the top deck. In the darkness a large, illuminated ship can be seen, passing in the distance, and far ahead the lights of Curacao indicate land. I brought a few biscuits to nibble and take care to put their empty wrappers securely in my pocket.

(*Cruiser's tip: For ecological and security reasons, it is forbidden to throw anything over board. Bottles with or without a message, sweets wrappers, food or even a cigarette end, flicked into the sea but sucked by a draft into the open cabin window below – each one could be your ticket to disembarkation at the next port.)

Almost alone in the restaurant for my early breakfast, I sit by the window and watch as another dawn breaks and Aurora approaches a new harbour. With a cup of green tea in one hand and a croissant in the other I survey the landscape as it unfolds slowly in the distance. Really, this has to be the most relaxing way to travel!

The morning is overcast, warm and very humid. As we are getting ready to go ashore, a heavy rain shower pours down, but then, by the time we are boarding our coaches, the sun breaks through the clouds once more.

Today we have a very pretty young black female driver who handles the large coach like a man. She is shy and quiet, but tour guide Carla is a stout, maternal and exuberant woman who clearly loves her job and welcomes us to Curacao with joy and pride. She will teach us many interesting facts about the island's colonial past as a part of the Dutch Antilles.

Our first stop is at a neat museum, housed in a colonial family mansion with wonderfully crafted baroque wooden door frames. There are household items, maps and pictures from colonial times on display, and an unusual instrument called a Carillion.

The main exhibit is housed in an outbuilding. It is the front part of the first Dutch aeroplane to cross the Atlantic in 1934 – a rather small and frail-looking piece of engineering. The account of this nerve-wracking flight is told on several panels that line the walls. It is hard to believe that this tiny plane survived a long-distance flight in one piece, braving weather conditions that were grim by all accounts.

We drive through Willemstad into the countryside. At a salt lake we can see a flock of flamingos that arrived from Venezuela and settled in these former Salinas.

"They tired of Mr Chavez, you know," Carla remarks with a mischievous smile.

But the highlight of our tour are the Hato Caves, carved into the coral rock of the former sea bed that rose in the course of geologic time to form this island. Tiny bats, hanging upside-down, cluster above our heads in family groups. Some begin to flutter about, disturbed by the torch and our presence.

These coral rock caves are very porous. Water trickles and drips through many fissures as another subtropical rain shower pours down outside. But although this cave system is comparatively small, it contains very good specimens of stalactites and stalagmites, as well as flowrock formations in the shape of giant jellyfish.

The local guide points out a series of rounded domes in the ceiling and explains that these are the signature of a sea cave, hollowed out by an endless succession of waves as they lapped against the cave's roof for thousands of years. In the outer cave, this roof has been blackened by smoke ... smoke from the torches and fires lit by runaway slaves who sought refuge here, some two hundred and sixty years ago, but even this hiding place underground could not save them from being captured and put to death.

We leave the cave and its reminder of a dark chapter in the island's history behind and get a good view over the wooded hillside that slopes down to the sea. At first glance the treetops look inconspicuous, but after a while and with some prompting from our guide we notice several iguanas. These large lizards are sunning themselves lazily on the top branches and look like miniature dragons. To Europeans, this is a fascinating sight.

And on we go, to the Chobolobo Liqueur Factory where we are shown how the famous Curacao is made from orange peel. We learn that the Dutch colonists were disappointed and frustrated when their imported orange trees would not produce sweet fruit in the perpetual heat. Nevertheless, they found a use for their harvest of bitterness and the result was this potent liqueur.

We are shown how heaps of orange peel are sliced, dried, boiled, fermented and distilled to a liquid, as clear as water but containing over 30% of alcohol. Food colouring is added for those well-known jewel colours, and all colours have the same flavour. I take Carla's word for it, for nothing could induce me to try them. I buy some 'Alcolado Glacial' instead, a mint-green mentholated splash lotion, advertised as "air conditioning in a bottle" and handy in the tropics.

Carla is a truly lovely lady, a reporter who also guides tours and educates tourists in the history of her homeland, and she is very pleased with me because I am able to answer any question she puts to us on various topics. (Oh, those teachers!) Now she exclaims with astonishment and praise because I supply the name of the highly toxic apple-like tree, the *Manzanilla*, and I am surprised myself that I remember it after all these years. (It had been one of the first things I was taught upon arrival in the Caribbean when Mother, sharing my fondness for plants, warned me of the deadly danger this innocent-looking tree brings to tropical beaches.)

After this comparatively short excursion I spend a few hours wandering the streets of Willemstad by myself. The Queen Emma pontoon bridge is an interesting feature: known as the 'Swinging Old Lady', she swings aside once in a while to let ships pass in and out of the inner harbour. Crossing over from *Otrobanda* – 'the other side' – I study the colourful rows of buildings and the high arc of the Queen Juliana Bridge, all of it neat and Dutch and picturesque, and photographed hundreds of times a day.

I decide to send a postcard to my son from every port stop on my journey around the world, as far as it is possible. The local post office is easily found and I think it best to post the card here, rather than risk missing the ship's mailbag. Because of the political changeover going on at the time of writing, the island does not yet have proper stamps and uses plain white stickers with a simple bar code instead. This is disappointing after the colourful and very appealing stamps of St Lucia, but hey – one cannot hurry the political process, especially in the Caribbean!

    I also learn that one may pay with US dollars on the island, although change is given in the local currency only. So, what to do with my fistful of guilders? I begin to look around for likely items, but nearly all the shops in the area sell trashy clothes and shoes at fairly steep prices. There is not much else of interest, but in the end I buy a lovely card that shows an antique map of the island.

Returning to the ship, I pass the stalls that line the quayside once more and buy a small, decorative metal gecko painted in iridescent colours from a dour-looking black woman. My efforts to chat are blocked by her deadpan expression. But when I offer her my remaining guilders on top of the asking price, her face breaks into a smile at last; she clasps my hand warmly with both of hers and nods wordlessly.

(*Cruiser's tip: As a rule, prices for items of the same kind will drop progressively as their distance to the dock area increases. When going ashore, don't buy at the first stall, but check out its prices and compare them to other stalls you will see along the way. That first seller will still be there when you return to the ship.)

Now I am hailed by a grey-bearded Rasta musician who has taken post in one of the stalls to sell CDs and pass the time of day with two companions and their instruments. He calls out to me, "Hello, lovely lady! I was admiring you when you walked by earlier. Where you from?"

    I reveal my origins, upon which he promptly bursts into music and improvises a flattering reggae song about my person. The wonky rhymes of his lyrics make me laugh out loud ... Well, what would *you* rhyme with Switzerland, off the top of your head? This is not a bad way to attract buyers, I think, and am pleased to detect some Caribbean spirit on this neat and sober Dutch island at last.

Back on board, I am suddenly feeling faint with tiredness and hunger. The largely sleepless night is catching up with me, and to wait until dinnertime, to dress up and be sociable does not appeal in this state ... Clearly the situation calls for another brush with Room Service!

But this time my order is delivered without a hitch and, tucked up in my comfortable bed, I soon enjoy another good meal. French duck terrine with salad and Melba toast, Spaghetti Bolognese with a sprinkling of parmesan, and then a heavenly slice of warm Dutch apple pie with thick cream: international comfort food for the famished sightseer!

Day 14 ~ Tuesday, 17th January 2012 ~ sunrise: 6.24am ~ sunset: 6.02pm ~ sea state: moderate ~ wind: E 6, strong breeze ~ weather: sunny ~ temperature: 25°C ~ time zone: GMT-5

Sleepless

Is it all this crossing of time zones that is messing with my sleep? I awake once again at five o'clock and lie in the dark, listening to the faint, quiet hum of the ship's engines somewhere far below.

(*Cruiser's tip: The progressive changing of time zones will naturally interfere with your sleeping patterns, but because this process happens so much slower than by air travel, there will be no jetlag. Just go with the flow and welcome bouts of insomnia as a chance to watch the night sky, to read, meditate, draw or write.)

It is such a unique feeling to wake up realizing that one has been moving steadily across an ocean all night and heading for distant lands – in this case, Panama.

Soon I am at my favourite spot on the top deck once more, ready to greet the day. But a look at the ship's clocks alerts me to the fact that it is even earlier than I thought, for they have been set back by yet *another* hour. How did I miss that? (Cabin stewards leave a little card on the bedside table to alert us to the changing of time zones, and it is mentioned in the daily newsletter too.)

Unsurprisingly, there is no one else about. It is still dark, but the pale sickle moon hangs overhead in a nest of small dove-grey clouds. The air is balmy, the breeze slight and the sea peaceful. Slowly the clouds take on a pink tinge as another rosy-fingered dawn, our ship's namesake, gathers strength on the eastern horizon. Today there is a particularly delicate and artistic array of feathery clouds, and they catch the light and play with its subtle colours in a kind of visual dance that holds my gaze spellbound.

How different each sunrise appears! Every morning there is a new arrangement, a slight variation in the choreography of an as yet untried piece of heavenly music. And in all the millennia yet to come, there will be no other sunrise exactly like this one. They are just as individual as humans are, but infinitely more beautiful ... Now the sun's luminous disc rises from the sea, striped by thin bands of cloud and magnified by its proximity to the horizon.

I meet a couple of dinner companions at breakfast, and they enquire at once after my wellbeing. It turns out they were concerned when I did not show up for dinner last night and wondered what had happened to me: Did I jump ship? Elope? Or catch the dreaded norovirus? – No, it was nothing more dramatic than the need for an early night.

(*Solo traveller's tip: If you are not part of a couple or a group, other people – passengers, staff and crew alike – will observe your movements onboard and ashore, so be prepared for a good deal of interest, speculation and gossip. It will of course be assumed that you are looking for a partner and you may find this tedious. Confound expectations by calmly and cheerfully going about your business or – in the case of a world cruise – your pleasure.)

After a spell of writing in my "hut" I attend today's lecture on 'Buccaneers in the Caribbean'. Gwen and her friend are there too and we use this opportunity to catch up. Then the visiting professor begins to explain the difference between

Buccaneers, privateers and pirates. Being of course relevant to the topic, a good chunk of colonial history is thrown in for free, and his trenchant observations and dry humour make me chuckle throughout.

(*Cruiser's tip: Any offered lectures by guest speakers who are acknowledged experts in their field are usually entertaining and informative, and another very welcome way to stimulate the mind. Enrichment is the new buzzword in the cruise industry, so prepare to be enriched.)

Lunching with a set of unfamiliar people, I find the general conversation dire. Aimed at the cruise line, it is a chorus of complaints about allowing the evil norovirus aboard and not allowing *us* to visit Acapulco. It really makes me appreciate our merry dinner circle! I remain silent, not wishing to give offence, though I am tempted to point out that toothpicks are available and there is no need to use one's fingers. How gross! Table manners seem to operate on the same level as the prevailing dress sense, for at lunchtime many passengers come to the restaurant in a T-shirt, shorts and flip-flops, in striking contrast to the beautifully turned-out waiters. This means that the restaurant personnel appears altogether more elegant and dignified than the clientele.

(*Cruiser's tip: Remember that your comportment automatically reflects on the image and reputation of your country, so strive to be a good ambassador.)

In the afternoon, as I wait for another ballroom dance lesson to begin, a dance partner appears unexpectedly. Lawrence must be in his late sixties. Of just the right height and nice-looking, he also has a calm and courteous manner. We move smoothly through the sequence of the square tango and enjoy it so much that we agree to make dancing together a fixture in our daily plan until he leaves the ship in Sydney. He informs me that his wife is with him, but is unable to dance for medical reasons; that she won't mind, and that his usual dance partner was unable to come on this cruise ... How perfect is that?

(*Cruiser's tip: Not everyone on a world cruise is actually going around the world. Only about a third of the passengers are in for the circumnavigation, so be prepared for early departures.)

After dinner I watch a film with Angelina Jolie and admire her remarkable beauty from every angle. I would say that she is one of the very few who can bear comparison with a sunrise. And yet, as we are leaving the cinema in a crowd, a woman remarks, "She has a weird chin."

How quick people are to find fault! Particularly with all that is great, or good, or beautiful ... and how reluctant they are to appreciate other people's gifts! It makes my heart sink with sadness.

Day 15 ~ Wednesday, 18th January 2012 ~ sunrise: 6.42am ~ sunset: 6.19pm ~ wind: NW 2, light breeze ~ weather: sunny ~ temperature: 29°C ~ distance travelled since Curacao: 687 nautical miles ~ in total: 5,148 nautical miles

Panama Canal

The wake-up call is set for five o'clock, but by three in the morning I am unable to return to sleep. The excitement of thinking about the imminent canal transit keeps me awake until, at last, the ringing phone signals it is time to get up.

(*Cruiser's tip: It is not necessary to bring an alarm clock. Your bedside telephone can be programmed easily with wake-up calls. But if you are using your mobile phone for this, make sure to set it to flight mode, for you don't want to incur hefty roaming charges at sea.)

By half-past five I am on deck and watch as Aurora heads for the lights of Colón. There are already quite a few people about, Gwen among them. She is a keen boatwoman and explains that in US waters the green and red buoys indicating starboard and portside are reversed. This is borne out by the lights that blink at the entrance to the Panama Canal, which we are now approaching. At a later date I shall request and receive more information on this point from the first officer:

"There are two buoyage systems in use throughout the world, both recognized by the International Association of Lighthouse Authorities. They are called IALA A and IALA B. The IALA A system, which is most common, has green buoys to starboard and red ones to port when entering port. IALA B, which is used by the USA

and Philippines (and a few others with strong US influence) has red buoys to starboard and green to port when entering port."

A nice gentleman is setting out chairs for his group in prime position and offers to fetch one for me as well. And so, as the sun rises and we enter the canal, I am seated in the front row above the ship's bow. All the while, more sleepy latecomers gather at our back and tetchy muttering is heard because they find themselves in the second or third row. (A saying about early birds and worms springs to mind.)

Now we draw near the Gatún Locks and are able to observe their workings closely as two very large vessels pass through ahead of us. One is an enormous automobile carrier of the largest size (called *Panamax*) that fits into these locks. I had never paused to think what kind of ships our cars might travel in on their way from one continent to another, and am amazed to see this huge floating box that only vaguely resembles a ship.

The time has come for Aurora to inch her way into the first lock chamber. I marvel at the fact that there is absolutely no waiting involved. Everything is so well planned and the ship's travelling speed so precisely calculated that it allows her to slot right into the endless chain of vessels that passes through this canal at every hour of every day throughout the year. This really is a place that never sleeps!

Now information on what is happening around us is broadcast from the bridge. We have already learnt quite a bit about the fascinating history of the Panama Canal from a port talk and a leaflet in our cabin, and now we hear more details of this unique feat of engineering. It is also interesting to learn about the transit fees. Each ship must pay according to its type and size. These transit slots are bought at auction and the starting price ranges from U$15,000 for 'regulars' to U$25,000 and U$35,000 respectively in the 'super' category. How much did P&O offer to secure our desirable daytime transit? This information is strictly confidential, but it is sure to be an impressive sum.

In a lecture at a later date, we learn that the Chinese are thinking of building another canal through Colombia, which would probably lower the cost through competition. But right now, Panama can ask pretty much any price – as long as it is less than the cost of a trip around Cape Horn.

In the meantime Aurora entered the first lock chamber and four 'mules' secured the ship fore and aft with steel cables, tied to their sturdy cabs. The big gates close behind her and water from the lock chamber ahead (recently vacated by the earlier ship) rushes down to raise us slowly to the next level. Inching Aurora into the second chamber, the dwarflike but powerful mules move alongside on rail tracks and keep her from bumping against the lock walls. The slots of space on either side of the ship are so narrow that, looking down her side, the water cannot be seen at all.

This process is repeated three times and heaves our vessel roughly twenty-six metres above the level of the sea. Now we pass out of the final lock and head into Gatún Lake. This lake had been dammed to form an integral part of the canal's artificial waterway, and at the time it was also the world's largest manmade reservoir. Gatún Lake is a calm, beautiful expanse of water, ringed with dense rainforest and dappled with small islands and big cargo ships.

(*World cruiser's tip: The ship's professional photographers alone may disembark to shoot the canal transit from land, and the photos and videos they produce make nice souvenirs.)

After a late breakfast I am ready to escape the fierce sun, the humid heat and the crowds on deck. But it must be said that we are very fortunate to have such clear skies, because it rains frequently and heavily in these parts.

The Crow's Nest bar has a splendid view across the ship's bow. Pleasantly cool and almost empty, it seems the ideal place to be. I settle down with my notebook, sipping tonic water and taking in the scenery as the ship finds its way through the maze of channels between wooded islands. Right now, this cruise is even better than I had imagined it!

We pass a boat service station and other buildings connected with the workings of the canal. An incredibly long freight train crosses a bridge that spans a sidearm of the lake and I count all of fifty wagons, each one loaded with two shipping containers and headed for the Pacific Coast.

Now the arc of the Centennial Bridge appears in the distance, built to relieve the bottleneck of the Pan-American Highway. Impressive numbers of vehicles cross over daily. This bridge spans the Gaillard Cut (alternatively called the Culebra Cut) – a channel that had to be blasted through the rocky neck of the Continental Divide.

We learn that, working here between 1881 and 1914, an estimated (because uncounted) 27,000 labourers lost their lives through either illness or accident. Malaria was a huge problem, and it was said that if you arrived to work here on Monday, you could expect to be dead by Friday. Such was the hardship of labour in those disease-ridden swamps.

Presently we come to the second set of locks, this time on the Pacific side. The skyscrapers of Panama City can be seen on the left, rising incongruously from the rainforest, and far ahead the Bridge of the Americas is traced delicately against the hazy sky. Once this bridge was part of the Pan-American Highway, but since the Centennial Bridge opened in 2004, the new bridge took over the official route.

The Bridge of the Americas, dating from 1962, is one of the most beautiful bridges I have seen. It is impressive to watch its graceful arc expand in size as we draw near, and to pass beneath it is also a thrilling moment. I indulge in the romantic notion that some of the cars overhead may actually be travelling from Tierra del Fuego to Alaska, or vice versa. (Only later do I find out about the sinister Darien Gap that interrupts the route in Colombia with a stretch of deadly and all but impassable jungle.)

An important fact is explained via broadcast: Here in Panama, the rainforest is strictly protected and preserved by the government. And why? Because the canal relies on the frequent and heavy rainfall its trees generate. Every day, gigantic amounts of water (somewhere in the region of fifty-two million gallons) leave Gatún Lake to rush through the locks, and they need to be replenished by the constant precipitation the country's rainforest provides. It is as simple as that: No forest – no rain, no canal – no business.

The opening of the canal in 1914 was overshadowed by the outbreak of the First World War, but it has been operating for almost precisely one hundred years at the time of writing and saves all transiting vessels a costly trip of roughly eight thousand miles around South America ... Indeed, Aurora made the voyage from Atlantic to Pacific in about ten hours.

Day 16 ~ Thursday, 19th January 2012 ~ sunrise: 7.17am ~ sunset: 6.42pm ~ sea state: calm ~ wind: 1, light airs ~ weather: sunny ~ temperature: 27°C

The Pacific

For the first time on this journey I awake *after* sunrise. From the breakfast table I look out on the Pacific Ocean which is doing its name justice today, being as calm and peaceful as the proverbial millpond. The only waves in sight are those spreading from Aurora's bow.

Then it is time for a special treat: a facial at the Oasis spa. Sandie is the senior beautician and her hands have the touch of a maternal angel. With gentle care she buffs, pats and massages my delighted and long neglected skin with scented lotions, creams and serums. Never having had a facial before, I see how one could get addicted to this kind of treatment, for I am soon drifting in a state of deep relaxation and bliss. The skin is radiant, and the mood is too.

By contrast, my first lunch at Marco Pierre White's much-hyped Café Bordeaux is rather disappointing. In the brochures one is told to expect nothing but the best, but the headwaiter places me at an uncomfortable table in the tight corner, and the table waiter splashes a copious amount of water beside my glass and does not bother to mop it up until I ask him to. The service does not compare favourably with the high standard I had encountered at the Medina and the Alexandria restaurant.

(*Cruiser's tip: Such specialty restaurants usually require advance reservation, though you may get a table at lunchtime if you are prepared to wait. Surcharges apply.)

Today's dance lesson is a considerable success, for I learn the quickstep sequence quickly from scratch, and this impresses Lawrence and moves him to sincere compliments. Maybe I missed my true calling as a ballroom dancer? Anyhow, it is really enjoyable and I wish I had started sooner.

On a sudden impulse I revisit the elegantly priced Mayfair boutique to try on the midnight-blue evening dress I have now been eyeing for several days. It fits perfectly, looks gorgeous and seems made for me, as a couple of other customers confirm with enthusiasm. Oh dear! This makes it almost impossible to return the garment to its hanger and walk away. But the price is more (and quite a lot more) than I ever paid for a dress, and how often would I be able to wear it? ... But in the end I decide to add it to my wardrobe. After all, it seems moderately priced when compared to the transit fee for the Panama Canal, and one does not often find something to wear that looks and feels so right. The ladies around the shop applaud my decision.

In one of his sardonic little alphabet poems, Hilaire Belloc pointed out that "living cheaply is its own reward." In the case of this lovely dress, and paraphrasing him, I would say that self-indulgence is its own reward too.

(*Cruiser's tip: There will be so many nice things to buy along the way that it will become ever more difficult to keep sight of the limits of budget and luggage. Unless money is of absolutely no importance, you will have much opportunity to practise iron self-control – and yet it is nice to treat yourself once in a while.)

Tonight there is a formal dinner, and a Black and White Ball in Carmen's. Dance partner Lawrence introduces me to two other ladies he has been dancing with on occasion, and then he dances with each of us in turn, according to our musical preferences. Yes, men who can dance are in great demand and short supply, here as anywhere.

Day 17 ~ Friday, 20th January 2012 ~ sunrise: 7.48am ~ sunset: 7.07pm ~ sea state: calm ~ wind: NE 5, fresh breeze ~ weather: sunny ~ temperature: 27°C

Hot Bamboo

Once again I am up at five o'clock for no good reason, and so I undertake the little bit of sewing that is needed to adjust another dress. That tedious task completed at last, I go up on deck to watch a sunrise over the Pacific Ocean for the first time. Then on to another spa appointment, for today I try the 'Hot Bamboo' massage that comes highly recommended. The physiotherapist Manuel (young, intelligent, gorgeous, Argentinean) begins the session by brushing my skin gently to increase circulation. He follows this with a massage and uses warm frangipani oil that has a sweet, enchanting scent. Then, finding just the right amount of pressure, he smoothes any knots, lumps and creases from my muscles with heated bamboo rods of various sizes. They roll on the planes of the body rather like a rolling pin on a lump of dough and their effect is deeply relaxing.

Manuel's trained hands move in a slow choreography perfected over time, the ancient body wisdom of the Far East flows through them, and the thoughtful towel-wrapping technique he employs means that his clients never feel chilly or exposed … What an extremely pleasant experience!

After fifty minutes of this mindful treatment he ends with a scalp massage and pulls strands of hair through his fingers, so that they may benefit from the precious oil as well. I find myself drifting in a state of such divine peacefulness that I can hardly bring myself to rise when the session is over.

As I had hoped, this cruise is proving a successful way of caring for body, soul and mind. "Indulgence is healing" is the motto of the Oasis spa. And indeed, after only a couple of treatments I notice that I have rarely felt so at home in my body, nor been so happy with myself.

Straight after the massage, still floating on a cloud of lovely frangipani scent, I flop into a seat at the Curzon theatre to enjoy another lecture by the knowledgeable and entertaining professor. Today he takes us through the early history of the Panama Canal ventures – all the ones that failed.

He is witty in an irreverent way and fond of acerbic remarks such as "But sincerity is no excuse for stupidity ..." regarding the way in which the celebrated French engineer Lesseps had approached the initial canal project.

Fortified by such healthy mental stimulation, I admit to myself that I have grown tired of the tediously repetitive lunchtime table talk and am delighted to find that the head-waiter is willing, upon request, to direct me to a small table where I can enjoy my meal without any company.

(*Solo traveller's tip: In the intensely social setting of a cruise ship you may have to make your need for solitude a priority at times. The staff aim to please and will strive to fulfil any reasonable request – so just ask.)

Day 18 ~ Saturday, 21ˢᵗ January 2012 ~ sunrise: 7.14am ~ sunset: 6.21pm ~ sea state: calm ~ wind: NW 3, gentle breeze ~ weather: sunny ~ temperature: 26°C ~ time zone: GMT-6

No Acapulco

I went to bed early and slept extremely well, quite possibly because of the deeply relaxing 'Hot Bamboo' massage, but the clocks have been set back by another hour and I awake at three o'clock precisely. Somehow I just cannot get into a normal rhythm – not that it matters much. And so, Mozart's string quintets plugged into my ears, I go on deck to watch another sunrise ... What a sublime start to the day!

After my preferred healthy breakfast I visit the gym. (Regular exercise has now become much less of a struggle.) After twenty minutes on a type of treadmill that works on thighs and hips (heart rate: 147) I join another 'Stretch and Relax' class. Already an increase in flexibility is noticeable and the scales register a definite loss of kilograms. I check this delightful fact several times, just to make sure that the ship's sway is not distorting the reading ... but no, the ship is not swaying today, for Aurora flies across the smooth and glassy sea like a bird on the wing.

(*World cruiser's tip: Yes, it is indeed possible to lose weight on a long cruise. Eat moderately and healthily, take the stairs instead of the elevator, make use of the gym equipment, the Jacuzzi and the pool, take part in those daily exercise sessions, walk or run laps on the designated deck – and after only a couple of weeks you will be thrilled to notice very motivating results.

If you really set your mind to it, you could use a cruise to get slim and fit, benefitting from the help of friendly fitness coaches at no extra cost. Alternatively, you might be one of those cruisers who gain 6-7 pounds per week on average.)

Now I swim a couple of lengths in the Riviera pool that is conveniently empty of people at this early hour. It is another bright morning and, since we have been steaming north for two days, the sun's rays are beating down with less force. Drying off in the sunshine is agreeable and I treat the skin to some fine St Lucian coconut oil.

But then the captain's voice addresses us from the bridge. He explains that there is a crew drill in progress and all passengers are requested and required to return to their cabins. We are to look out for suspicious parcels and report any sightings to Reception. A bottle of champagne will be awarded to whoever finds such a parcel, planted around the ship by security officers so that the crew may rehearse the proper procedures.

To most passengers this is a nuisance, but – in view of Costa Concordia's tragic accident – it is reassuring to see that the ship's safety is being taken so seriously.

(*Cruiser's tip: No matter how irksome such requests may seem to you – remember that on any ship the captain's word is the law. Therefore comply graciously and don't grumble.)

My cabin turns out to be without parcels of any kind, and so I am free to return to my sunlounger. The captain's voice keeps us informed of the exercise in progress while groups of the ship's staff and crew in lifejackets make their way to various assembly points.

At eleven o'clock I attend the astute professor's next talk. Today he is treating us to an outline of the "murky and dark" political and financial dealings in connection with the construction of the Panama Canal. He has many a trenchant comment on the imperialism of the United States, but states in fairness that no other nation could have built the canal at that time – this being "one of the largest and most difficult engineering projects ever undertaken."

After thus exercising body and mind, it is time to cater for the soul with a choir session. 'I will follow Him' and 'One Voice' were tricky to learn but are beginning to sound much better. These melodies, sure to remain in my head for the rest of the day, are not nearly as annoying as that old chestnut 'Delilah' – a song seemingly designed to make one want to leap overboard.

We were scheduled to visit Acapulco today, but this port stop has been cancelled. A letter announcing this change of plan was sent to every passenger before the beginning of our cruise, but many have still not come to terms with the fact. The letter had stated that it was "due to security concerns" – a wording that was possibly a bit too sparse, given the upset this cancellation was likely to cause.

Upon receiving the letter, I googled 'Mexico News' and gathered that this place is going to the proverbial dogs, its social fabric, economy and tourism industry effectively destroyed by brutal drug wars.

Violence and killings in and around Acapulco during several months prior to our cruise made P&O deem a visit unsafe, yet passengers still complain about the loss of this port stop on a daily basis, seemingly unable to follow the cruise line's reasoning. But is it not entirely understandable that this risk cannot be taken? Imagine the hail of complaints if any passengers should get hurt, or killed …!

Besides, such cancellations are a clear signal to countries in violent turmoil that they have to get their act together before other people will come and visit.

(*Cruiser's tip: In the case of such cancellations, do swallow your disappointment and count your blessings. Changes to the initial itinerary are likely to occur on any voyage of great duration. There will always be a valid reason, dictated by circumstances beyond the cruise line's and the captain's control, so it is best to accept any change of plans without complaints.)

In today's dance lesson we learn the Mayfair Quickstep. It is good fun once our feet have mastered that lively sixteen-bar sequence, and before long our steps and movements match the music smoothly. We all glide around the dance floor and enjoy this informal taste of the magic of ballroom dancing with happy feelings.

As I return to my cabin-hut to get ready for dinner, I notice a suspicious parcel, placed squarely on my bed. What could it be? I am not expecting any deliveries. Is this the work of a tardy security officer? Should I report it to Reception?

Closer inspection reveals that this dark-blue box of elegant design is sporting the P&O crest, so I cast suspicion to the winds and look inside. The parcel contains a stylish porcelain tea set for two, a present from P&O to their world cruisers ... What a nice gesture – and how perfectly timed to smoothe Acapulco-ruffled feathers!

Day 19 ~ Sunday, 22ⁿᵈ January 2012 ~ sunrise: 7.32am ~ sunset: 6.56pm ~ sea state: slight ~ wind: N2, light breeze ~ weather: sunny ~ temperature: 22°C

Ocean Thoughts

Peaceful sleep was enjoyed, and for much longer than usual. Maybe a more normal rhythm is setting in at last?

At breakfast I look out across the smooth surface of an ocean that reflects light like a gigantic mirror, and as my gaze is drawn towards the horizon, I try to imagine that half a planet of water is lying before me – a hemisphere of ocean, its vast plane stretching out almost forever ... but the mind, as they say, boggles.

"And on all sides nothing but the bloody ocean ...!" is how someone expressed it who was probably travelling in less favourable circumstances.

It occurs to me that we human beings in our frail and vulnerable condition have found ever better ways of taking the environment that is essential to our lives into those realms that are by their very nature inaccessible and hostile to us; that the ships we build are little crusts of 'Earth', of home, carrying adventurous travellers over the death-plains of oceans or into deep space ... how staying at home and tending the garden has never been enough to quench man's thirst for the Great Unknown.

I do not think that the German poet Goethe ever crossed an ocean, yet there are lines in 'Faust' (his most famous drama) that capture the essence of what I see before me perfectly, and so I recite them to myself as I wander around the deck, my eyes trained on those vast spaces:

Mephistopheles:
"Und hättest du den Ozean durchschwommen,
Das Grenzenlose dort geschaut,
So sähest du doch Well' auf Welle kommen,
Selbst wenn es dir vorm Untergange graut.
Du säh'st doch etwas – sähest in der Grüne
Gestillter Meere schweifende Delfine;
Säh'st Wolken ziehen, Sonne, Mond und Sterne –
Nichts wirst du seh'n in ewig leerer Ferne.
Den Schritt nicht spüren, den du tust,
Nichts Festes finden, wo du ruhst ... "

Faust:
"Nur immer zu – wir wollen es ergründen.
In deinem Nichts hoff' ich das All zu finden!"

My translation would be:

Mephistopheles:
"And had you swum across the ocean,
Perceiving the infinite there,
Still you would have seen wave after wave approaching,
Even as you dreaded your doom.
You would see *something* –
Dolphins roaming calm green seas;
Clouds drifting by, sun, moon and stars –
But you shall see nothing in eternally empty space.
Not feel the step you take,
Nor find firm ground on which to rest ..."

Faust:
"Well then – we shall fathom the mystery.
In your Great Void I hope to find the All!"

It is time for my third session with the acupuncturist. Now that we have met a few times, we talk on a less formal note. Rodrigo tells me more about the points he is treating, and without attempt at flattery observes that the condition of my skin and body make me appear about ten years younger than my actual age. How cheering! So it seems that although teaching has taken its toll, the ravages of stress and self-neglect may not be irreversible.

Upon request and for the record, Rodrigo takes a few pictures of me as a 'Pacific pin cushion'. After the session we sit and chat for a while, and he relates how a sudden onset of excruciating back pain completely changed his life. Major surgery loomed, scary but inevitable as he believed. Just in time, a friend told him about Chinese medicine, and there he found a non-invasive cure of his problem. This life-altering experience made him quit his job as a well-paid high-level accountant to train as a healer, for he wanted to help other people with the same treatments that cured him.

In turn, I tell him how I come to be travelling around the world at this point in my life. Rodrigo shares my opinion that the fact that I will have neither home nor job nor money when I return from this cruise is really nothing to worry about, for things will happen if given the chance and "it is important to have time for yourself."

Having plenty of time for myself is indeed the true luxury of this cruise, and being free to decide at any moment what I would like to do (or not to do) is an unaccustomed pleasure. Nothing at all is dictated by the needs of other people, and no other routine is given than the one I choose to invent for myself, according to the promptings of the moment and my inner voice.

Day 20 ~ Monday, 23rd January 2012 ~ sunrise: 7.15am ~ sunset: 6.16pm ~ sea state: rough ~ wind: NW 7, moderate gale ~ weather: cloudy ~ temperature: 19°C ~ time zone: GMT-7

Chinese New Year

After a long spell of calm seas, a Beaufort force 7 gale throws up white-crested waves that rock the ship and once again induce motion discomfort. I hold out through another talk by the witty professor – 'Why Buccaneering never took off in the Pacific' – but then I withdraw to my homely cabin-hut, swallow some tablets and lie down in the dark.

Another sleep-deprived night is making itself felt and I decide to spend the rest of the day in bed, even though this means I shall miss the final rehearsal of the Aurora Vocalists before our performance tonight. A brief phone message left for Lawrence informs him that I am unable to dance today. A great shame really, for it is to be one of those Latin Jam sessions I enjoy so much.

A long spell of sleep does the trick and when evening comes I am feeling quite recovered. We celebrate Martha's birthday with champagne and some professional group photographs, and then a bevy of waiters gathers to sing 'Happy Birthday'. I enjoy dinner despite the heaving of the ship, and our choir performances also. Carmen's is packed with an enthusiastic audience at six and eight o'clock and our choir pulls out all the stops. – 'Delilah' never sounded better!

(*Cruiser's tip: Each ship has a team of commercial photographers who will take pictures of the passengers at dinners, birthdays and events unasked, and special portraits upon request. They also take

shots of the ports on your route. All of these pictures are exhibited in their gallery, but you are under no obligation to buy any unless you really like them. This photo service does not come cheap, but it is good value should you want professional pictures to show your friends and family later.)

Day 21 ~ Tuesday, 24*th* January 2012 ~ sunrise: 7.53am ~ sunset: 6.20pm ~ sea state: rough ~ wind: NE 6, strong breeze ~ weather: cloudy ~ temperature: 18°C

Sea Legs

Finally, a whole night of unbroken sleep! Other passengers tell me that rough seas and the attendant noises kept them awake, but thankfully I missed all that.

The Pacific, roused from its somnolence, continues to give us a bumpy ride. The great ship is heaving, thudding and shuddering in a manner that feels entirely familiar by now, but I am able to get up and move about without feeling nauseous. Have I found my sea legs at last?

At the shop I buy a set of the much-recommended acupressure wristbands, even though I no longer feel sick, for there could always be a next time.

(*Cruiser's tip: If you are prone to sea sickness, equip yourself with recommended tablets, with candied ginger or ginger sweets, with acupressure wristbands and so forth. They will all help to ease the initial misery, and eventually you too should get used to the ship's motion in all but the worst storms. Sniffing the rind of a freshly-

peeled orange may bring relief, and eating green apples is said to be a miracle cure – so be sure to stop by a fruit basket in good time.)

After eight consecutive days at sea, I find that I am looking forward to feeling solid ground beneath my feet. We have been steaming north for days now and the temperature has dropped quite noticeably. There will be no more sunbathing or swimming at present, but there are plenty of other things to do and to see, so boredom is not an option.

At dinner, another bottle of champagne graces our table. This time it is by courtesy of P&O, because Beryl is one of those passengers whose cabin has been soaked by the most recent leak. Water from other leaking pipes also drenched the Axminster of the corridor leading to my cabin, but this carpet has already been taken up and will soon be replaced with a dry one. On this ship, pipe leaks are apparently a common occurrence and no cause for concern or panic. (In these early days, complimentary champagne is awarded to sweeten the mood of those affected, but this will no longer be considered necessary on the later legs of the journey.)

Rows of suitcases and bags are lining the corridors today. Many passengers, Gwen and her friend among them, have reached their final destination and are going to disembark tomorrow. I feel sorry for them all and am glad that my own journey continues. Occasionally rough seas and frequently leaking water pipes are as nothing compared to the joys and pleasures of this cruise, and I really do not want to dwell on the unavoidable moment when it must come to an end.

Day 22 ~ Wednesday, 25th January 2012 ~ sunrise: 7.20am ~ sunset: 5.26pm ~ weather: cloudy ~ temperature: 16°C ~ time zone: GMT-8 ~ distance travelled since Panama: 3,286 nautical miles ~ in total: 8,434 NM

San Francisco

We reach San Francisco and pass under the subtly lit Golden Gate Bridge shortly after five o'clock, well before dawn, but of course I am on deck to see this impressive sight.

Maybe it is the cooler weather that makes me change my usual breakfast of fruit and yoghurt to one of scrambled eggs, sausage and baked beans on toast – or maybe I need to fortify myself for the scheduled US immigration procedure with face-to-face interviews. Spectacular rumours circulate the decks. Apparently once, on another cruise ship, bored passengers began to sing "Why are we waiting" – and this resulted in an eight-hour lockdown with iris scans and body searches. We have been earnestly advised not to make any kind of comment and to keep things running smoothly, for no one will be allowed to go ashore until the entire ship has been checked and cleared by the immigration officials.

(*Cruiser's tip: Take immigration formalities seriously and follow instructions to the letter. In this matter, more than in any other, consideration for others and compliance with requirements are of paramount importance.)

On my way to Reception to buy US stamps I notice a team of black-clothed police officers traversing the Atrium, complete with bulletproof vests, combat boots and stony expressions. This is clearly most serious business! Hopefully the Brits will be able to contain their raucous humour for a while, because

I recall Bill Bryson's observation that an attempt to joke with US immigration officials will lead straight to being escorted in handcuffs to a cell ... Speaking of which, ship's gossip has it that a couple of passengers are even now being held in the cells below deck. Their violent behaviour (a punch-up in the launderette, apparently) means that they are going to be set ashore in San Francisco and have to make their way home. Cruise ships have a zero-tolerance policy in such matters, probably to stop passengers from behaving like children in the playground.

(*Cruiser's tip: Be on your best behaviour! Any form of vandalism, violence, intimidation, stealing, verbal or sexual abuse, as well as insulting or impersonating the captain and his staff has immediate, serious consequences. Likewise all inappropriate pranks, sitting or standing on the railing, jumping from deck into the sea, scaling the facade to get into other people's cabins – basically, anything illegal or just being rowdy will see you escorted off the ship.)

But in the end I find the US immigration formalities not that intimidating. The whole process is meticulously organized and moves along smoothly. Yesterday, all passengers had received a letter of guidance, including a personal 'manifest number', and now we are called in groups of one hundred people to queue outside Vanderbilt's with our paperwork. US immigration officials are seated at little tables and check our passports and visa waiver forms. Both are inspected and stamped, and then the officers wish us a pleasant stay in the United States of America.

By half-past ten in the morning, all 1,850 passengers and about 850 crew members have been cleared and are free to go ashore.

My first tour of the day takes us through the city, over the Golden Gate Bridge and into the hills to visit the 'Muir Woods National Monument'. It is one of the last stands of uncut redwoods and is named after John Muir, the Scottish conservationist. The most ancient of these big trees are more than a thousand years old!

We learn about the lack of adequate technology that made logging in this steep-sided valley impossible in the days when all local redwood forests were converted into the booming town of San Francisco. And so a few redwood trees survived – unlike the town built from the precious wood, for its buildings went up in flames when earthquakes struck.

It is very still between these trees whose great trunks soar heavenward like the pillars of ancient cathedrals. Few shafts of sunlight filter down to the damp, dark and cool floor of the valley where they dapple sculpted bark and webbed layers of branches, twigs and needles.

"This is the best tree-lover's monument that could possibly be found in all the forests of the world. You have done me great honour, and I am proud of it ..." wrote Muir to William Kent, who had bought these woods and named them after the popular conservationist.

The gift shop here is a pleasant surprise. It stocks a range of unusual items, all made from responsibly sourced redwood, even the jewellery, but I cannot resist the beautiful cards, stickers and posters that bring back memories of my first career as a graphic designer.

We drive on to Sausalito and hear about its colourful history in which brothels, saloons and the smuggling of alcohol figured prominently during the days of the Prohibition. We are given time to wander about by ourselves, and I admire gorgeous handcrafted items with hefty dollar price tags that are displayed in the shop windows. Here, shopping seems to take place on a different level altogether!

Across the bay Aurora is be seen, berthed on Pier 39 and framed by the prison island of Alcatraz, the Bay Bridge and the attractive skyline of the city. I am pleased to see her white hull in the distance, and it makes me realize that I feel strongly connected to my floating temporary home.

Returning to the ship after my first tour, I have no more than forty-five minutes before my second tour of the day departs to explore 'Chinatown by Night'. Quickly I transfer my new photographs to the laptop and recharge the camera's battery while nipping upstairs to the Orangery for a quick bite to eat. The self-service buffet is absolutely perfect under the circumstances! But before leaving the ship once more, I pay a brief visit to the Medina and explain the reason for my absence to my dinner companions, so that they won't worry or overspeculate.

*(*World cruiser's tip: The ship usually spends two days in those major harbours that conclude each segment of the journey, and so it is possible to enjoy several excursions in these places.)*

A coach ride takes us through Little Italy and the Financial District into Chinatown, and there we leave the vehicle to wander around on foot. Our guide tells us about the city's historical background and points out things of interest, but these hardly rival the colourful, gaudy splendour of Chinese shops that display treasure troves of oriental artefacts, fit to furnish palaces: jade carvings, crystal goblets, silk hangings and satin cushions, bronze dragons, stone lions and ivory

Buddhas ... It really is a sight to behold and, illuminated, all the more dazzling at nighttime.

Then we are shown an ambitiously named 'Fortune Cookie Factory'. Our guide tells us that it was actually the Japanese who had invented the fortune cookie in the early twentieth century, but their attack on Pearl Harbour made a renaming of this popular product necessary.

A single downtrodden Chinese woman is working at a primitive machine that turns out heated roundels of wafer dough, which she bends into the familiar shape around each slip of printed paper. Three of her kinsmen hang about the dingy shop, leaning on crates and gossiping idly while they watch the woman at work. Shelves all around are piled high with transparent bags that contain the fruits of her labour. This is a dispiriting place, painted a ghastly shade of green and lit with flickering neon. I am glad to leave it behind and feel sorry for the poor woman who cannot do the same.

As we are returning to our coach, we pass a statue of Robert Louis Stevenson and are told of this English poet's connection with San Francisco. He fell in love with a married American woman ten years his senior and followed her here, hanging around, seriously ill, until she consented to become his wife ... And on across the Bay Bridge to Treasure Island, named in honour of Stevenson's famous adventure story. From this little island, the twinkling lights of the city and the illuminated bridges can be admired.

Our ship in Fisherman's Wharf is glittering festively and I look forward to getting back on board. It is so nice to return at the end of an eventful day to one's comfortable, cosy cabin with its freshly made bed and spotless bathroom, cleaned by invisible hands. Grateful thanks to you, Leandro, my marvellous cabin steward!

(*World cruiser's tip: To express their appreciation, some people pack a gift bag filled with specialities from their home region and present it to their cabin steward at the beginning of the journey.)

Day 23 ~ Thursday, 26th January 2012 ~ sunrise: 7.20am ~ sunset: 5.26pm ~ weather: dense fog, later sunny ~ temperature: 16°C

Monterey & Carmel

Today's excursion is a day trip down the coast to Monterey and Carmel, and this requires an early start. Leaving the city shortly after eight o'clock, our coach takes the scenic coastal route, but unfortunately its splendour is shrouded by thick and famous fog that rolls in from the ocean and hangs about until the sun succeeds in burning it off.

By that time we have already reached the little town of Davenport, where we enjoy a coffee break. Then, as we drive on, the Californian hills are revealed at last. We see fields of artichokes and strawberries stretching out on either side of the road and our guide lists the superlative amounts of fruit, nuts and vegetables that are produced by this sunny state.

Driving on through Santa Cruz, I am struck by the pleasing architecture of its houses. Though vaguely similar in style, all are individual and attractive. There is not a single breeze-block building anywhere ... in fact, I have not seen an ugly building yet, not even in the city, and this impression is confirmed in Monterey. Every aspect of the town proclaims an ambition to make the urban space look good. The streets, walkways and buildings have nothing cheap or shoddy, haphazard or derelict about them. All this obvious care has such an uplifting effect, it reminds me that the Austrian philosopher Rudolf Steiner had already pointed out, early in the twentieth century, that the state of our surroundings is intimately connected to our morality; that the quality of the outer space affects our inner attitude directly. Universities, schools, hospitals and even prisons would benefit from the understanding that beautiful and harmonious surroundings produce joy, respect, care and responsibility, whereas ugly surroundings, such as sink estates and slums, spawn and perpetuate depression, disrespect, vandalism and crime.

With such thoughts I wander up and down, exploring the high street by myself while the group follows our guide around. Soon I discover another little print of that delightful series first encountered at the Redwood gift shop. This one is of Monterey and features perching seagulls, and I just *have* to add it to my collection.

Cannery Row is our next destination, made famous by John Steinbeck's novels. There we have lunch at the Fish Hopper, a restaurant built above water at the end of a pier. It offers great views of seafront buildings, circling pelicans and the waves as they crash onto the rocks of the bay. The seafood pasta is excellent, and the conversation at my table revolves around yesterday's dramatic happenings aboard our ship, for two ladies are able to provide a more informed version of the current rumour: A younger passenger was arrested by US police after they found a considerable amount of cocaine in his cabin, stuffed inside a teddy bear. (The ladies had this news from someone who actually witnessed the man being led off in handcuffs.)

I decide to skip dessert in order to have some private time to explore Cannery Row. I had devoured Steinbeck's novels in my youth and now welcome this chance to see their actual setting. Earlier we learnt from our guide that Monterey Bay is attractive to marine biologists (such as Steinbeck's Doc) because a deep-sea trench is found just outside the bay. It brings the conditions of the wide ocean conveniently close to shore for investigation and allows the scientists to be back home in time for supper.

We continue along the 17 Mile Drive, a stretch of coast known for its scenic beauty. In former times, the rich and celebrated members of society used to drive in horse-drawn carriages to picnics on Pebble Beach. These days, they come here occasionally to live in secluded rows of very expensive villas (upwards of ten million dollars) behind the smattering of exclusive golf courses that line this privileged strip of coast. The area is gated for the protection of its rare plants, its wildlife and its millionaires, but visitors may also pass through after buying a ticket that opens the gates, and so we are able to take a look at this curious sanctuary.

We stop at Bird Rock where sea lions perch among sea birds on rocky outcrops that rise from the thundering surf. Cute chipmunks nibble snacks, offered by Chinese tourists who seem unable to make sense of the picture signs that ask visitors not to feed the animals.

At the next stop we admire the poetic setting of the Lone Cypress. Perched on a crag in the sea, this ancient tree is estimated to have withstood the elements for roughly two hundred and fifty years. Nowadays, the venerable conifer is secured with steel cables and even guarded as a registered trademark, and it is hoped that it will live to be at least three hundred years old.

Carmel, our final stop, is a little bijou town. Boutique after luxurious boutique lines the peaceful, wide and tree-lined main street that dips down to a lovely beach. Here, shopping turns into an almost religious experience, for these shops are like temples. Their treasures, devotedly displayed on altars and tastefully lit, are guarded by young, priestess-like sales assistants in a reverently hushed atmosphere; and though I buy nothing, I take many photos of these shrines of colourful perfection and abundance that are second to none.

Wandering down to Carmel Beach, I find the mood on this late winter afternoon captivating. Pines rear into the pale sky, interspersed with grotesque sculptures of lifeless bleached wood, and the hazy grey crescent of waves that are breaking in the background completes a living Japanese ink painting. A delicate coral skeleton, lying in the sand at my feet, echoes the shape of the trees all around.

Our return journey takes us inland through an area that was once known as Santa Clara, famous for its orchards. Clouds of blossom petals on the wind used to look like a snowstorm in spring, but the orchards are long gone and now the area is called Silicon Valley, renowned as a hotbed of cutting-edge technology. (From apples to Apple ...)

Darkness falls swiftly and turns the five-lane freeway into a stream of white and red light. It floats us back to the city and Fisherman's Wharf, where Aurora awaits our return. Feeling less tired and more adventurous today, I use the remaining hour before we have to be back on board to explore Pier 39, California's most popular attraction after Disneyland and Disneyworld. It turns out to be yet another amalgamation of stunning shops and eateries, and I am pleased to find one more poster of the same lovely series – this one showing San Francisco's cable cars.

And soon I return to the ship in an excellent mood. After enjoying a light meal and some quiet time in my cabin, I mount a display of my collection of posters and cards on the walls. These prints instantly add a more personal touch to my hut and make very pleasing souvenirs.

(*Cruiser's tip: Bring mounting squares to fasten cards, prints and posters in a way that will make them easy to remove without leaving messy traces. Alternatively, you can use magnets on those metal cabin walls, which is also a great way to organize your notes and invitations.)

Getting ready for bed, I watch Aurora (via TV screen) as she puts out to sea and passes underneath the Golden Gate once more, accompanied by the classical music that comes with this particular channel.

This day, so full of new and interesting impressions, concludes the first leg of our cruise around the world, and I am very happy that the journey continues.

~ ~ ~

~ The Second Leg ~

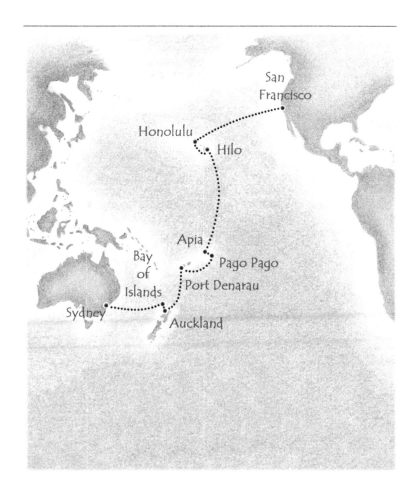

Day 24 ~ Friday, 27*th* January 2012 ~ sunrise: 6.30am ~ sunset: 5.01pm ~ sea state: choppy ~ wind: N 5, fresh breeze ~ weather: cloudy ~ temperature: 18°C ~ time zone: GMT-9

Rough Seas

Now Aurora is heading straight into the Pacific, bound for the Hawaiian Archipelago, and choppy seas make our ship dance to their lively rhythm. Nevertheless, I am feeling fine as I make my way to the gym for another morning session of exercise. Working on upper-body strength with Jovan is fun, and the beneficial effects of regular exercise are showing. Then choir rehearsal, learning that 'Any Dream Will Do'.

In the afternoon's dance class we are grappling with the Social Foxtrot. The smooth dancefloor demands extra balance today, for it tilts with the ship and causes hilarious moments among the swaying couples.

Wearing my recently bought acupressure wristbands, I am relieved to find that I feel quite all right, despite the heaving surroundings and no view at all of the horizon. Am beginning to feel more like a sailor – progress indeed!

The rest of the day is spent updating my travel journal with memories of my excursions in and around San Francisco. Whenever I leave my cabin-hut to take a break, I find a few newly embarked passengers in the corridor, looking lost and bewildered as they try to figure out which way to go. And although I am new to cruising myself, today is the first time I feel like an experienced hand, for I am able to help out with directions to the restaurant, the launderette and the library.

Day 25 ~ Saturday, 28*th* January 2012 ~ sunrise: 6.53am ~ sunset: 5.42pm ~ sea state: calm ~ wind: SE 2, light breeze ~ weather: sunny ~ temperature: 16°C

New Captain

As I awake this morning, I notice that all earlier movements and noises are missing. Has the ship stopped somewhere? It seems completely still. Hurrying to the top deck, I find the ocean calm once more. Aurora sweeps along as if on rails, and this is how I like it best.

But later, updating my journal on deck in the chilly breeze, I catch a cold that makes my nose drip and snuffle. Though this is annoying, the day passes pleasantly in its familiar pattern, with an additional salsa class that proves very enjoyable.

In the evening, all world cruisers are invited to a pre-dinner party in the Crow's Nest bar to meet the new captain. He took over from the previous one in San Francisco and will command the ship until our return to Southampton.

As befits the occasion, every lady is sparkling and glittering, every gentleman smartly suited and bow-tied. The mood is festive and free drinks flow freely as our captain makes an amusing speech that earns appreciative laughter from the crowd.

Seated comfortably with a complimentary drink, my eyes sweep the Pacific horizon that is lit by a faint and dusky afterglow. I think of my colleagues, and also of dear former pupils far away, and wonder what these pupils would say if they could see their teacher now ... Something including the words *not fair*, no doubt!

Day 26 ~ Sunday, 29th January 2012 ~ sunrise: 7.14am ~ sunset: 6.19pm ~ sea state: slight ~ wind: E 4, moderate breeze ~ weather: partly cloudy ~ temperature: 16°C

Cold Misery

I awake in a fragile mood because my head cold intensified during the night. Feeling unusually vulnerable, I decide to keep all contact with the outside world to a minimum and to make the most of my cosy cabin-hut.

Breakfast at the Medina with simultaneous work on the journal finally brings my travel report up to date. But then, feeling weak and feverish, I return to bed for more rest. Later in the day I change my mind, pull myself together and attend choir practice and a dance class, but despite my best intentions and efforts I am unable to enjoy either one. All of a sudden, everyone and everything feels much too close for comfort, and as we sing 'You Are My Sunshine', my eyes well up with tears. Our cheerful choir leader, convinced that this is a happy song, would be surprised at such a reaction; and yes – it is a happy tune, though the words are anything but and hit the old scar hard today.

During the dance lesson, Lawrence shows concern because I am not feeling well. Though he is all consideration and kindness, his fussing just adds to my already severe irritation and, impatient to leave, I gladly withdraw from human contact once the rumba session is finally, *finally* over. Hurrying back to my cabin and bed, I feel like an unhappy creature of the deep sea, head dim with slime and lack of air.

(**Cruiser's tip: Being ill on a cruise is no fun. Of course there is a doctor on board, but, unless you are rolling in money, you will not* want to bother him. The list of prices for medical services may not exactly give you a heart attack, but it will make your eyes water. Comprehensive travel insurance usually covers such medical fees, though normal health insurance likely won't. Another point: If you are on regular medication, be sure to bring enough and don't rely on the ship's medical staff for replacement.)

Day 27 ~ Monday, 30th January 2012 ~ sunrise: 7.10am ~ sunset: 5.54pm ~ sea state: calm ~ wind: E 3, gentle breeze ~ weather: cloudy ~ temperature: 18°C ~ time zone: GMT-10

Tropic of Cancer

After a restful sleep and a hot shower, my spirits revive. The sea remains calm as Aurora makes her way briskly towards Honolulu, and our new captain announces that we shall be crossing the Tropic of Cancer at two o'clock this afternoon, with about six thousand metres of water beneath our keel.

At breakfast, Gilbert tells us from his ample cruising experience that this captain always announces indifferent or good news with the preamble "This is the *cap-taín,* speaking from the bridge ..." and this peculiar way of pronouncing his title signals instantly that there is nothing to worry about. But if he should use the customary "This is the *captain* ..." to begin an announcement, it means the news will not be good. Oh boy – or rather, oh *cap-taín!* We hope in vain that we will get no proof of it on our journey.

My headcold is still hampering me, so I take this day off from my usual activities in order to look after myself. It is indeed a privileged situation when one can ditch any part of the day's programme that does not suit one's mood! Instead of exercising at the gym, I now visit the Oasis spa to try the 'Catalonian Mud Foot Soak' that detoxifies and supplies essential minerals to the skin. It is also good for tired legs. The treatment is carried out on small groups of clients at the same time and is just the right thing today, for it warms my chilly feet and noticeably improves my state of wellbeing. It is also interesting to observe the procedure:

First our lower legs and feet are scrubbed gently with a mixture of rough sea salt, lime and ginger to exfoliate the skin and stimulate circulation. Then our feet are placed in individual bowls of special Catalonian mud diluted with hot water, and they soak for twenty minutes while the assistant spreads more mud along our shins. Once legs and feet have been rinsed and dried, she applies some nourishing lotion to finish. The treatment is very agreeable, and I am struck by the Christian image of a young woman washing and salving our feet, just as Mary Magdalene did to honour Christ.

Feeling refreshed, I walk around the Sun Deck for about fifteen minutes as recommended, so that the beneficial effects of the mud application may be transported around the whole body. An appetite for life and food returns with this walk in the sea air and I decide to have lunch at the buffet instead of the restaurant, because I too have grown fond of the Orangery. Those quick plates of steamed rice and vegetables appeal to me, garnished with tender pieces of fish or meat according to the inclination of the moment. Healthy salads and a light dessert also support the ongoing weight-reduction. It pleases me that I can sit and contemplate the ocean all by myself, without any need for smalltalk, and this reminds me that, as a child and even then attracted to sea and silence, I dreamed of becoming a seafarer or a hermit ...

And now it seems that – even if only in a very approximate way – I have achieved both ambitions at once, though in a setting that is not really conducive to either ideal.

After a long siesta I am off to the spa once more, for Tony and Jovan both insisted that I just *had* to go and sit in the steamroom to cure my cold. I follow their advice and do not regret it. Spending time in the steam unblocks my nose, and the sauna's dry heat clears my head miraculously.

Day 28 ~ Tuesday, 31st January 2012 ~ sunrise: 7.10am ~ sunset: 6.21pm ~ wind: S 3, gentle breeze ~ weather: partly cloudy ~ temperature: 24°C ~ distance travelled since San Francisco: 2,083 nautical miles ~ in total: 10,517 nautical miles

Honolulu

From my breakfast table I have a splendid view of the skyscrapers that mirror the sunrise in Honolulu harbour. It is a thrilling sensation to have made it at last to Hawaii; that the lonely speck on the world map is about to reveal something of its true nature.

Then, on my way to the assembly point for our shore excursions, I encounter one of the ship's most high-ranking officers. He is leading a line of police in black combat gear and his expression is most serious. This time I have an idea what is going on: These officers are searching the ship for drugs, and it will be talked about at the dinner table tonight.

After a delay of more than half an hour, my group is called to board a coach for the 'Coastal Explorer' excursion. Our tour guide greets us with a lot of forced jollity and loud merrymaking. His approach, geared towards an American audience, seems peculiar and annoying to us more reserved Europeans. It takes him a while to notice this, but then he changes his manner, calms down and starts doing a good job introducing us to the sights and the history of O'ahu Island.

First we are taken to Diamond Head Crater and learn about the geology, the plants and the wildlife to be found there. We also hear that this volcanic crater with its large and level central plain has been a sacred site to the people of Hawaii since ancient times.

Then we drive along a dramatic stretch of tuffstone coastline and stop at Halona Point to view its famous blowhole: a small opening in a low shelf of rocks that is battered by the waves. When the tide is right, water is forced through this hole and shoots up like a geyser – but sadly not today, though we witness a few timid attempts, as if a baby whale were trying to produce its first little plume of spray.

There are no whales either; but, driving along Sandy Beach, we can see scores of youngsters bodysurfing on the crashing waves. Here, the red flags are always out.

Then we stop at Kaona Beach, a quiet bay which our guide calls paradise. Indeed, its white crescent of soft sand between beach-almond trees and the turquoise, crystal-clear water is very attractive, and also completely deserted at this time of day. We do not have time to go for a swim, but most people dip their feet in the water or do some beachcombing, for scattered on the fine sand are pebbles of black lava, tiny branches of polished corals and rosy beach almonds.

From Makapu'u Lookout we see Rabbit Island, and volcanic rock formations that drop in craggy cliffs down to the sea. The remains of a war temple at a sacred site prove that the early Hawaiians were not ambitious builders. Those rocks they amassed were simply heaped up loosely to create large, tiered platforms, and from these the priests addressed the people. Our guide explains that the concept of work was entirely foreign to native islanders, everything they needed was provided by Nature for free. When the first sugarcane and pineapple plantations were set up, a suitable workforce had to be imported from elsewhere; and that is how Chinese and Japanese, Filipino and Portuguese workers from around the South Pacific came, saw and settled, contributing their part to the huge cultural diversity of these islands.

From Pali Lookout high in the Koolau Mountains we can see far across the land. The view is impressive, but even more intriguing are little groups of wild chickens that are scratching and roosting in the bamboo forest. They have a happy, truly free-ranging life here, and hardly any predators to worry them.

After this interesting half-day excursion I return to the ship for a quick self-service lunch. Then, water bottle replenished, I venture forth by myself. There are many attractive stalls in the harbour area that invite the visitor to browse. Among the appealing items on display, I search for things to wear in the tropics and try on a row of flimsy and colourful garments. In the end I buy three of these outfits from hardnosed and unsmiling Chinese businesswomen who allow no haggling. But one of them, kindlier than the rest, drops the added tax and throws in a lovely shell necklace for free.

Usually, our ship's security officers keep a stern look on their face when checking passengers out or in, but today I am greeted with a smile and a cheerful "Welcome home!" upon my return. Is it the relaxed Hawaiian atmosphere that has effected this change?

On our excursion, as we captured a flavour of this island's easygoing approach to life's demands, we also observed the hand gesture that accompanies the Hawaiian exhortation to "Hang loose!" – Could this possibly have rubbed off on our stern security staff too?

Onboard, I make a dash for the launderette because those nice new clothes need a quick rinse. Luck is with me and I am able to secure a machine at first try. Lately, the launderettes had been so busy that I found it impossible to get any washing done.

(*World cruiser's tip: Port days are favourable for doing laundry because most people will be occupied elsewhere. However, on some ships the laundry facilities may be shut when in port.)

Aurora is reflected on the glassy sides of skyscrapers amidst the colours of the sunset, and the tall buildings are grouped in such a happy way that I do not tire to look at them. As the sun goes down, our ship leaves the pier. She swings around and heads out to sea again, gathering speed towards Hilo. We shall arrive there tomorrow morning.

Our dinner table is decorated with balloons, for it is Beryl's birthday, and all the waiters in the proximity gather round to sing 'Happy Birthday' to her with joyful vigour. And then there is indeed talk of the black-clad port officials I passed early this morning. Rumour claims that they are still on the ship, searching our cabins with sniffer dogs.

(*Cruiser's tip: Be sensible and don't bring any drugs on your cruise, for even one little joint may see you escorted ashore and turned over to the local authorities; and of course there will be no refund for the part of the journey you will have to miss.)

Day 29 ~ Wednesday, 1st February 2012 ~ sunrise: 6.57am ~ sunset: 8.11pm ~ wind: S 2, light breeze ~ weather: partly cloudy ~ temperature: 21°C ~ distance travelled since Honolulu: 219 nautical miles ~ in total: 10,736 nautical miles

Hilo

The second month of my journey begins with a tour around the 'Highlights of Hawaii'. First we are driven from Hilo to Onomea Bay to explore its sights. Here, large and beautiful botanical gardens were carved from the dense jungle by Dan and Pauline Lutkenhouse, a Dutch couple who dedicated their life to this project.

A boardwalk takes us down the valley – past a lovely waterfall and a collection of more than two thousand kinds of tropical plants – to the bay with its twin rocks of myth and legend. We walk through groves of huge palm, mango and monkey-pod trees. Ginger, bromeliads, heliconias and orchids mingle with giant tree ferns, and these are reflected in the waters of a peaceful pond in which lazy Koi carp float, golden-red and silver … It is incredibly beautiful, calm and serene, and the tropical vegetation's vigorous and abundant growth evokes distant aeons of evolution.

In connection with more recent history, we visit a park that harbours the statue of King Kamehameha the Great. At nearly seven feet tall he was a veritable giant of a man and, by all accounts, had a character to match. In 1810 this king unified the islands under his rule – mostly by the tried and tested method of having anyone killed who opposed him. But the great Kamehameha was a crafty diplomat as well. He admired King George III and befriended the British, thus obtaining the firearms he needed for his conquest.

We stop for lunch at a hotel that overlooks Hilo Bay, and we can see our 'Great White Canoe' at her berth in the distance. The buffet lunch is excellent and plentiful, but once again I skip dessert in order to gain a bit of time to wander around by myself, exploring the area.

(*Solo traveller's tip: In this way you avoid gaining weight and are able to escape the herd for a while without taking the risks of solo land excursions. The guide will naturally be anxious about losing you, so promise to be responsible and make a point of returning in good time.)

Huge Banyan trees line the street and spread out canopies that provide pleasant shade. These trees were planted in the nineteen-thirties by famous people of the time, for example Amelia Earhart, Richard Nixon, Cecil B. DeMille and Louis Armstrong, and that is why Banyan Drive became known as 'Hilo Walk of Fame'. Fifty trees marked with name plaques still survive, but many others have been lost to tidal waves and tsunamis over the years.

    I see that a variety of smaller plants is living as lodgers in the magnificent web of branches and dangling air roots. Banyan trees are like vertical gardens that provide dwelling places for birds, insects, frogs and rodents. These amazing trees are luxury hotels for a type of client that would not feel at home in the grand hotels that line this pleasant street, nor be so welcome there.

    In a cove behind a derelict parking lot I find a lovely stretch of beach. Strewn with black lava pebbles, tiny green coconuts and sea shells, it lies shaded and peaceful in the midday heat. Oh, wouldn't it be nice to spend the afternoon sitting here, toes dipped in the water, just hanging loose!

But it is time to visit the volcanic region of the island. Here, plumes of steam and evil-smelling gases rise from the shrub that stretches out across the highland plateau near the crater, and a vaporous column of similar gases rises from the deep crater of Mt Kilauea. Though very quietly active at present, its caldera can only be viewed from a distance. The Jaggar Museum offers a good view from its elevated location, and detailed information on all aspects regarding the volcanic origins of the Hawaiian island chain. This Museum is named after Thomas Augustus Jaggar Jr., the renowned American volcanologist who had founded and directed the Hawaiian Volcano Observatory. He studied the earth's crust almost his entire life, attempting to learn more about our lively planet's "subterranean machinery totally unknown to geologists."

Although we have a mountain of fire beneath our feet, it is surprisingly cold up here and I seize the opportunity to buy a long-sleeved T-shirt at the gift shop. It will make a nice present for my son and ward off the chill on this outing. The T-shirt says: "Advice from a Volcano: – Stay active! – Keep your inner fire burning! – It's ok to let off steam! – Go with the flow! – Be uplifting! – It's all a matter of time! – Have a blast!"

(*Cruiser's tip: Be prepared for changes in temperature and take something along to keep you warm, especially in higher regions. Alternatively, you may treasure a growing collection of T-shirts and sweaters. They will remind you of chilly excursions or make nice presents for friends and family at home.)

Now we go for a short, leisurely walk through a cave-like lava tube, named after the Hawaiian lawyer, politician and businessman Lorrin Andrews Thurston who had explored it.

Thurston was also a keen amateur volcanologist, befriended Jaggar, helped to fund his observatory and was instrumental in establishing the Hawaii Volcanoes National Park.

'His' lava tube lies hidden in the ground, extending its tunnel beneath a forest that consists of an attractive mix of tree ferns and ohea trees, whose wood was once used by native warriors to make spears. Created by lava as it drained away, this natural tunnel is some 600 feet or 182 metres long and, according to our local guide, a natural wonder that is "unique to Hawaii".

But this claim turns out to be untrue. Looking it up on the internet later, I find that there are lava tubes in all the volcanic regions of the world, especially in Iceland, Portugal, Spain, Korea, and of course the USA.

(*Cruiser's tip: Take the things you are told by enthusiastic local tour guides with the proverbial grain of salt. If any such facts seem important to you, check them out before passing them on, to avoid embarrassment.)

It is late afternoon by now, and yet we still have one more attraction to visit: The Mauna Loa Macadamia Nut Factory. There we are treated to free samples of a delicacy that comes in a wide variety of flavours, from sweet to very spicy.

Wandering around the factory's shop and admiring all those tastefully boxed nuts, I suddenly spy a beautiful beach bag displayed above the merchandise. Its printed design in faded tones of yellow and ochre shows an antique sea chart of the Hawaiian Islands, and this I cannot resist. The appeal of old parchment maps gets me every time! This lovely bag will be useful on my upcoming beach excursions, and it also makes a very nice souvenir.

Upon our late return to Hilo's harbour, a US security official boards our coach to check our passports, and with no more than ten minutes to spare we enter the ship's security zone for the usual procedure of x-raying and metal-detecting. We are sternly instructed to drop our 'US exit card' into a box in the Atrium, and then we are free to enjoy the evening.

(*Cruiser's tip: It is recommended that you return to the ship at least fifteen minutes before the given departure time. The computer logs everyone's return, and tannoy calls for certain passengers to contact the purser's desk may mean that they are still unaccounted for. Be aware that your ship is obliged to keep to a strict time plan and cannot wait for tardy passengers.)

I drop my things off in my hut (as Martha and I now call our cabins, in the Dutch tradition) and hurry to the sauna to warm up, hoping to counteract the effects of those relentless streams of cold air on coach and volcano. Only one other person is in the sauna, a youngish chap from the Isle of Man. (I believe I met his father earlier.)

We chat about the day and our respective excursions while admiring a view of the sea from the sauna window. Suddenly he exclaims that he saw whales in the bay outside the harbour, but as he tries to point out their location among the waves, they disappear.

Humph ...! By now I have grown quite accustomed to my lack of luck where wildlife-watching is concerned. Other passengers have spotted dolphins, turtles, whales and flying fish, and some claim that they caught a glimpse of crocodiles when we were passing through the Panama Canal ... but as far as my own observations go, the seas might as well be empty of life.

(*Cruiser's tip: You may want to pack a good pair of binoculars for wildlife watching, sightseeing and pirate-spotting, for some of the most interesting sights will be at a distance.)

Day 30 ~ Thursday, 2nd February 2012 ~ sunrise: 7.11am ~ sunset: 6.44pm ~ sea state: slight ~ wind: E 3, gentle breeze ~ weather: partly cloudy ~ temperature: 23°C

Cruise Fitness

I resume my early-morning exercise routine with a spell on two different kinds of fitness equipment, followed by a good workout with Jovan. We are using dumbbells for resistance training and the lighter ones have already been taken. Only weights of four kilos are available and are a bit heavier than I would like, but I struggle manfully through these exercises without dropping the weights on my toes.

Then a relaxing half hour is spent in the Jacuzzi and the pool – both free of people because of a sudden tropical rain shower. Floating in a pool on the ocean and showered by large, warm raindrops, I am once again radiantly happy, delighted with this treat I bestowed on myself in reward for years of tireless work and parenting.

(*Solo traveller's tip: Recently widowed women enjoy a long cruise after the strain of being a fulltime carer for an ailing spouse. So do ex-wives after a gruelling divorce, empty-nesters after their brood has flown, and burnt-out teachers after years of being tied to the timetable and harassed by unreasonable parents.)

The theme of tonight's Black Tie evening is 'James Bond', though not one of the tuxedoed gentlemen is remotely like Connery, Brosnan or Craig. But the concert by a duo of girl-violinists is impressive. They perform with amazing verve and skill and make us marvel at their virtuoso playing as they dance across the stage in matching sparkly ball gowns, backed by an orchestra.

It is an enjoyable performance, though I am compelled to imitate one of those famous monkeys again, covering my ears because they hurt from the high volume of amplified sound. By contrast, the piano recital later in the evening is purely acoustic, and what a relief it is to hear the instrument speak for itself! An appealing selection of piano pieces from the Romantic era ends with a favourite by Schubert.

A late turn around the top deck – completely bare of people at this hour – concludes the evening. Wandering the length of the ship, I delight in the quiet darkness, the warm breeze and the stars of a tropical night.

(*Solo traveller's tip: If you are looking for contemplative solitude and comparative silence on a cruise ship, you will find them on the top deck during those final hours of the day, and the early hours of the morning.)

Friday, 3rd February 2012 ~ sunrise: 7.13am ~ sunset: 5.06pm ~ sea state: slight ~ wind: E 4, moderate breeze ~ weather: partly cloudy ~ temperature: 27°C

Past & Present

Instead of exercising, I pay an extended visit to the sauna and the steamroom early this morning, and afterwards go for a swim. The sauna proves very beneficial for my blocked nose and is no longer a place of pure, hellish heat to me now. From this experience I learn how useful it can be, once in a while, to try out certain things I could not cope with at an earlier, more sensitive stage in my life, and thus give myself a chance to find out that I have grown in strength, resilience or acceptance over time.

Today I brought waterproof earplugs to the pool, and with their aid I now swim and dive underwater just like I used to do as a child. It feels unexpectedly liberating to move in the mermaid-ways of so many years ago, delighting in the same fluid underwater manoeuvres.

It occurs to me, in continuation of the earlier thought, that it may be equally enriching to try out some of the things I had once loved to do, but that are no longer part of my life because I outgrew them.

(*World cruiser's tip: Use the special setting of a long-term cruise to think about every aspect of your life – past, present and future. Experiment with the boundaries of habits old and new, because you need not feel restricted by your normal life, status and persona and can make the most of this glorious spell of freedom. What other circumstances afford such liberty?)

Day 32 ~ Saturday, 4th February 2012 ~ sunrise: 7.16am ~ sunset: 5.27pm ~ sea state: calm ~ wind: E 4, moderate breeze ~ weather: sunny ~ temperature: 28°C

Equator

Upon leaving my cabin this morning, I notice a large folded towel on the carpet outside. It has been placed there by the cabin steward to catch a regular drip of water from the light fitting above my door. Oh *no!* I really don't want my homely hut to get flooded like so many others, but my cabin steward is unworried. Leandro assures me that the leak has already been reported and will be taken care of immediately.

What is the matter with this ship's pipes? In the past weeks plumbers were seen, repeatedly dismantling walls or ceiling panels and poking around in the dark spaces beyond as they searched for the source of yet another leak.

Fortunately, Aurora's hull is sturdy and more waterproof than its delicate insides ... or so one hopes. For what do passengers know of what goes on below decks? Precisely nothing, and it is surely best that way!

(*Cruiser's tip: In circumstances such as these, there is nothing to do but to keep calm and carry on, trusting that those in charge will take competent care of the problem.)

There is no time for exercise sessions this morning, because I am about to have a fourth and final acupuncture treatment with Rodrigo. As soon as I walk in, he diagnoses a difference in my appearance and changes his approach accordingly. He taps a needle into my inner forearm and a dull pain shoots along the meridian. It feels like a weak electric current and makes me wince, but Rodrigo is pleased. "That was right on target!" he declares, and explains that he aimed for a point that corresponds to the female emotional life, if I understood his words correctly.

His perceptive assessment is impressive, because there is indeed something going on. As yet I have no idea what it could be and did not think it showed; but by the end of the day I will have realized that I miss a friend to talk and laugh with, a kindred spirit of similar age and background with whom I can be myself without always guarding my words and feelings; someone who doesn't have to call me *madam* – that polite form of address, constantly used by the Indian staff, which makes me cringe inwardly every time.

Feeling restless and impatient, for the first time I find it quite impossible to relax during the treatment. The insipid meditation music gets on my nerves, my nose is blocked and the constant sniffling doesn't help. What a bother!

Rodrigo hands me a tissue and applies tiny plasters in my ear to relieve the cold. At their centre is a tiny mustard seed, particularly good for stimulating the relevant points, and their effect can even be measured by a subtle change in the pulse. But despite it all, my mood remains irritable.

Aurora reaches the equator after lunch and I join the excited crowd to witness the ceremonial 'Crossing of the Line' that is celebrated by the Terrace pool on the aft deck.

Last night, Gilbert told us that King Neptune usually comes aboard with his court of marine creatures to baptize those crew members who have not crossed the equator yet. Among other things, they are dunked in the pool and given a certificate to prove that they have been to 'The Other Side'. In theory it sounds like a charming pageant to celebrate the occasion, but in practice the event is seriously disappointing. The ceremony turns out to be nothing more than a custard fight in the pool between Neptune's team and a P&O team. The King of the Oceans has no central ceremonial role, and a sense of occasion is definitely lacking.

Four first-timers of crew and staff are roped together, have to sit by the edge of the pool throughout the fight and are shoved into the messed-up water as an afterthought; but at that point the entertainment manager already dismissed the audience. King Neptune never thought to address them, the fact of their first-time crossing was ignored and they played no part at all.

What a let-down! ... Really, *any* celebration, serious or funny, is handled much better in all Waldorf schools around the world and I may have become too used to our standards, because it seems to me that the ship's entertainment team is as clueless as it is cheery. All they achieved was to distract from a unique occasion with irrelevant silliness, gallons of soiled water and much vacuous noise. As mighty Neptune, Ruler of Oceans, I suspect that I would feel strongly moved to sink this ship right here and now.

Can an acupuncture needle in the right place be held responsible for this onrush of dissatisfaction with people in general and their actions in particular? I think not. It is just another case of not infrequent disappointment that arises at yet more evidence that the realm of coherent thought is *terra incognita* to so many, and that this privileged lifestyle seems to produce nothing more than mindless folly.

But on the positive side, I now succeed in changing the music files on my MP3 player after nearly deleting them all by accident. Yes, I admit to being more familiar with Greek mythology than the mysterious ways of electronic gadgets.

And what a great pleasure it is to hear Mozart's 'Requiem' again! It is a piece of truth and sanity in a crazy world, proof that heaven is there, behind the distractions and the noise, waiting to be heard by those who are willing to listen.

Day 33 ~ Sunday, 5th February 2012 ~ sunrise: 7.20am ~ sunset: 5.48pm ~ sea state: slight ~ wind: N 5, fresh breeze ~ weather: partly cloudy ~ temperature: 27°C

The Dress

Up at six o'clock, I find that interesting things are happening in the corridor, for crew members have assembled a laundry tub on coasters, stepladder, bucket and drill to deal with the water still trickling from that central light outside my room. I take a picture of this thrilling scene before I leave, hoping that all this water shall be promptly contained.

At a small table by the eastern windowfront of the Orangery I listen to the 'Requiem' once more, but this time it is accompanied by my first sight of a sunrise in the South Pacific. To me, the only word that sums up the effect of this particular mix of sunrise and music is *happiness*.

Today, all passengers who are going around the world are invited to a special lunch at the Alexandria restaurant with the captain and the officers. Our circle of dinner companions is joined by Walter, a charming elderly American who joined the cruise in San Francisco. He is given Martha's place at our table, because she is seated with her Dutch friends on this occasion. The meal is delicious, the conversation animated, and from our table at the stern window I get a splendid view of the ship's receding wake. Looking out at the seemingly endless vista of water, I imagine our position on the map and recall that my pupils and I had studied this remote part of the globe last year. Little did we realize what adventures my world geography lessons would lead to!

It is another Black Tie evening and time to put on The Dress. Wearing it, I feel oddly transformed, like Cinderella on her way to the ball. This gown is right for me in a way clothes so rarely are. Indeed, it feels like a sartorial soulmate.

At dinner, the ladies express their instinctive understanding of this fact frankly and tell me that I look beautiful. How very nice of them! ... The gentlemen, being British, say nothing, though their looks speak. And the Indian waiters, Francis and Marcus especially, smile and nod appreciatively.

Once I return to my normal life on land, there will be no opportunity to wear this dress. My string of pearls can confirm it. But incidentally, those pearls go extremely well with the sparkly midnight-blue of the dress's fabric, and so, all things considered, I do not regret buying it. If nothing else, The Dress shall be a memento of this journey and a tangible reminder of a unique adventure.

Day 34 ~ Monday, 6th February 2012 ~ sunrise: 7.24am ~ sunset: 7.55pm ~ sea state: rough ~ wind: NW 7, high wind ~ weather: heavy showers ~ temperature: 26°C ~ distance travelled since Hilo: 2,288 nautical miles ~ in total: 13,024 nautical miles

Apia

We approach the independent Samoan island of Upolu in choppy seas. At breakfast, expecting to see boundless ocean as usual, I am surprised to find a large landmass looming dimly under the clouds, insubstantial as a promise. The little boat of the pilot bounces wildly on its way towards us. After taking him aboard, Aurora completes a slow circle outside the atoll's narrow entrance to the harbour, waiting for things to improve. The wagging tail-end of a cyclone with its low pressure system is making its influence on the weather felt, and an announcement from the bridge about the difficult sea conditions (with a worried undertone) leaves us wondering if we shall be able to make landfall at all. But then the wind eases off just enough to allow our great ship to be squeezed into this tiny harbour, very slowly and carefully.

Boats of all sizes rise and fall alarmingly along the pier, and a large tarpaulin, put up to welcome us, has been blown over and lies in a sad, tangled heap. On top of this, tropical rain begins to lash down in great torrents, drenching anyone still out on deck. Who would have pictured a South Pacific island in such British weather?

In due course, Aurora is made fast alongside her berth and we are free to go ashore. But my group is offered a refund for our planned beach excursion because the weather forecast is pessimistic. Quite a few people return their tickets and I think of doing the same, but then decide to go ahead anyway, for a first visit to a South Sea island ought to be memorable even in tropical rain ...

And our small group of intrepid explorers shall not regret this decision, for the rain stops as we drive along the north-western coast and across the Le Mafa pass. I am enchanted by steamed-up glimpses of this tropical paradise with charming little houses, abundant flowers, and friendly free-roaming dogs, pigs and chickens. Large, happy-looking people smile and wave as we pass, and I realize that *this* is what I imagined Hawaii to be like.

The Sopo'aga waterfalls are on truly splendid form, nourished by the downpour of a wet season that lasts from November to April. We are given a 'coconut demonstration' at the botanical gardens nearby. Experienced hands de-husk coconuts at a stake and split them open by tapping the right place expertly with a flat stone. The nut is scraped out of its shell on a small, anvil-like tool, and then a milky liquid is pressed from the grated flesh by twisting it in a dense mesh of washed coconut fibres. The coconut cream thus produced plays a big part in the daily diet of Samoans. And not only that: every part of the palm tree is useful, which is why the people of these islands call it the 'Tree of Life'.

Tafatafa Beach is where a barbeque buffet lunch is served. The meal, prepared locally, is excellent and plentiful. The roast chicken is tender and tasty, the lemonade made from a tropical fruit is divine. We enjoy our meal in neatly lined-up beach huts that are simple open platforms with a thatched roof of palm leaves and a magnificent view of the lagoon. How glad we are that we did not return our tickets! The surf is breaking along the coral reef of the atoll, far out to sea, and we listen to its distant roar and thunder.

While others are swimming or snorkelling, I wander along the waterline. The weather is warm and pleasant now, and for a while it looks as if the sun might break through. But the clouds keep the upper hand and before long another shower patters down on sea, sand, palm trees and beach huts. With an umbrella, offered by a kind lady, I continue my stroll and enjoy the little tapping sounds the raindrops produce on its screen and on the clear wavelets that roll around my ankles. Tiny fishes dart like shadows past my toes as I dig them into the watery volcanic sands. It is all utterly blissful!

Two hours later we are moved on to admire an even bigger waterfall that thunders into a volcanic crater. Rain turned the impressive Papapapaiuta falls a muddy brown, but we only leave the coach for the briefest of looks because another torrential downpour is about to break. The roads are now flooded in parts, but there is so little traffic that this is not a problem. Our driver, a very large and calm Samoan, handles every obstacle in a skilful manner.

It had been mentioned in a port presentation earlier, and now we can see for ourselves that Samoan people are mostly large, tall and well-built. Traditionally, Samoan men are known as good sportsmen and wrestlers, and they are fervently religious. About 98% of the population is actively Christian, and this little island is reported to boast more churches than all of Rome. Now we pass some of them, lined up almost side by side along the road. They are dedicated to *Iesu Keriso* and some of their facades are decorated with red hearts or a painted cross.

Our tour guide tells us that discipline and respect for one's elders are important in Samoan society. Children are expected to do as they are told. Should they answer back or be naughty, it is considered quite all right to smack them.

But the children I see on the beach and by the roadside look sweet, unspoilt and unlikely to misbehave. What would it be like to be a teacher here, in paradise?

And now we cross the path of Robert L. Stevenson once more, for he settled with his wife on this very island after touring the South Pacific for almost three years. The couple bought a plot of land in the village of Vailima, and their residence is now a museum. Stevenson was admired by the islanders as a gifted storyteller. They adored him, and the verse he wrote as his epitaph was translated into Samoan and is sung as a folksong to this day.

Back on the ship I should like to lie down for a while, but there is no time to rest after this all-day outing because Beryl has invited all her dinner companions to the Pennant Grill. She was hoping to celebrate her birthday on its terrace, but the relentless rain removes us to the inside.

There, not one table is big enough for us all and we have to split up. The waiter places Gilbert, Martha and me at a table beneath the sound system's amplifiers that spout a recording of crashing waves, interspersed with the shrieking of seagulls. (The sound of ceaselessly rushing water cannot be considered pleasant on such a wet day.)

Eventually, the rushing and gushing above my head irritates me so much that I ask the young waiter if the sound track could be changed. His reluctant response indicates that he is out of his depth; but later, after being asked a second time, he obliges and puts on some music.

Regrettably it is no real improvement, for a loud and percussive invasion of sound hinders our conversation. Do I grit my teeth and bear it, or do I complain for a third time? Isn't it somebody's task to make sure that dining here is a pleasant experience? Martha endures the discomfort with stoicism, while Gilbert (who disapproves of my complaint) states proudly that none of these soundtracks bother him. Well, there are certainly occasions when a tin ear is a great advantage – though I refrain from saying so.

Our waiter serves the first course and soon returns to ask if everything is alright. I mention that music is too loud. (In fact it is superfluous, but I know better than to ask for silence.) He goes to reduce the volume, and now it looks as if the meal might become enjoyable at last. The dishes are very attractively presented, but my roast lamb with its aristocratic title unexpectedly makes the keen steak knife seem like a blunt saw. Soon enough the waiter returns to enquire if we are enjoying our meal. I inform him reluctantly that the meat is rather tough. Hearing this, he looks surprised and walks away without a word.

Tired after the long excursion, I instantly decide to let it go and not make a fuss, disliking the role of dissatisfied client which I am forced to assume here. Having arrived in a good mood and ready to enjoy Beryl's treat, I can't help but find this whole dinner experience disappointing. Had I come here by myself, I could – and certainly would – have left the place by now; but because I am here as Beryl's guest, this is unfortunately not an option.

The manageress, hearing from the waiter that I am not happy, comes to the table and puts her arm comfortingly around my shoulders. I find this inappropriate. She asks why I had not said anything. This amazes me. What more could I have said? Does she expect me to point out that I had informed the waiter of every one of my complaints, thus putting him on the spot? Not knowing what to reply, I say nothing and wait for the earliest possible opportunity to make my excuses and slip away from this disagreeable situation. To compound the unpleasantness, Beryl is sure to take my unhappiness with her treat as a personal affront, for Gilbert is even now recounting my issues to the others at the large table. From his earlier comments it seems reasonable to assume that he is not taking a sympathetic view. – What a distressing end to a lovely day!

Day 35 ~ Tuesday, 7th February 2012 ~ sunrise: 6.19am ~ sunset: 6.56pm ~ wind: SW 5, fresh breeze ~ weather: sunny spells ~ temperature: 26°C ~ time zone: GMT-11 ~ distance travelled since Apia: 160 nautical miles ~ in total: 13,184 nautical miles

Pago Pago

Getting up early, I describe my dining experience in a letter and give it to the restaurant manager at breakfast, assuming that this will lead to a discreet talk, as happens at our school when someone is unhappy for any reason. But the manager approaches me at the breakfast table where Gilbert is eager to chime in with his contrary opinion. The manager says he had not been informed at the time that anything was amiss, that the sound track is standard and they serve a lot of lamb without getting complaints. – And that's that.

    Hard to believe that someone in his position should have so little skill in dealing with a complaint. Surely all that is needed is an acknowledgement of the issues, an apology on behalf of the restaurant and a small gesture of goodwill to show that the client's satisfaction matters. Why does the manager seem personally affronted? Now he departs, saying that he will pass my letter on – which is the last I ever hear of the matter. It leaves a bad impression, but I do not want to spoil the day by pursuing this any further.

We arrive in Pago Pago on the island of Tutuila with a slight delay due to a passing squall. It is tricky for a big ship like Aurora to enter such a small harbour. There is little water and less room for manoeuvre, but probably some very tense moments on the bridge.

When the time comes, we passengers assemble in the Curzon theatre to collect our tour stickers. Expecting to go ashore presently, we wait for our groups to be called up to head down to the gangway, but after some fifty minutes of tedious waiting an announcement is made via the PA: "This is the captain ..." (Oh *dear!* Oh *no!*) ... Well, the captain has to inform us that there are unforeseen difficulties with the paperwork "due to miscommunication", and that they are "working closely with the authorities" but need to contact Honolulu to resolve the problem – hopefully within the next hour. We don't get more information, but I suspect at once that we ought not to have handed in our US exit cards in Hilo, because we are now back in US territory and probably without the necessary papers.

With a collective groan we leave our seats and seek more agreeable ways to spend an hour of waiting. At the Crow's Nest, where I go for a view of the harbour, I meet Walter again (that nice cosmopolitan American who joined our table for the World Cruisers' Lunch), and time passes much more quickly in congenial conversation.

At last we are cleared to leave the ship and make our way to the line of waiting island tour buses. They seem to be handmade, mainly of wood, and have a fret-sawed interior unlike any we have ever seen. Their windscreens are headed with painted mottoes such as 'Believe in Life' and 'God is Awesome'. In sharp contrast, their sides are decorated with pictures of rugby teams and ugly robotic monsters.

Our driver is another large Samoan, wedged tightly into his seat behind the wheel, but our tour guide Aleki is a slender youth with a shy, affectionate sunshine-smile. He explains that he guides tours to raise funds for his stay in the United States where he plans to study engineering, and he engages our attention easily without having to resort to silly jokes. As we are driven along the coast, and then inland to the village of Leone, Aleki points out government buildings and traditional assembly houses with many pillars, as well as a great variety of churches. He is a Methodist himself, and the distinction of his native village is that it can boast the greatest number of guesthouses.

Leone is the place where a hugely successful British missionary by the name of John Williams landed in 1830. We visit the splendid Zion Church, built in 1900 by the London Missionary Society and still a thriving place of worship. Williams, however, met a sticky end after years of spreading the Word of God throughout these scattered islands, for he and a fellow missionary were killed and eaten by the gospel-resistant inhabitants of another island group.

On these islands, the influence of the church is clear and life seems the better for it. The actively Christian ethos, combined with strong and time-honoured tribal traditions, makes for an ordered, peaceful and hospitable society. Those disparate religious communities seem to coexist without too many problems, and their different churches are built almost side by side along the roads.

Surprisingly, American Samoa has a more dilapidated look than the independent Samoan island we visited yesterday, but both places have a problem with litter. Accustomed to nothing but biodegradable waste for centuries, people here seem unable to grasp that plastic, glass and tin cans will not be reabsorbed by nature's cycles, and that responsible waste management is urgently required.

But who would blame the Samoans for their lack of action? Our scientifically enlightened western civilization has only fairly recently become conscious of this fact, and the problem is far from being solved.

Viewing with dismay the rubbish strewn amongst tropical vegetation everywhere, I imagine how easily church and school could combine to address the problem. Together they could teach children a proper awareness of this issue: Explain the possibilities of recycling, draw before-and-after pictures, organize litter-picking parties in the communities and thus spread the message to the adults.

(In fact, I should like to be involved in such a project myself, for I treasure memories of a weekend spent cleaning up a deserted and rubbish-covered beach on a Greek island single-handedly. Viewed with suspicion by passing locals, it is anyone's guess what they did, after my departure, with that enormous pile of rubbish I had assembled.)

We have reached the beautiful coast and stop at the Vaitogi cliffs. These are essentially great boulders of black lava, and we see how its roping flow-patterns once met the sea, aeons ago. Their brittle hardness resists erosion even now.

On top of the highest cliff, locals have gathered to perform a ritual chant for us. With this chant they are calling the turtle and the shark, according to an ancient legend.

While everyone else is crowding onto the cliff to wait in vain for a glimpse of shark or turtle, I absent myself to study the lava patterns. The tide has swept them clean of debris, and despite a soft, porous look their substance is hard as glass. Aleki comes over to check what I am doing and, hearing of my interest in lava, he at once begins to search the ground. A short while later he hands me a lump of his native island's geological foundations with a beaming smile.

So far, we have smiled at each other quite a bit out of mutual sympathy, and now we use the moment to exchange fragments of personal information: How he comes to be at home on two neighbouring islands – and how I come to be travelling around the world by myself.

I assume that such solo adventures are not done by women of his culture, and that female wanderers would be frowned upon or condemned by the very traditional Samoan society. But Aleki is of a new generation and clearly has an open mind. He is a truly lovely person and radiates youthful promise – that rare quality which makes us trust that the evolution of the world will not have been in vain, and that one day all of mankind shall be good and wise and beautiful and true. – May Life treat him kindly!

Although the day began with heavy showers, the sky has long since cleared up and the sun is shining with tropical might. We are shown a mound of loose rocks at the edge of the rainforest and are told that it marks the site where, once upon a time, pigeon-hunting competitions were held among the young men hoping to marry the chief's daughter. As in Hawaii, heaps of rocks alone mark formerly inhabited sites. There are never any ancient ruins, for none of these islanders erected stone buildings.

At the former residence of the late Governor Tauese Sunia, a cooling drink is served and we learn about this much-loved 'father' of his people. Sunia had been an eminent politician and, judging by the photographs, an astute, kind and gentle man with the best interests of his country at heart. His tomb is seen on the veranda in a prominent place, for in Samoa the dead are buried at home. Family tombs are a feature of all yards and gardens, and so the ancestors are always close by, watching over their descendants.

Our last stop is again at the coast, and there we are shown the Flowerpot Rocks, a little way offshore. They are huge boulders with steep sides, and their tops are covered in miniature jungles that give them the look of an unruly hairdo. According to legend, these rocks are a husband and wife awaiting permission to come ashore, having fled from the cannibalistic king of neighbouring Upolu. Their little son is represented by a smaller rock farther along.

After the tour we still have plenty of time to look around the little harbour town of Pago Pago by ourselves. I post a card to my son, visit the indoor market and chat with the friendly ladies at the stalls. They are selling jewellery, bags, sarongs, and a range of artificial frangipani flowers to wear behind the ear: On the left side if you are taken, on the right if you are available, or – according to a joke by our guide in Apia – in the middle if you happen to be undecided.

At dinner, the most popular topic is our imminent crossing of the International Date Line. Tomorrow we shall be losing a day and go from Tuesday, the 7th directly to Thursday, the 9th of February. Surprisingly, many people have no idea why this happens. "Where does the day go?" they ask.

Day 36 ~ Thursday, 9th February 2012 ~ sunrise: 6.33am ~ sunset: 7.30pm ~ sea state: slight ~ wind: NW 4, moderate breeze ~ weather: sunny ~ temperature: 27°C ~ time zone: GMT+13

Date Line

Today, a humorous version of our daily newsletter is titled 'The Day That Never Was' and gives an absurd programme of activities and events under the missed date of the 8th of February. The lost day continues to be a favourite topic at our lunch and dinner tables, and possibly missed birthdays appear to be the main concern.

Had I continued to teach my class for another year, our curriculum would have included a look at the way in which time is measured around the globe; at the system of time zones devised in modern times, and the fact that it is nothing but a universally accepted convention to facilitate worldwide communication and trade. Before the continents became linked by these threads, no such system was needed. The cycle of the rising and setting sun, though variable, had always sufficed each local community.

The independent Samoan Islands demonstrated the arbitrary nature of our time system just a few months ago (in December 2011) when they decided to put themselves on the other side of the International Date Line. They chose to align themselves with their main trading partners Australia and New Zealand, rather than America, and so they dropped Friday, the 30th of December from their week, went from a Thursday to a Saturday and from GMT −11 to GMT +13. American Samoa did not participate in this time-travelling and remained, politically correct, on the same calendar date as the far-distant United States. And now the islands of the

Samoan group, although side by side in space, are separated in time by being on different days of the week.

This ought to be sufficient proof (if such proof were needed) that the measuring of time is entirely in our hands and is *not* dictated by the universe. The annual grumbling about the supposedly "unnatural" British Summer Time is brought to mind. Teaching point: Why there can be no such thing as 'natural time'.

Viewed from a practical angle, changes such as this Samoan one must be a veritable windfall for all makers of maps, charts and atlases! Now new editions of *everything* are required to remain up to date, and business is good.

On our tour around the world, and setting our clocks back successively by one hour every few days, we have now reached the antimeridian at 180 degrees longitude – on the other side of the globe and opposite the prime meridian in London; have reached that imaginary line where the time differences to Greenwich Mean Time (GMT) of minus twelve and plus twelve fall into one and become the same. It is this insubstantial place that swallows up a day in our reckoning: Having arrived at twelve hours *behind* London time, we find ourselves all at once twelve hours *ahead* on a day that is yet to dawn in Britain, rather than sailing on into the past ...

In effect we are not losing a day, but a date, since the sun will rise and set in an unbroken pattern, and not until we reach Southampton again on our course due west shall we have 'lost' twenty-four hours – or rather twenty-three, for we shall be arriving in British Summer Time, at GMT +1.

Yes, this is indeed a topic that can make your mind spin! The cruise log passengers receive at the end of each leg will state that "The ship's clocks were advanced by 24 hours as Aurora crossed the International Date Line" – but these clocks do not show the date, and so I wonder: Did the crew member who advanced them have any thoughts on the utter pointlessness of his action?

Day 37 ~ Friday, 10th February 2012 ~ sunrise: 6.04am ~ sunset: 6.46pm ~ wind: NE 2-6, strong gusts ~ weather: heavy showers ~ temperature: 28°C ~ time zone: GMT+12 ~ distance travelled since Pago Pago: 787 nautical miles ~ in total: 13,971 nautical miles

Port Denarau

Port Denarau is the first harbour on our world tour that is unsuitable for a ship of Aurora's size. Anchor is dropped off Viti Levu, amidst little islands scattered around the lagoon. Pontoons are rigged with tenders, but boarding is tricky in these choppy sea conditions. Today's weather is cloudy once more, laced with heavy showers at frequent intervals.

My excursion to a 'Beachcomber Getaway' at a resort on a tiny island of the Mamanuca Group requires a boat trip of more than an hour. The catamaran's Fijian crew entertains us with songs to a vigorously strummed guitar, and by and by the dark grey skies are lightening.

Like Aurora, this catamaran also needs to keep a safe distance from the shore, and so passengers are transferred to smaller boats. Under the circumstances, this is a challenge. Big waves make the vessels bounce and crash against each other and the procedure takes time, but the moment my feet touch the coral sands of this miniature island, the sun comes out. We are welcomed in an attractive open-plan restaurant and served drinks and muffins.

The day's programme is outlined, and then we are free to do as we please. While others go snorkelling or swimming, I set out to explore the island. Wandering flat rocks of compacted corals, shells and sand, I scan the surf line for treasure. There are thick layers of coral debris and shells to sift through, and I become enthralled by those beautiful shapes and patterns Life invents below the waves.

On a cable that stretches out to sea between lopsided poles, black birds with white faces are sitting in a neat row, like pearls on a string, facing me. As I try to get closer with my camera without scaring them away, the first raindrops fall and develop into a copious downpour that makes me run for shelter. Hastily I stuff the camera into my Hawaiian beach bag and put it under a structure nearby that is covered with tarpaulin. Waiting for the shower to pass, I notice with dismay that what I took to be tarpaulin is really a fine mesh. It covers a pond containing baby turtles and does nothing at all to stop the rain from dripping through.

Oh *bother!* ... To protect my things from the rain, I approach the nearest beach residence and put my things in a little pile on its roofed veranda. At once the door is opened and a man comes out. What am I doing on his porch?

I explain the situation and he gives permission to leave my things sheltered under his roof for a while. That taken care of, I am free to resume my island expedition in the rain. These rain showers are warm and pleasant, even though the downpour is so strong that it pricks like needles. To breathe without inhaling water, one has to turn one's head aside.

Before long I have circled the island. Everyone else is huddled inside the restaurant where live music is played at a deafening volume. I walk on by and begin another circuit of the island. There are so many pretty shells to collect that it is necessary to be more discriminating. In passing I check on my things and the baby turtles that are floating leisurely in their net-protected enclosure. They do not seem to mind the constant spray of droplets, and neither do the white-faced birds, now almost obscured by a dense veil of rain, for they continue to perch on that same cable.

Upon reaching the restaurant once more, I go to Reception, poke my head through the door to avoid making puddles on the floor and ask for some plastic bags to put my belongings in. After rummaging in a backroom for a while, the friendly receptionist hands me suitable covers.

With my things collected from the porch and securely wrapped in plastic I feel easier, but the heavy rain shows no sign of letting up. Anyway, it is nearly lunchtime by now, time to go to the restaurant. At a table in the roofed outdoor area I use my damp beach towel for a general mop-up, and under the sign that states *'No Wet Clothes in the Restaurant!'* I pull my dripping beach dress over an equally waterlogged bikini. Then I join the queue for lunch, and no one comments on my rule infringement because nearly everyone is sporting wet clothes today.

Fijian dishes are beautifully presented and served by the amiable staff who are apologetic about the weather and assure us that this relentless rain is most unusual. It never lasts more than twenty minutes at most, they state with a sorrowful shake of their heads. But the food is delicious, and afterwards we are treated to a show of the traditional and famous hula dance by two girls with incredibly mobile hips. A martial dance follows, performed by two men. It features vigorous canoe-rowing ("Are we in Hawaii yet?" I imagine) and fierce grimacing with an outstretched tongue.

Finally, the younger of the two men shows us a Samoan fire dance. He is a youth of good looks and perfect physique, and his performance is breathtaking and jaw-dropping in its energetic and daring accomplishment.

As we are sheltering from the rain under the same tin roof before my departure, I get a chance to have a brief chat with him and ask some questions. For how long has he been practising this skill? For four years, he says. And how come the fire does not burn his skin when the flames touch it? "One gets used to it, but at first it is painful." He does have a few burn marks. And what made him, as a Fijian, learn this Samoan dance? He points out a friend, a Samoan who came to live here and asked if he wanted to learn it.

In turn, he is surprised by the fact that I am travelling around the world by myself (aren't they all?) and would like to hear more about my adventure, but the time has come to leave. Our group is assembling to board the small boats that await us at the beach, and he waves goodbye with a sincere "It was nice to meet you!"

I am intrigued by this tradition of dancing with fire, which is so clearly about man's mastery of a dangerous element. This kind of dance is practised on many of the islands along the Ring of Fire, so their male inhabitants must feel a real need to demonstrate their ability to handle the element's powerful destructive force.

But dancing with fire is also a convincing metaphor for the human capacity to tame volcanic passions and master flame-like desires within the soul, and this fact is eloquently expressed in the striking image of a young man who tames flames in a daring act of remarkable self-control: a dance in which he does not get burnt.

The time of our return trip passes in musing on the appeal of Polynesian men. Here, male good looks appear to be more common than elsewhere. And, quite apart from being handsome, they seem to be completely at ease with themselves – which makes them even more attractive. Of course I have had only the briefest of glimpses and am therefore in no position to judge, but the gentle, openhearted friendliness I witnessed here is appealing.

The young girls who performed the hula dance with an endearingly shy, self-conscious air were also lovely and a pleasure to observe. After weeks spent among the cruising crowds, I notice that I am becoming increasingly sensitized to the state of the human form. There are so many crooked and bulging shapes to be seen all around that they inevitably make me more aware what a rare and precious thing human beauty is – beauty, scattered like these coral islands in a sea of decrepitude and ugliness.

Day 38 ~ Saturday, 11th February 2012 ~ sunrise: 7.01am ~ sunset: 8.00pm ~ sea state: slight ~ wind: NW 3, gentle breeze ~ weather: sunny ~ temperature: 27°C ~ time zone: GMT+13

Cyclone Detour

The captain informs us that a new cyclone is heading our way. It makes a detour necessary for our comfort's sake and will add about another hundred sea miles to our route, but it ought not to delay our arrival in Auckland on Monday. It is of course imperative that the ship arrives on time and does not lose its prearranged slot in the harbour. The captain adds that our new course will take us "back across the Date Line which, I know, you all like so much!" This humorous hint refers to the fact that he received many questions and queries about that crossing earlier. And so we find ourselves back on GMT +13 for a while.

At the dinner table, I am being pointedly ignored by Beryl, Gilbert and Amanda, who obviously consider it the height of ingratitude that I did not enjoy myself at the Pennant Grill the other night. But Tony continues to laugh at my remarks and makes me laugh in turn, and dear Martha proves a loyal friend. Our table waiters, Francis and Marcus, are always friendly and kind, and they are also keenly observant. Now and again I notice that they are covertly glancing at my face, as if they knew and understood everything.

Day 39 ~ Sunday, 12th February 2012 ~ sunrise: 6.56am ~ sunset: 8.14pm ~ sea state: lively ~ wind: SE 8, gale ~ weather: heavy showers ~ temperature: 21°C

Well of Sadness

Today I visit the library for a closer look at the island groups of the South Pacific. Studying world maps in a large atlas always has a calming effect on my mind and puts any minor irritations, such as the behaviour of my dinner companions, into perspective.

Then I give the 'Chocaholics' event with its fabled chocolate fountain a miss because today's dance lesson runs through all the Latin dance sequences we have learnt so far.

It is very enjoyable, and afterwards Lawrence introduces me to his ailing wife. If she minds at all that her husband likes to dance with me and several other ladies, she hides it well. Anyhow, I for my part have no intention of giving her cause for jealousy.

There are several things to take care of at this point, such as buying the next round of postcards and stamps, and changing British pounds to New Zealand dollars for our next port of call. Then it is time to get changed for another dinner. Today's dress code is 'smart casual', which means that some passengers will aim for a smart, and others for a casual look.

My favourite place at table is next to the window. Here I can watch the waves from the ship's bow as they run into the oncoming swell and throw up an impressive curtain of foam; all the while pondering those feelings of sadness and disconnectedness I often feel when surrounded by people. There is nothing for it but to receive this pain that wells up like the ocean swell, welcome it into my heart and let it dig that deep well which, according to a Persian legend, joy will come to fill, God willing.

How is it that, touring the Scottish Highlands alone for weeks, I never suffer a moment's loneliness? Walking the hills and moors in perfect solitude, I felt deeply connected to my surroundings; but on this ship, with its crowds in a jolly mood as they chatter on their rounds, moving from social events to companionable meals to collective entertainments, I usually feel alone. Astute minds might argue that these are obviously not kindred spirits, and they would be right. But why do I find it so hard to hold on to my habitual state of calm contentment in these gregarious circumstances?

Day 40 ~ Monday, 13th February 2012 ~ sunrise: 6.48am ~ sunset: 8.21pm ~ wind: 2, light breeze ~ weather: partly cloudy ~ temperature: 21°C ~ distance travelled since Port Denarau: 1,250 nautical miles ~ in total: 15,221 nautical miles

Auckland

This summer morning in New Zealand is as wet and grey as any in Great Britain, but the forecast from the bridge seems confident that we shall have sunshine later. Stepping out on deck this morning, I have Auckland's skyline of glass-and-steel office towers right before me, and though it is not yet seven o'clock, traffic is already bustling busily. Ship-to-shore gantry cranes along the docks awaken and lower their long necks towards the water like prehistoric animals. Yes, this is civilization as we know it – and yet such a modern city feels strange after time spent among Polynesian islands.

Today, the usual security procedures are enlivened by the appearance of a sniffer dog – a light-coloured, tail-wagging Labrador. This dog follows its trained nose purposefully along our line of bags and exudes exuberant friendliness. Tempting though it is, I am sure it would be a mistake to pat it, for immigration officials in New Zealand look just as stern as any we have seen to date. It is not just drugs they are screening us for, but also any kind of food. Nothing edible is to be brought ashore, and only commercially bottled water is allowed – somewhat grudgingly, one feels.

Our tour takes us through Auckland, the City of Sails, and over the Harbour Bridge, nicknamed the 'Nippon Clip-on'. Why? Because about ten years after the original bridge was built, it was no longer able to cope with the traffic across the bay and a Japanese firm landed the contract to extend it by clipping two extra lanes onto either side. But Auckland's volume of traffic has again outgrown the bridge's capacity, and now a tunnel under the bay is planned.

We reach the Sky Tower and take a speedy elevator to its viewing platform. Thick glass panels in the floor make for exciting and lofty views of the streets far below, but they are not for the fainthearted. The panorama is impressive. Aurora can be seen in the distant harbour, and for the first time she appears dwarfed by her surroundings.

Then we visit the 'Antarctic Encounter & Underwater World', a project realized against all odds by a man called Kelly Tarlton. Unfortunately he did not live to see his dream project completed, which – despite the initial scepticism – became one of Auckland's main attractions.

Here we see a lovingly constructed replica of Robert F. Scott's hut from the base camp of his ill-fated expedition, complete with a science lab and piano of the era.

A snowmobile on a track takes us around a colony of two kinds of small penguins that live here in precariously simulated Antarctic conditions. Many forms of marine life are displayed, among them the gruesome but fascinating specimen of a pale and slightly flaking giant-squid baby in formaldehyde. – Wouldn't my class have loved to see that!

The last half hour is spent on a sunny wall by the quayside, writing postcards:

"Dear Everyone, this is as far away from it all as I can get on the globe. From here onwards I shall be returning. Not sure that I'm ready yet; am rather enjoying this lovely life of luxurious leisure and world-viewing."

This half-day tour over, I use the afternoon to explore the wide and busy streets of Auckland by myself. Numerous souvenir shops are selling an assortment of sheepskin boots, lambswool clothing, seashell jewellery, woodcarvings in the Maori style, gaudy fridge magnets, and appealing ranges of cosmetics featuring kiwi fruit, Manuka honey and Rotorua mud.

Back on the ship, a special treat is in store, for I had taken up the 'Valentine's Day Offer' and booked a spa appointment. Now I get a Swedish back-and-neck massage, an ankle-and-foot massage, and a facial with special attention to the skin around the eyes – all for just fifty-nine pounds. I enjoy these harmonizing treatments a lot and am surprised, once again, by how much better my skin looks and feels afterwards. Having always been dismissive of beauty treatments in my tomboyish manner, I am on the road to my personal skincare Damascus. ("Road to Damascus moment: used in reference to an important moment of insight, typically one that leads to a dramatic transformation of attitude or belief.")

Evening comes, and I take pictures of Francis and Marcus, our lovely team of efficient waiters who make dinner such a pleasant experience each day. It is Francis's last week with us, because his contract ends in Sydney and he will be going home to Mumbai. It has been an inspiration to observe him perform his daily duties with such good humour, dedication and precision. He added a touch of class to the restaurant with his personality, and his quietly caring manner made me think of Mother Teresa, who reportedly said: "Not all of us can do great things – but we can all do little things with great love."

Day 41 ~ Tuesday, 14th February 2012 ~ sunrise: 6.54am ~ sunset: 8.20pm ~ wind: 2, light breeze ~ weather: sunny ~ temperature: 26°C ~ distance travelled since Auckland: 148 nautical miles ~ in total: 15,369 nautical miles

Bay of Islands

By the time I step on deck, Aurora is already lying at anchor off shore. Two hundred metres of cable are keeping her steady in twelve metres of water beneath the keel, as our "cap-tain" announces from the bridge. The waters of the bay are smooth and boarding the tenders is easy today.

My excursion has the off-putting title 'The Maori Experience' but turns out to be the most rewarding tour yet. In the course of half a day, we are taught to row a double canoe Polynesian style, responding to traditional calls and chanting "paddle-and-tap, paddle-and-tap" in time with the rhythm and in perfect unison.

Our instructor is a chief of the Ngapuhi tribe and an impressive man of stocky build; charismatic, loud-voiced and adorned with traditional tattoos. Incredibly good with words and fond of talking, he confides that his nickname is Big Mouth, before narrating New Zealand's history from his people's perspective. His son-in-law (whom he frequently interrupts) tells us about the plants we see as we paddle up the beautiful Waitangi River towards the Haruru Waterfalls.

Then the chief calls upon his grandson, sitting at the back of the canoe, to recite his ancestral genealogy for us. The boy is a youngster of about fourteen years and complies without shyness. Working alongside grown men and learning the ropes, he knows his place and has no discernible teenage attitude. He is the little one who has much to learn, and he knows it; but what he has learnt, he displays without embarrassment. In the following Q&A session, I ask what it means to poke out one's tongue at an enemy, and the chief explains: In former times, when warriors customarily ate the slain bodies of their foes, there was no worse insult than to tell a man by showing him your tongue that he would soon be no more than your excrement, for your wagging tongue signalled that you could already taste his flesh.

The chief dismisses the notion that warriors ate their enemies to assimilate their spirit or their power. It was all about reducing their opponents to dung.

"We are a pragmatic people," he claims with pride.

Standing tall and naked (except for a feathered loin cloth) at the carved prow of his canoe, the chief tells us about the swirling tattoos that cover his chest and shoulders. As he aligns himself with the cardinal directions of the compass, each blue-black line tells a story about the geography of the land around him: Over his breastbone there rises a hidden spring that feeds the sacred lake. From it, two rivers run east and westwards across his shoulders. One of these rivers flows calmly into the Bay of Islands, as shown by a repeating pattern of lines, while the second river, more turbulent, is represented by large swirls. – It is true earth-writing, etched onto the living skin.

Ngapuhi – the name of his tribe – has been translated by anthropologists as 'People of the Land', the chief tells us; though he himself would say that it means 'We People who *are* the Land'. This subtle distinction is illustrated by his own tattoo, for the hidden spring of life that rises within his chest and spreads in waves through his body is depicted by the swirling pattern on his skin – a pattern that traces the life-giving streams of his homeland at the same time.

I am touched by the beauty of his summary that makes me – in this instance only – able to appreciate tattooed skin.

At the end of the excursion, the chief asks if one of us would like to say a prayer to our god(s) in gratitude for our journey together. Because, as he puts it, "Wherever canoes are tethered, conversations take place and enlightenment happens."

A gentleman rises to the occasion. Standing up in the canoe, he speaks beautifully and from the heart as he expresses his special thanks in all our names. Then we climb out of the canoe one by one and strip off our lifejackets. These are now drenched with perspiration, for the sun is shining mightily and the day is hot. The chief shakes our hand in farewell and offers those who are willing the traditional Maori nose-to-nose gesture of friendship. And his straightforward, genuine humanity and spiritual awareness make this moment of stillness, affection and true listening to the other's presence a perfect embodiment of all that I have lately begun to miss.

In the afternoon I visit the small local town and spend my NZ dollars on the poster of an antique New Zealand map, some beautiful cards and a sarong, printed with elephants. Then I return to the landing place to catch a tender to the ship, but all other passengers have had that very same idea, apparently: The queue is long, the sun is hot, and it seems quite pointless to stand in line for hours.

Instead, I sit down in the shade of a tree nearby and watch the tenders as they come and go. Large shuttle buses come and go as well, disgorging more and more passengers who keep the queue at a constant, enormous length, and so I decide to wait until most people have gone, content to sit in the shade and absorb the beauty of this place.

The afternoon's canoeing group returns from their outing, receive the traditional farewell and leave to join the queue. I observe the chief and his kinsmen as they clean and tidy their canoes with care, collect paddles and lifejackets and, supervised by the chief's managerial wife, pile it all into two large and gleaming white vans. Then the men exchange their traditional wraps for contemporary shorts and pull on aqua socks to fetch their Yamaha outboard engine before driving home, possibly to check their emails or update their website. Clearly, the Maori inhabit two very different worlds at once; but, as the chief remarked earlier: "Why shouldn't we use all that wonderful technology?"

I turn my attention to two little girls who are playing on a strip of sand by the water and am touched by their earnest engagement with the natural world, their graceful movements and the unspoilt beauty of their human form that seems like a seed, a message and a promise. At times it can be distressing to see how many adults have not fulfilled this potential. The seed fell on stony ground and grew up twisted, the message went unheeded as the mind narrowed, and the early promise of childhood was broken or lost ...

To witness it is to feel sad, and at times disheartened.

At ten past six I board the last tender. The sea is choppy now and my fellow passengers are crabby, angered by the long wait. They report that two of the ship's tenders developed engine problems which put them out of action and caused a cumulative delay. Once we are all back on the ship, there is barely enough time to get changed before dinner is served.

My arms and shoulders are a bit burnt from rowing in the sun, but I am very pleased with this beautiful day and in a contented mood that tides me over the frosty ambience now hanging over the dinner table. My formerly so friendly dinner companions are determined to punish me. And what for? ... For not being like them, presumably. I pretend not to notice and gaze quietly out of the window. Unexpectedly, a dolphin jumps from the waves right beside our ship, arches its back in the evening sunshine and dives back into the sea, leaving a flash of joy and gratitude in my mind that is like a greeting from a better world.

Day 42 ~ Wednesday, 15th February 2012 ~ sunrise: 6.16am ~ sunset: 7.51pm ~ sea state: slight ~ wind: S 3, gentle breeze ~ weather: sunny ~ temperature: 24°C ~ time zone: GMT+12

Tasman Sea

Exhausted by yesterday's vigorous Polynesian-style rowing in the heat, I plan a day of nothing but journal-writing and rest. Conveniently, Lawrence rings with apologies. Because he and his wife will be leaving the ship in Sydney, they need to prepare for the end of their cruise and do some packing. And so there is ample time for an extended siesta, followed by tranquil hours in which to write and draw.

Aurora is steaming straight across the Tasman Sea, heading for Australia. It is sunny and hot on deck, and rather windy. My sunburnt arms are very grateful for this restful day spent indoors, and also for a generous lathering of Manuka Honey Regenerating Cream, bought in Auckland and working like pure, cooling magic.

Day 43 ~ Thursday, 16*th* February 2012 ~ *sunrise:* 6.55am ~ *sunset:* 8.26pm ~ *sea state: slight* ~ *wind: SE 3, gentle breeze* ~ *weather: sunny* ~ *temperature: 25°C*

Keeping Busy

In this morning's exercise class, Britta is homing in on our abdominals. Afterwards I seek out the launderette to tackle a bit of unavoidable ironing. The launderette's confined space is hot and steamy like a sauna from all the ceaseless activity, but one ironing board is available and I set to work. Doing laundry on a cruise is a healthily grounding experience, a bit of hands-on work to contrast all that leisure and pampering. But ironing has never been a favourite activity of mine, and eventually the humid heat becomes so overpowering that I flee to my cool cabin, those freshly pressed clothes fluttering in my wake.

Working on the journal keeps me busy until lunch, which I usually have upstairs in the Orangery these days. Going there early helps to avoid the rush, and not being waited on saves a lot of time. After the meal I watch the lengthy but strangely entertaining film 'Australia', shown in preparation for our arrival there tomorrow.

Earlier, I asked the waiters for permission to sit in the empty restaurant at five o'clock, for I would like to draw the view from my place at table as a frame for the jumping dolphin. The waiters, happy to oblige, are intrigued by my request but let me get on with it as they go about setting the tables for dinner. The atmosphere is peaceful and work progresses well. As I get ready to leave, Marcus and a few others come over to take a look at the drawing, and their interest leads us to flick through the whole book. They seem so pleased to see this journey (for which they are working so hard) recorded in words and images, and their faces are beaming as they identify each place and picture.

It is Francis's final day on duty and, dinner over, we take turns at shaking his hand in farewell. In reward for his first-class service, he now receives generous tips in the customary envelope, with words of heartfelt thanks and best wishes for the future. We are all saddened by his leaving and agree that we shall miss his kind and competent presence.

(*Cruiser's tip: The giving of tips and gratuities remains a highly contentious issue, but do take it very seriously. Before embarking on your cruise, study the company's policy for tipping the staff. Different cruise lines have different regulations, though all of them pay very small salaries to remain competitive.

Their hopeful reasoning is that your generosity will make up for their costiveness, but it means that those workers who have little or no contact with the clientele – hardworking cooks and cleaners, the engineers and maintenance workers below decks – do not benefit from such gratuities. And so some of the cruise lines have begun to add automatic gratuities at a per-day rate to their passenger accounts, to be shared out later among the crew. These charges are optional and are removed upon request, should you wish to handle the matter at your own discretion.

The fact remains that tipping in some form is essential on a cruise, therefore budget a generous amount and be aware that the ship's crew and staff work diligently for your personal comfort at the sacrifice of their own. Their willingness to provide excellent service for a minimal salary ought to be rewarded.)

Day 44 ~ Friday, 17th February 2012 ~ sunrise: 6.30am ~ sunset: 7.47pm ~ wind: E 3, gentle breeze ~ weather: sunny ~ temperature: 26°C ~ time zone: GMT+11 ~ distance travelled since Bay of Islands: 1,163 nautical miles ~ in total: 16,532 nautical miles

Sydney

Our arrival in Sydney really could not have been better, for we approach the harbour at sunrise in calm, clear weather. The view of the skyline with its iconic opera house and the Harbour Bridge is spectacular!

Martha and I meet on deck, admire the sights and take scores of photographs in our intense enjoyment of the lovely scene. Even from our breakfast table we have a good view of Sydney's signature landmarks, for Aurora is berthed in prime position on Circular Quay. I am thrilled to be here!

Today, our local tour guide is a more mature lady – elegant, distinguished and quite unlike any of our previous guides. She shows us around Sydney and outlines its historical progress from convict colony to "the most happening city in the world" (according to a recent survey).

Maybe it is this reputation that attracted the fruit bats? Thousands of these creatures have come to settle in Sydney's botanical gardens and their colonies wreak havoc in old and precious trees. Nothing that has been tried will scare them away, and because these fruit bats are a protected species, the options are limited and the park wardens in despair.

Furthermore, a long spell of drought has brought large numbers of ibis from the wetlands. They too settled happily in the urban centre of Sydney, where they pick through the rubbish. We are told that the city council had to commission special ibis-proof litter bins to stop these birds from making a mess everywhere. Add to that the aggressive bull sharks now populating the harbour, and it is clear that this splendid place is enjoyed by a wide variety of species.

It is a flawless morning with blue skies and abundant sunshine as we drive out to Bondi Beach. Owing to a recent row of rainy days, the coast is lush and green and looks its best. The famous beach is loosely populated on a Friday morning. Its white sand is soft and deep and of astonishing fineness. Tanned surfers with bleached locks huddle around their boards, children paddle in the shallow water, beach babes in mini-bikinis stroll up and down, and I collect a handful of lovely periwinkle shells.

And now, finally, it is time for a tour of the opera, or 'The House' as it is affectionately called. This is a building to fall in love with! It looks stunning from every angle as the light plays on its white surface in the changing moods of the day and holds the curved shells of its structure in dreamlike, silent motion, like the feathered pinions of birds, the wings of butterflies … I am smitten! Has there ever been a building that comes so close to expressing poetry and music in its cadence, its rhyme and its rhythm?

We are shown the inside of this fascinating building by Jon, a guide who is clearly in love with The House himself. With several informative stops along the way he steers us through interlinking stairwells, hallways and foyers to the enormous concert hall with its steep tiers of seats and the famous stage where practically all of the music world's great names have performed over the years.

And then we sit in the opera theatre and listen to our guide's narration, all the while looking at the black, yawning cavern of the bare stage. In a little while, the set of tonight's 'Magic Flute' will be brought up on an enormous platform elevator at the back of the stage ... and I have a ticket!

On this tour, the story of The House's building project is told from hopeful start to controversial finish, a process that was fraught with difficulty and dramatic twists. And, as seems inevitable wherever something so outstanding is conceived, there had been dissent, opposition, intrigue and heartache. Imagine how the Danish architect Jørn Utson must have felt when he was forced to leave the completion of his visionary work to others! He left Sydney in bitter disappointment and never returned to see the building completed.

But, in a happier ending, Utson's son is now working with the management of The House on the conservation and development of his father's magnificent monument to the creative human spirit.

All too soon this enthralling tour is over and everyone heads for the gift shop. It yields a nice poster, appealing postcards, another T-shirt, and a lovely little book that tells the story of The House and its architect.

Comparing prices, I notice that some of the tags show amounts that cannot actually be paid in Australian Dollars, for these have no small units like pence or cents. And so the T-shirt, priced at 29.99AU$, in actual fact costs thirty dollars. I bring this matter up at the till and am informed that "it is customary to round up".

Raising a Swiss eyebrow, I enquire if this variation on a familiar pricing theme is even legal, for surely it must be considered quite unethical to announce prices that are not matched by the local currency ...? At this point it becomes clear that there is indeed a limit to the laidback attitude of those easygoing Aussies, for the sales personnel suddenly displays distinct signs of tetchiness. And, seeing that no good will come from pursuing this fascinating question further, I hand over thirty dollars, grab the T-shirt and leave The House behind.

After a good meal and some rest on board, I dash off another postcard to my son, who works at another opera house.
"Today we had a spectacular arrival in Sydney at sunrise. Then a tour of the city, Bondi Beach, and the fabulous opera where you were constantly on my mind. Tonight I shall see 'The Magic Flute' there, in a production of the New York Met. How lucky am I? But hey – *I* may have been there, but I got *you* the T-shirt."
The postcard, dropped in the mailbox, begins its long journey to the other side of the world, while I get ready to go out and visit The House for a second time.

It is no more than a short stroll around Circular Quay, yet we are taken to the opera by coach. Arriving at the meeting point exactly on time, I learn that my group is already gone. *Bother!* ... I rush down the stairs, over the gangway, into the terminal and down the escalator, just in time to be counted as the last member of the group. The coach departs at once and the lady in charge addresses us with welcoming words that end in "... and you have all got your tickets."
What? *Tickets?* – What tickets, I ask, greatly surprised, for I remember reading that we would receive them on the coach, in exchange for the tour ticket I now hold out to her.

Did I not see the desk in the foyer where we were supposed to pick up our tickets for the performance? No, I did not, for I was in a hurry and worried about missing the group. With a sigh the lady rings her colleague and asks for my ticket to be delivered directly to the opera.

Gilbert and Amanda are making snarky comments at my back, but I take no notice. Instead, I am wondering why this group had left early: Before every excursion, passengers are requested NOT to show up early at the assembly points, and advised to keep STRICTLY to the given time. Until now, respecting these instructions had never caused me problems. And why inform passengers that their tickets will be handed out on the coach, if they are then to be collected inside the terminal? ... Could it be that our tour organizers expect their explicit instructions to be ignored by all and sundry, or why else do they seem surprised that I took them at their word?

Now our coach turns into a side street. It is blocked by police cars with flashing lights, a crowd has gathered, and these onlookers gape at a businessman who is lying on the tarmac, right in front of a car. To our relief he is conscious and there is no blood, but the coach driver mutters in exasperation, for he knows that we shall remain stuck here.

After a long wait, an ambulance arrives and we get to witness extremely unhurried Aussie emergency assistance. Then nothing more happens for quite some time, until the unfortunate man is bundled off to hospital at last.

We make it to the opera in good time, reminded of the lethal power of cars and the importance of caution for pedestrians. The group goes inside, but I am told to wait for my ticket at the entrance. There I am joined by a petite, elegant American lady in her sixties who is also ticketless, for she too trusted the instructions and had overlooked the desk at the terminal. Her name is Norah and we take to each other instantly. Soon enough our tickets arrive and we go inside to find our seats. How *exciting* to sit in the Sydney Opera House at last!

Here, Mozart's music has to rise from a Wagnerian pit. The fact that the orchestra is hidden from sight takes away an important part of opera's fascination. Aware of this, the conductor performs a charming little act to make up for his invisibility: A handpuppet, smartly dressed as a conductor, appears over the parapet and takes a bow in his place – to great hilarity and general applause.

After the *ouverture*, the curtains rise on Julie Taymor's acclaimed production. It plays with visually appealing Asian imagery, provides magical moments and works especially well for the animals, from birds to bears.

Pamina's voice is strong and beautiful, and she carries her part with convincing loveliness. Monostathos, *not* black, is exquisitely revolting, and Papageno plays on a blatant Aussie-ness that earns him the warmest applause. But above all, Mozart's musical mastery triumphs once again.

The performance over, I stroll along Circular Quay by night and by myself, preferring not to return by coach. Aurora lies on the opposite side of the bay, fully illuminated and reflected by the dark water. She looks wonderful anywhere, but this setting is more splendid than most.

The bars along the waterfront are bustling with people in a party mood – mainly young, tanned and good-looking urban professionals who are making the most of the happy circumstances that placed them in this particularly vibrant spot on the face of the earth. Music is everywhere, sparkling drinks, splendid food and carefree laughter ... Yes, life is good in Sydney!

The summer night is warm and the harbour with its myriad lights a heartlifting sight, framed by the big Harbour Bridge, our white ship, and the opera house that is even now spreading its sails to catch the breeze.

The House remains anchored to its idyllic location, but Aurora will be sailing away to new shores at midnight – by which time I am, regrettably, fast asleep.

~ ~ ~

~ The Third Leg ~

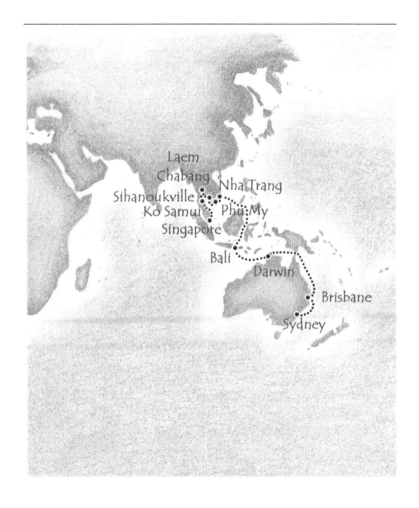

Day 45 ~ Saturday, 18th February 2012 ~ sunrise: 5.30am ~ sunset: 6.26pm ~ sea state: calm ~ wind: NE 3, gentle breeze ~ weather: sunny ~ temperature: 25°C ~ time zone: GMT+10

Limitless Spaces

My core muscles are still smarting from Britta's efficient workout last Thursday, and so a day of rest and journal-writing is most welcome. At a shaded table on the sunny side of the Promenade Deck I write all day, sheltered from both wind and heat as we sail along the eastern coast of Australia towards Brisbane. The sea is calm and glitters in the strong sunlight like smashed glass. In the hazy distance, the coastline is faintly visible.

A sudden announcement is broadcast from the bridge and addresses queries and complaints regarding the intense interest shown in our ship by local police, port and customs officials. Now it transpires that passengers' cabins had been searched once again (to the annoyance and upset of those concerned) but the captain's words make it quite plain that this is an investigation with which he – and therefore all of us – must comply.

Though he has one of the coolest jobs in the world, in moments like these I do not envy him. Does the complaining and rumour-mongering of his passengers get him down at times? In any case, this captain has admirable control, not just of his ship, but also his voice, and if he feels annoyed at the hassle, it is impossible to tell.

The time has come at last to carry out something I have long been looking forward to. My plan is to gaze at the stars of the Southern Sky while listening to Mozart's 'Requiem'.

After dinner I go to the deserted top deck and stretch out on a stack of sunloungers above the bridge. As Aurora glides through the darkness on her steady course, I study the night sky with the MP3 player attached to my ears. I have been looking forward to this moment since last June, when I first imagined it, but now that it is here and real, I find that much of this singular situation has to be pictured actively in the mind, since the human eye is unable to take it in: neither the true expanse of the ocean around, nor its depth below; not the extent of the continent lying at some distance to the left, nor limitless space as it rises above.

The mysterious ciphers formed by these southern stars are unknown to me. The only familiar figure is Orion, the Hunter, standing upright and still to the west. And all of these features – land, sea and sky, and the unnumbered stars – extend over distances that defy comprehension, for they fade beyond the radius of the beating heart and the watchful mind; but what an immense joy it is to be that tiny speck of consciousness in the midst of it, beholding this wonder!

Tingling with the splendour of all this vastness, I sing familiar notes of sublime music over the hum of the ship's engines: *"Pleni sunt coeli et terra gloria tua ..."*

Who but Mozart could bridge the distance between the stars and the human heart?

Day 46 ~ Sunday, 19th February 2012 ~ sunrise: 5.34am ~ sunset: 6.29pm ~ wind: 2 ~ weather: sunny ~ temperature: 32°C ~ distance travelled since Sydney: 491 nautical miles ~ in total: 17,023 nautical miles

Brisbane

Aurora makes her way up the Brisbane River in the early hours of the morning, her great propellers churning its silt to muddy clouds that swirl about her white bulk.

Sydney is a tough act to follow, and unsurprisingly our arrival in Brisbane is devoid of magic or excitement. The industrial estates that are dotted along the riverbanks, the pair of stark Gateway Bridges and the city's distant skyline have nothing captivating about them. But even so, Brisbane might be a very nice city – though I shall never know, for my excursion is taking me away to the Gold Coast. This is where Steve Irwin's conservation park is located, better known as 'Australia Zoo'.

Queensland is nicknamed the 'Sunshine State' and today's weather proves the point, for the air temperature is already above thirty degrees Celsius by the time we arrive at the zoo. This means of course that all animals are having an extended nap. Koalas snooze in their favourite tree, dingoes, kangaroos and wombats are stretched out on shady ground below. Snakes, large and small, sleep in tidy coils, like ropes on a quayside. Crocodiles float in their pools, basking in the sun and demonstrating that a motionless state of complete stillness is the only one that makes sense in such heat.

But an animal show at the 'Crocoseum' temporarily moves a variety of birds and beasts to a display of liveliness. Fed in public by a courageous keeper, the fierce snapping of the great crocodile's jaws can be heard all around the arena.

Australia Zoo is a lovely place, dedicated to the education of the public and the preservation of endangered wildlife. An exhibition of all things concerning crocodiles is particularly interesting, and I am fascinated by the fact that croc's skulls are riddled with air holes like a Swiss cheese or a sponge.

All around the walls, Steve Irwin's life and work is documented in pictures and articles. He was the Australian version of Gerald Durrell, with a similar passion for animals. Like Durrell, Irwin was concerned with preserving them for future generations, but one unfortunate day, snorkelling at the Great Barrier Reef, he met with an irritable stingray and an early death. Ever since, his wife and children have cared for the zoo and carry on his inspiring work.

Despite the intense heat of midday, it is enjoyable to wander around the beautiful grounds with a cooling cone of ice cream while observing unfamiliar animals. Some people even pay to have their picture taken with a cuddly koala that was dragged from its siesta for this purpose.

A long return journey and a cooling shower later, people congregate on deck, mostly in swimwear, to enjoy the mild evening sunshine with a drink and a chat while watching Aurora's departure. The river seems barely wide enough for the great ship to swing around, assisted by a tugboat at her stern. The captain calls it his "handbrake turn" and executes this challenging manoeuvre neatly. Now Aurora is heading downriver, bound for Cairns.

At dinner, there is general speculation about Tony's disappearance. We have not seen him since Sydney and cannot imagine that he would leave the ship without saying goodbye. It seems so unlike him! Enquiries by Amanda and Gilbert at Reception yield the information that "There is no passenger by this name aboard." Which is more mysterious still ... Whatever happened to him?

Day 47 ~ Monday, 20th February 2012 ~ sunrise: 5.43am ~ sunset: 6.36pm ~ sea state: calm ~ wind: E 2 ~ weather: sunny ~ temperature: 29°C

Great Barrier Reef

This morning, shortly after nine o'clock, Aurora passes her sister ship Oriana which is heading in the opposite direction. Both blow their horn in salutation, and crowds of passengers throng the railings to take pictures. Meanwhile I enjoy a swim, pleased to have the pool to myself.

The pool is usually too crowded for swimming these days, and I avoided it since I noticed that nobody bothers to shower before they go in. *Ugh!* Isn't a preliminary shower a matter of common courtesy? A notice on the wall requests it plainly – but does anyone read the pool rules? Since there is no one around to enforce these points, most passengers, just like little children, ignore them.

(*Cruiser's tip: The pool rules are few and have been established for good reasons. It is a matter of individual responsibility to respect them.)

Now the captain informs us that we entered the waters of the Great Barrier Reef around three o'clock this morning, and that a local pilot has come aboard to assist Aurora for the duration of her transit. How exciting!

Looking over the ship's side, I spot a long, light-coloured sea snake that swims towards our vessel in a movement as fluid as the surrounding waves ...

Wow! I am delighted to have seen a creature of the sea at last, and a fairly unusual one at that. It makes me look forward even more to tomorrow's excursion. This outing is the most expensive one on my list of bookings, but the Great Barrier Reef has intrigued me for years and I am keen to get a glimpse from a floating platform, an underwater viewing chamber and a semisubmersible.

Day 48 ~ Tuesday, 21st February 2012 ~ sunrise: 6.13am ~ sunset: 6.47pm ~ sea state: calm ~ wind: SE 3, gentle breeze ~ weather: sunny ~ temperature: 30°C

Bad News

Never before have I seen the ocean as calm and still as this morning. Like a dull mirror, it reflects the light playing on cloud formations. Here and there, isolated cloudbursts veil the coastline with rain showers. It promises to be a splendid day – until, over our breakfast, we hear the ominous words: "This is the captain, speaking from the bridge ..."

Oh *no!* Hearing it, we know that we must brace ourselves for bad news. And it is bad news indeed! The captain regrets to inform us that, despite the best efforts of his team and the cruise line's port agents, the local authorities will not consent to clear our ship for disembarkation at anchorage at Yorkey's Knob, but *only* and *if* we go through the established procedures at the harbour terminal in Cairns.

But 1) Aurora is unable to dock there at such short notice, 2) it would mean a twenty-eight-mile roundtrip by tender for hundreds of passengers, 3) this would take most of the day and 4) not leave enough time for the booked excursions ... and for all these reasons he, as captain, decided to cancel our stop here and head straight for Darwin.

Hearing this, about two thousand passengers catch their breath in disbelief. Surely this *cannot* be happening! But by and by, stark reality sinks in and I feel an overpowering wave of disappointment. My one chance of ever visiting the Great Barrier Reef just evaporated in a flash, even though we are *so* close! Extending beneath our feet and Aurora's keel, it remains as inaccessible as ever, and there is nothing for it but to accept what cannot be changed.

Trying to keep calm and not feel too bitter about the situation, I go and distract myself with a session at the gym. (Since I don't drink any alcohol, it is the best I can do.) Jovan tries to lighten the gloomy mood and attempts a feeble joke about it all, but our glares put him on guard. To us, this is no joking matter!

Later, on deck, I breathe calmly as I attempt to relax on a sunlounger, but now and again I wander to the portside rail, look at the islands and bays along the coast, imagine the wonders beneath the sea's surface and feel cheated. And in all the faces and conversations around me, sentiments are expressed that echo mine. After a light meal at the Orangery, I withdraw from this disappointing day to have an extended siesta. Then I busy myself with some sewing, adjusting the hemline of a beach dress while watching a port presentation of Darwin on the TV. It helps to occupy my mind with other thoughts than those still circling the Great Barrier Reef and the missed chance to see it.

At dinner, the commonly held opinion is that we must have acquired a reputation as a drug ship. Surely this must be the reason for the sternly unyielding attitude of the Australian port authorities! Rumour has it that Aurora was mentioned on Sky News earlier, and some people maintain that there are customs officials aboard even now, searching cabin after cabin with their sniffer dogs ...

However that may be, all are agreed that it is awful to have our plans spoilt by a few passengers involved with drugs, and the big question is: Will it cause more problems in other ports?

Day 49 ~ Wednesday, 22nd February 2012 ~ sunrise: 6.23am ~ sunset: 6.53pm ~ sea state: calm ~ wind: E 3, gentle breeze ~ weather: sunny ~ temperature: 31°C

Low Point

So the proverbial honeymoon is over! Halfway through this cruise, the experience has reached what I assume must be its lowest point, and as yet I cannot see how it will recover. For one thing, there is the growing list of places we have to miss: first Acapulco, then the Great Barrier Reef, and now, as we have just been told, Cochin as well. And then there is a sense that something unpleasant is going on behind the scenes – something that will have an impact on our cruise, but about which we must be told nothing ... and as a result, one feels horribly like cattle awaiting its fate.

On a daily level, things are also looking rather bleak. Many familiar faces have disembarked in Sydney, our lovely dance instructors among them. They made their lessons such fun, but the new couple has a teaching style that is much less appealing. My dance partner Lawrence remained in Sydney too and no suitable replacement came aboard there. The new girl in charge of the Aurora Vocalists has never led a choir before and is out of her depth – and so I decide to drop both dance lessons and choir singing, because their earlier light-heartedness is gone and it just isn't fun anymore.

Martha, who often attends concerts, plays and shows at home, agrees that the evening entertainment acts are dire and the volume is much too loud. Not even the films that are being shown these days provide a welcome distraction, for I know them by heart. And although Jack Lemmon, Marilyn Monroe and Audrey Hepburn have a timeless appeal, I am in no mood to watch them again right now.

And so I stick to my usual morning exercise routine with the lovely, professional gym team (who are fortunately with us for the whole journey) and continue to work on my journal, which keeps me sane. Right now, it is necessary to envisage my blessings to ward off feelings of frustration and gloom – until I hear from Lucy and Tom that they have just missed the Great Barrier Reef for the *second* time. On their earlier world cruise, a violent earthquake in Chile sent such enormous waves across the Pacific that boarding the tenders became quite impossible. – What rotten luck!

As our ship glides along the coastline, I look for Australia's northernmost point, Cape York. At the same time a message, broadcast from the bridge, informs us at last of certain facts. The captain confirms that three of Aurora's passengers were arrested by local authorities in San Francisco and charged with possession of Class A narcotics. Since that date, port officials everywhere have kept a close eye on our ship, the captain says, but he does not expect this to have any further impact on our future ports of call – none other than that we shall continue to be thoroughly screened.

Late as it comes, this statement clears the air, though there is no mention of what happened in Sydney. Where, for example, is Tony? There has been neither sign nor news of him. Did he fall overboard? Has he missed the ship? Or – horrible thought – was he arrested?

Evening comes, and with it a change of plans. It had seemed so appealing to sail into the sunset and not be heard of for three months, but now I break my resolve not to be in touch with Britain for the entire duration of this trip. Let's send a few emails home ...

But wouldn't you know it – the internet is down! Not because there is no satellite coverage, as an apologetic note outside the Cyb@study's door claims. No, the satellite dish is not working and cannot be fixed until we get the defective part replaced in Darwin.

I learn this straight from the technician whom I find grappling with the problem and ready to answer questions, and therefore I don't give credence to the latest rumours that are flying around Aurora's decks like startled starlings. They claim indignantly that our internet connection to the outside world has been deliberately cut by the cruise line. Why? So that no passenger is able to tell their families, and the world at large, about the ship's problems with drug smuggling, of course!

Day 50 ~ Thursday, 23rd February 2012 ~ sunrise: 6.49am ~ sunset: 7.24pm ~ sea state: calm ~ wind: E 4, moderate breeze ~ weather: sunny ~ temperature: 30°C

Passenger Arrested

Today marks the end of the first half of our journey around the world, if everything goes according to plan. And now we get more information from our beleaguered captain. He has permission to inform us that another passenger had been arrested in Sydney for possession of drugs. He can say no more than that; but rumour has it that it was a middle-aged man who went ashore with bags of cocaine stuffed into the wetsuit he wore under his clothes. Even so, the cunning ploy did not fool Sherlock, the sniffer dog!

Everyone is now convinced that it must have been our cheerful Tony, but I still find this hard to believe. He may not be the sharpest tool in the box – but would he really do something so stupid?

To soften the blow of our missed visit, the local pilot gives a talk today and we learn some interesting facts: The Great Barrier Reef lines the top part of Australia's east coast for about 2300 kilometres. Freshwater from numerous rivers prevents the coral reef from expanding towards the shore and keeps it at a distance, and so, as its name indicates, this reef forms a great barrier against the tides of the Coral Sea. The waters of the resulting channel are extremely calm, and ships like to use this tranquil sea lane even though scattered reefs, hidden atolls, shoals and shallows make it a difficult route to navigate. In the past, accidents happened and ships ran aground on occasion, but then local pilotage was made compulsory in 1991. Given the reef's delicate and unique eco system, it is surprising that there is no restriction on the type of vessel that may use this passage. As long as a local pilot is aboard, even oil tankers are allowed.

It is the longest singlehanded pilotage anywhere in the world, and naturally the pilot will get tired towards the end. His fatigue could become a problem, and so the duration of each transit has to be managed very carefully.

Someone asks if he is in command of the vessel during his pilotage. He declines, saying that the running of a ship is always "to master's orders and pilot's advice".

Walking turns around the top deck, I stop here and there to spend time in pleasant conversation with acquaintances old and new, and begin to feel more upbeat as a result. Then a couple of agreeable hours are spent with the big atlas in the library, sketching a map-like impression of the coastline we are travelling along. This also helps to lift the mood.

The sea in the reef's channel is so calm and smooth, it looks as if it had been oiled. There is not a wrinkle on its glossy surface. A line of repetitive cloud formations sits low on the horizon, resembling a row of chorus girls in fluffy skirts and sending mirrored streaks of reflected light across the shimmering water.

At dinner there is only *one* topic, for Googling passengers confirm that it is indeed Tony who was arrested in Sydney, with about thirty kilograms of cocaine. The silly man! He is probably having dinner in prison as we speak. Now there will be no more of the spa treatments he liked so much, no bottles of fancy wine or T-shirts for his grandchildren. And although we all liked him, we are now very cross, because it is due to his antics that we had to miss the Great Barrier Reef. Well, the mahogany tan he was so proud of will have faded considerably by the time he is seen outside prison walls again! (A news article will later reveal that he is facing a charge of life imprisonment and a fine of 80'000 dollars. Certainly not the retirement plan he had in mind!)

Day 51 ~ Friday, 24th February 2012 ~ sunrise: 6.47am ~ sunset: 7.11pm ~ wind: N 2, light breeze ~ weather: sunny ~ temperature: 32°C ~ time zone: GMT+9.5 ~ distance travelled since Brisbane: 1,990 nautical miles ~ in total: 19,013 nautical miles

Darwin

I collect my tour sticker and wait on the Promenade Deck for the appointed time, only to find that this group left early too and is already disembarking. Rushing ashore to catch up, I am once more the last person to board an already full coach.

As I sit down in the second row of seats reserved for disabled passengers, I sense a wave of animosity directed at me by the elderly couple at my back. They seem displeased with me for some reason, but I ignore their dark mutterings and turn my attention to the local tour guide who is now introducing himself. Jake is a tough and lean Aussie in his sixties, charming, tall and well-spoken. Commendably, he also refrains from cracking silly jokes, and as we are driving through the city, he tells us about the World War II bombing raids on Darwin by the Japanese – sixty-four in all!

It is a two-hour drive to Litchfield National Park and I am glad to be sitting at the front of the coach. Prone to travel sickness, I have to keep my eyes fixed on the road ahead at all times. In my childhood, the family car had to be stopped regularly on outings, so that I could be sick by the roadside, but occasionally dad's collar suffered misfortune. What a great relief it was to find that car journeys were no longer a problem once I could steer the car myself! And that is why, as an adult, I tend to forget about it; but on long coach drives in hot weather, such as this one, those familiar and dreaded feelings of nausea rise up once more.

(*Cruiser's tip: If overly sensitive inner ears make you suffer from travel sickness in general and car sickness in particular, be sure to get a letter stating this fact from your doctor before the cruise. This letter will prove your need to sit at the front of a coach and should spare you much aggravation.)

Amongst the abundant greenery of the monsoon rainforest, Jake points out various plants. For example, there is a type of eucalyptus tree that produces a black stocking of furry bark around its lower trunk as protection against wildfire. There are also delicate little fan palms, Australian Box with silvery stems, termite-resistant Northern Cypress and lush sugarcane grass. The droppings of free-roaming donkeys and horses decorate the road, and as we drive deeper into the national park, we see reddish termite mounds scattered between the trees. Crouching low among the shrubs, they resemble wild beasts on the prowl.

We stop at the Magnetic Termite Mounds. These are not in fact magnetic, but aligned to the North-South axis of the compass. Moulded from minuscule specks of soil, they are constructed in such a clever way that they catch as little heat as possible during the day. Their inside temperature is always agreeable, and these clay structures, hard as rock, withstand floods as well as wildfires.

Even more impressive are enormous clay heaps placed in close proximity, called the Cathedral Mounds. At almost three metres high, they are estimated to be between fifty and seventy years old. They tower above us like indestructible fortresses, and it is amazing to think that they were created by such frail, tiny creatures as termites. The original termite colonies have long since abandoned their former homes, but one of these mounds has now been taken over by meat ants. Bustling in and out of their tiny holes, they make us wary of getting too close in our sandaled feet.

The humid heat is intense and it is a relief to get back on the air-conditioned coach. But the hostile couple at my back are muttering that the guide is not doing his job properly and is "easily distracted". It seems to annoy them greatly that Jake, seated across the aisle, had fallen into conversation with me earlier. (The drive was long, his info-talk was done, and he was eager to try some of the German words he is learning). What makes people so judgemental, petty and spiteful?

Suddenly, a bird of prey flies up from the roadside, a black snake writhing in its claws ... The brief glimpse of this powerful image burns itself into my memory, for it has the vivid quality of an omen – of heavenly powers triumphing over evil. How thrilled the great Alexander would have been to see it on the eve of battle!

I wish I could have captured the moment on camera, but the startled bird was gone in a flash. Jake thinks it may have been a whistling kite, quite common in these parts.

Then he explains the plight of snakes and other wildlife now threatened with extinction by the toxic cane toad. Tragically, this disagreeable amphibian had been imported from South America in the fond hope that it would fight the sugarcane beetle in the plantations. No preliminary studies were done at the time, and so it was not discovered until much too late that the beetle (high up on the stalks) and the toad (staying on the ground) never met. Instead, being easy prey, the toxic toad entered the food chain and killed off lizards and crocs, iguanas and snakes, birds, cats and dogs. The slow but steady spread of the cane toad throughout Australia seems unstoppable, and no way has yet been found to reverse this ecological disaster.

This information bothers me intensely and I question Jake: What is being done to find a solution? Should there not be a scientific contest to search for the best approach, with a sizeable reward from the government? (I am thinking of a substantial prize here – like the one that had been promised by the British Parliament for a reliable way of establishing the correct longitude at sea, for this was a matter of national importance in the eighteenth century.)

How is it possible that this obvious problem has been allowed to continue unchecked for so long? Jake is happy to discuss this matter, for it is of great concern to him too, both as a farmer and a lover of wildlife.

We arrive at the Wangi Falls that plunge from the Tabletop Swamp over a steep, rocky cliff into a pool. Usually, visitors may swim in this inviting basin, but today the swimming area is closed. The water level is high and there is danger of crocodiles sneaking in. A large poster reads:

"OBSERVE CROCODILE WARNING SIGNS! Estuarine crocodiles (salties) inhabit the rivers throughout the Top End region. Incidents have caused serious injury and fatalities. The crocodile management programs in Darwin Harbour, Katherine River, Wangi Falls and Manton Dam reduce the risk of crocodile attack, but crocodiles may move into these areas without being detected. Be aware – and ALWAYS take notice of warning signs!"

A boardwalk leads across the flooded river and on into the rainforest, and now we are free to go exploring by ourselves. I have never walked through rainforest (except the botanical garden variety) and savour the experience.

The hot, humid closeness and the abundant greenery recede into dim darkness on all sides, and as I walk slowly and steadily uphill, I study the upthrust of a wild profusion of shoots, stems and trunks, veiled by dangling curtains of vines or lianas. From rotting layers of leaves on the ground, fungi are sprouting, moistened by the perpetual drip from large leaves that keep out the sunlight.

A platform, halfway up the cliff, affords a good view across the treetops below. One could do a circular walk over the cliff and around the waterfall, but that would be pushing it. It is hot, the remaining time is short, and it seems prudent to turn back at this point.

After a short drive, the coach stops at a roadside café. Half of the place is a building site because it was hit by lightning not long ago. For lunch we are offered a choice between chicken and a local fish, and as we drive on after the meal, Jake tells us interesting facts about the lifecycle of this Barramundi, also known as Asian sea bass:

Barramundi are hatched in the brackish water of estuaries or marine bays, and all those little fishes mature as males, swim upriver and live in freshwater; but then, when the monsoon season begins, they return to the estuaries to meet and mate with older, and much larger, females.

They participate in several spawning seasons, mature in age and grow in size, and then these Barramundi males undergo a sex change. By the next spawning season, they become fully-functioning females for the rest of their lives, and this amazing life-process is known to biologists as being 'sequentially hermaphroditic'.

Not only is this large, tasty and sexually versatile fish popular with both scientists and fishers – Barramundi is also a great favourite with the saltwater crocodiles.

Our tour now takes us through the former mining township of Batchelor, attached to Australia's first uranium mine, and here a "rest stop" (meaning toilets) is scheduled.

(*Cruiser's tip: When going on shore excursions in undeveloped countries or rustic areas such as the Australian outback, be sure to equip yourself with paper tissues or even a toilet roll. You will be glad of it on a trip to what is called the restroom. But it will hardly be a room, there won't be much rest, and there certainly won't be any toilet paper.)

A lady would like to buy a few things that are not available onboard, nor in the gift shops we normally visit, so she asks Jake if he would take her to the local store. The main body of our group, also keen on this opportunity, accompanies them, and I am pleased to find the laundry liquid I need, as well as a proper spool of black thread for my sewing.

(*Cruiser's tip: Be sure to take your favourite laundry liquid on a long cruise, for the kind that is for sale onboard is too harsh for fine garments. You might also need a little sewing kit, since sufficient thread of the right colour is hard to come by.)

Most people are pleased to be in a 'normal' shop at last, and delighted to purchase everyday items, but some members of the group grumble about "half an hour lost" as we queue at the till. Gilbert, who had complained earlier that the termite mounds were not spectacular enough, is particularly vocal about the perceived "waste of time" and seems to hold me personally responsible for it. – What a grouch!

The long return drive to Darwin causes queasiness again, even though I keep my eyes on the road all the time. Jake, seated across the aisle, tells me about the Northern Territory and its beauty, and describes his experiences as a tour guide in the Kakadu National Park. It all sounds spectacular and helps to take my mind off the increasing nausea, but it also makes the critical couple livid with barely supressed rage.

Our final destination is the Crocodylus Park, a research and education centre with a large crocodile farm attached. From the safety of a roofed boardwalk above the enclosures, we watch separately penned crocodiles as they are being fed. The keeper dangles a piece of meat above the pond, attached to a string at the tip of a pole like a primitive fishing rod. The animal moves into position and, ever so slowly, raises the front half of its body from the water. Keeping absolutely still, it fixes its prey … Then a sudden flash of movement, a rapid leap and a terrifying snap of its jaws – the meat is gone and the crocodile's bulk flops back into the water.

We have a prime view of the rosy inside of those tooth-lined jaws and cannot help but imagine ourselves in the place of that hapless piece of meat which is about to begin its journey through the crocodile's digestive tract. – No, one would not want to see this at close range in the wild!

Back on board at the end of the day, it is a relief to strip off the perspiration-damp clothing and have a cold shower, but dinner turns into an unpleasant test of my fortitude.

It turns out that Gilbert, Amanda and Beryl blame me for taking a reserved seat at the front of the coach, and once the first course has been served, they blast me with furious indignation. (Beryl, who had not been part of this excursion, must have been briefed by the other two.) Their accusations make it clear that they know nothing at all about travel or car sickness, and they do not want to believe me when I try to explain. In their view, I had wilfully taken away the seat of a disabled person (never mind that there weren't any), and they exclaim that "poor Nigel" (who walks with a cane) had to sit *at the back* of the coach. It does not seem to matter that Nigel was on a different coach altogether, nor that he is making every effort to avoid the 'disabled' label.

Red-faced with anger, Beryl shouts across the table, "You are just selfish! That's what you are!" and it is obvious that this pronouncement gives her tremendous satisfaction. Amanda and Gilbert then combine forces to trounce me for "wasting their time at the rest stop" – and in these waves of high emotion I sense the jaws of large beasts snapping at me.

Again I am surprised that people can be so malicious, and so enamoured of their own opinion that they disregard the facts entirely, as Gilbert now does when he dismisses my repeated efforts to explain as "Rubbish!"

I manage to finish the main course, (not easy with shaking hands), make my apologies to Martha (who is sympathetic) and forego dessert, withdrawing instead to the safety of my cabin to deal with the hurt.

Of course it is impossible to find sleep in this agitated state, and I lie awake for a long time, wondering what to do. Our erstwhile so jolly dinner table companionship has fallen apart quite spectacularly since Tony's arrest; and, unwilling to tolerate the ignorance and unkindness of these people any longer, I resolve to ask the restaurant manager if he could move me to another table tomorrow.

I am tired of listening to their mean-spirited gossiping about other people, tired of being friendly and pretending that I don't mind. Beryl in particular has never forgiven me for saying that their sport of 'Simon-bashing' (which took place every day, as soon as the man had left the table) was not acceptable to me. And I am glad that I spoke up, even though it has made me their next target.

What makes them so sure that they know my motives? Is it really selfish of me to look after myself, if nobody else does? Would Gilbert and Amanda really have preferred it, had I thrown up unselfishly at the back of the coach? And do I have to justify my actions to these people who are so entirely incidental to my life? – No, of course not!

Pondering how life always finds ways to stage its little dramas, even in this most pleasant and carefree of settings, I eventually fall asleep.

Day 52 ~ Saturday, 25*th* February 2012 ~ sunrise: 6.23am ~ sunset: 7.04pm ~ sea state: calm ~ wind: 2, light breeze ~ weather: sunny ~ temperature: 29°C ~ time zone: GMT+9

Problems to Solve

Awaking sad, but in survivor mode, I list the things I need to do today, so that I may carry them out one by one without getting paralyzed by unhappiness.

Step 1: Fill in Indonesian immigration card and drop it off at Reception. (First things first!)

Step 2: Have a late and solitary breakfast upstairs.

Step 3: Book a hair salon appointment to lift spirits.

Step 4: Speak to the restaurant manager about moving tables. (This proves unexpectedly easy – no questions asked; or he may have been alerted to the situation by waiters who were silent witnesses ... Anyhow, we agree that I shall dine at the Orangery until he has sorted out my move.)

Step 5: Put laundry in miraculously free machine and return to cabin to write journal. (On the way, I pass Gilbert in the corridor. He is clearly gossiping about me to a woman I don't know, because he stops short as soon as he sees me, with a sheepish look of guilt on his face.)

Step 6: Have hair washed and trimmed. (The view of the Timor Sea just beyond the mirror is spectacular. I enjoy it consciously, fully aware that I shall never have a haircut on the Timor Sea again.)

Step 7: Return to cabin to wash out weird blow-dry hairstyle and make alterations with own scissors, as always. (At last I am pleased with the result and notice that I look and feel a lot happier already. Oh, for the miraculous effect of haircuts!)

Step 8: Have lunch early and watch 'Eat, Pray, Love'. (Martha is at the cinema too and I take this opportunity to tell her that I shall be leaving our table. She replies that she is very sorry but totally understands. Dismayed by what she terms the small-mindedness of Gilbert, Amanda and Beryl, she asks if all English people are like this. I assure her that indeed they are not.)

Step 9: Sit in queue at tour desk and wait to speak to manager. (I describe my trouble with car sickness, and that my way of dealing with it angers other passengers. He tells me that there is absolutely nothing wrong with taking one of the reserved seats if they remain unclaimed, and he offers to help me out by showing me to one of these seats himself.)

Step 10: Go to gym for a workout with Britta. (Happy with the way I have addressed my problems, I can focus on the physical exercise and feel relieved.)

The evening brings a new, pleasant sense of freedom, since having a buffet dinner at the Orangery means that I can go there anytime I like, as long as it is before nine o'clock. Also, following tonight's Black Tie dress code is not required.

At my table by the window I enjoy a generous helping of tasty fish and chips, the informal ambience and the total absence of dinner companions.

After the meal I go on deck to watch the setting sun for the very first time on this journey. The evening sky with its delicate range of luminous colours is spectacular. No matter how ugly the minds of people – the natural world remains a creation of supreme and comforting beauty! And, watching the sun as it dips into the sea, the lyrics of 'Time' by Pink Floyd come to my mind, echoing from a hidden place that belongs to the past:

"And you run, and you run to catch up with the sun, but it's sinking, / Racing around to come up behind you again. / The sun is the same, in a relative way, but you're older, / Shorter of breath, and one day closer to death ..."

Day 53 ~ Sunday, 26*th* February 2012 ~ sunrise: 6.58am ~ sunset: 7.28pm ~ sea state: calm ~ wind: NW 2, light breeze ~ weather: sunny ~ temperature: 29°C

A Little Kindness

This entire day is dedicated to the journal, for there is much to write about. In between chapters, I take a break to deliver envelopes with tips and personal messages of thanks to the Medina, addressed to Marcus and Oliver, the waiters of my former dinner table.

(*Cruiser's tip: Pack some thank-you cards and use them to reward good service, giving your tip a personal note. It will brighten the day of any member of staff.)

At the restaurant, I give my envelopes to the manager with a request to pass them on, because handing them over myself would expose my premature departure to their kindliness and their respectfully expressed regret – the mere thought of which makes me feel tearful right now.

Oliver, who took over Francis's duties in Sydney, is a quiet Indian with the kindest face imaginable. I never knew that eyes could express such a mild and loving tranquillity. These particular windows to the soul are suited to the image of a saint; so unlike the embittered flints of Beryl, Amanda, Gilbert and their ilk. Why is it that the people I would like to know better cross my orbit distant as shooting stars, whereas the others stick around like burrs? ... Bad karma, I suppose! But then I see Norah outside the restaurant and am pleased to meet her again. Her husband Bob arrives on his mobility scooter and, introductions completed, Norah suggests that we should have lunch sometime. – Now *that* is something to look forward to!

(*Solo traveller's tip: Prepare a few calling cards with your cabin and phone number and give them to potential friends at your first meeting, because you may never again meet them by chance – especially on very large cruise ships.)*

In the afternoon I attend a 'Speed Spa' session: Seventy-five minutes of massages, nail-filing and buffing, a mini-facial – and all for just forty-five pounds. I am looking forward to this treat and feel fairly cheerful, but the moment Manuel's hands set out on the paths of a gentle shoulder-and-neck massage, I find myself fighting back tears. During Natalya's relaxing foot-and-ankle massage I can stop them no longer, and I weep quietly through Cindy's soothing scalp massage too. The therapists are of course concerned, but I ask them to ignore the waterworks and carry on with their treatments.

Although I had not expected these tears, they do not surprise me at all. Being tough and determined in the face of adversity and fairly skilled at presenting a brave front to the world, I know that it only takes a little kindness to make my tears flow – even the professional kindness of therapists. The pleasant touch of their trained hands is an embodiment of true kindness, and it is even more powerful than kind looks or words. But Sandie, having finished the facial and listened to a brief account of my troubles, has kind looks and words as well: "Whenever I see you around the ship," she tells me, "you look so happy and so beautiful – a real lady!"

I wish we could be friends ...

After the spa session and the tears I feel calm and relieved, and since I enjoyed yesterday's sunset so much, I now attend a repeat performance. And as I watch the sun's slow descent into the Indian Ocean, I try to picture this event in its actual reality: as the horizon rising up and incrementally covering the sun's fixed position, while the slow spin of our planet tilts us away from its light ... but my efforts at matching this known fact with the scene before me fails. To the eye, the sun is sinking into the sea as always, and I know that I am too close to see the reality.

The Orangery is agreeably quiet and I enjoy another pleasant, solitary dinner. (One could easily get used to this!) Then I return to my new favourite place, that stack of sun-loungers on the top deck. There, stretched out comfortably in the darkness, I sing German evening songs to the stars and the sickle moon that hovers above the ship's bow. These songs have also lain dormant for many years, but they too remain unforgotten. Is it not remarkable that the German language is so rich in moving songs that glorify the evening, the rising moon and the stars, while English folk songs tend to praise and celebrate the morning?

Gazing at the starry constellations far above, I try to envision the night sky's immense three-dimensional depth, but the eye insists on seeing a dark plane with tiny lights sprinkled across it ...

Well, this time I am too far away to see the reality!

'So sind wohl manche Sachen, die wir getrost belachen, weil unsre Augen sie nicht sehn ...' (Thus there are some things we laugh at indulgently, because our eyes are unable to see them ...) Dad liked to sing us traditional evening songs, such as the 'Abendlied' by Matthias Claudius. Leaning in the door frame, silhouetted by the light, he sang softly while his children fell asleep. And after all these years, the familiar lyrics impart the depth of their meaning to my adult mind, like a seed planted long ago that grew to reveal its potential.

Day 54 ~ Monday, 27th February 2012 ~ sunrise: 6.23am ~ sunset: 6.40pm ~ sea state: calm ~ wind: W 4, moderate breeze ~ weather: sunny ~ temperature: 32°C ~ time zone: GMT+8 ~ distance travelled since Darwin: 961 nautical miles ~ in total: 19,974 nautical miles

Bali

Hundreds of passengers are waiting to go ashore, but there is only a single pontoon at the pier. This means that only one tender can dock there at any time, and this fact slows things down considerably. In the end, our coach sets out on a tour of 'Scenic Bali' an hour later than planned.

My first impressions of Bali are jaw-dropping. Everywhere I look, idyllic and picturesque scenes captivate the eye. I wish that we could linger and look for longer, wander around and take a few pictures – but the coach zips along, expertly driven by a small, wiry and surly Balinese. Traffic is dense. There are more lorries than cars, and a large number of little motorbikes. Everyone seems to rely on these as their main mode of transport: families, grannies and teenagers, some of them considerably younger than the legal minimum age of seventeen. Our local guide tells us that accidents and fatalities are frequent, and that the majority of these involve, unsurprisingly, overconfident young men. The coach driver weaves his vehicle daringly between all the obstacles in his path, and we catch our breath repeatedly.

First we are shown a family compound in a village, so that we may see how people traditionally live in Bali. Crafts like woodcarving and mat-weaving are demonstrated, and then a delicious snack is served by shy, smiling women and their lovely daughters. Meanwhile, a group of men on a dais play Balinese music with blank, stony faces.

I begin a little chat with three girls in school uniform, hovering on the fringe of the crowd, and we get on famously once they overcome their shyness and try out a few words of English they learnt at school. Younger children join us. They look up at me with dark, smiling eyes and I am touched by their loveliness.

Tasty banana fritters are served at long tables, and we are shown a performance of traditional Balinese dancing. A graceful woman in colourful robes and theatrical makeup performs this ritual set of movements for us. Every aspect of the dance is prescribed; even the smile on the dancer's face is not her own. She makes herself into a vessel through which something older and greater than her temporal earthly form is transmitted: a sacred spiritual message. Its content may no longer be fully understood in our times, but its form remains unchanged, touching and beautiful.

We walk along footpaths to the rice paddies and see how these flooded fields are ploughed with a team of oxen. Rice is being planted, and the workers' backs are bent under a high and fiercely hot sun. "These farmers won't be making love tonight!" comments our guide with a grin.

A young man demonstrates how to climb a coconut tree with bare hands and feet, and a humble woman poses at her outdoor stove for our cameras. Some children who came with us from the village are now pounding rice to flour with gleeful smiles, taking turns with the mortar and pestle. To them, this daily chore is still play, and not work.

This country is truly a photographer's dream! Wherever one looks, there is beauty: in the scenery, the buildings, in tools and children and shrines – and in a way of life that is as old as it is aesthetic, despite the palpable poverty.

Our guide remarks that Indonesia competes with Nigeria for the title of 'World's Most Corrupt Country', and he says that the great wealth of his nation is in the hands of a few, while the rest of the population lives in poverty. This is borne out by the desperate tenacity of the vendors of fans, sarongs, woodcarvings and postcards who cleave to us as we make our way back to the coach.

Our next stop is the Pura Kehen temple, built in the 13th century. In the inner courtyard, dragonflies dart around us in larger numbers than I have ever seen, seemingly the silent spirits of this place. A giant banyan tree offers shade and shelter from the hot sun, and a wizened old lady with a tiny boy peeks over the upper temple wall and begins to sing *'Au clair de la lune'* in a reedy voice. As she sings, she waves the beaming toddler's hands at us, clearly hoping for a reward in dollars.

Our local tour guide in national dress is a lively and intellectual man who is eager to share his knowledge. As we drive into the hills, he explains the beliefs and principles of

Hinduism. It is obviously a subject that is dear to his heart. As he talks of the Vedas, the sacred syllable AUM and the divine trinity of Brahma, Vishnu and Shiva; of reincarnation, karma and the caste system, and the daily offering of gifts to the gods in the pujah ritual, I am reminded of studying all of this with my class, and how much we had enjoyed learning about the culture of Ancient India.

Lunch is served at the Mahagiri Hotel, high up in the hills, with a view of the ancient terraced rice fields that meander along the steep sides of the valley. We are told that President Obama ate here once and enjoyed it very much. We enjoy it too – the food just as much as the lovely garlanded space.

Returning to Klungkung, we visit the Royal Court of Justice, *Kertagosa*, also known as *Taman Gili*, 'the floating garden'. Dating from 1710, these halls are constructed from carved wood and raised high on stone platforms above the beautiful watergardens. Both meeting halls are painted with graphic murals that show the dire karmic punishments for a catalogue of human sins.

Despite this grim topic, it is another glorious place. Our guide is set to deliver yet another history lecture, but I wander off by myself to take a look at the lovely grounds. The intense heat is getting to me and I need a break, a spell of solitary quiet time. Unfamiliar plants grow behind walls carved with sculptures of horses in bas-relief, and in a corner I find a small, discarded offering basket – a precious little object, woven from bamboo leaves as testimony of a creative mind and nimble fingers.

Our last stop is at the secluded village of Tenganan where the Bali Aga, original inhabitants of the island, live. They preserve their ancient pre-Hindu culture, rarely marry outsiders and own no personal property. Yet they are well off by local standards, for their community owns a large area of rice fields and has begun to profit from increasing tourist interest as well. Not that you could tell this prosperity from the way things look; it is like having arrived at a settlement in the distant past.

We walk around the village and admire its houses and yards, its shops and stalls, until a sudden shower of rain drives us back to our coach, pursued by an army of vendors. Earlier, I bought stamps on the ship, and now I buy another postcard for my son. Our kind guide offers to post it for me, aware that by the time we shall return to the ship it will be much too late for mail. Though we return to the harbour with a delay of forty-five minutes, there is no hurry, as a call from the tour operator had informed him earlier.

(*Cruiser's tip: Never miss the ship, for it must leave on the dot. If you booked an excursion via the cruise line and your group gets delayed, the ship has to wait for your return. But if you head out by yourself and miss the appointed time, you will have to make your way to the next port of call to catch up with your cabin, at your own cost. So keep an eye on the clock and be punctual. Don't become a 'pier runner' for the amusement of the fellow passengers whose hobby it is to watch out for panicked latecomers and cheer them on from the Lido Deck.)

The queue at the pier seems endless, for in our absence the tender operation met with misfortune: a squall arose, a rope broke and the pontoon was swept away. Rather than wait for the Balinese to decide on a course of action, members of our ship's crew set about fixing the pontoon themselves, but the restless sea made this difficult.

Meanwhile, the local taxi drivers took industrial action and blocked the complementary P&O shuttle buses in a bid for business. This angered the passengers, who in turn refused to hire any of the taxis ... and that is why a large number of people remained inside the harbour terminal the entire day, unable to see Bali or return to the ship.

Accounts by various eyewitnesses allow us to piece these events together as we stand in the queue for an hour, shaded by the colonnade of the terminal, with toilet facilities alongside. Increasingly vociferous expressions of anger and complaints erupt from seething passengers and are aimed at any busy member of staff who is hurrying past. I should like to remind those exasperated people that a cooling shower, a good meal and a freshly-made bed await us; that *we* had not been stuck in the harbour terminal for hours, nor were we blown up by extremists; that it is pleasant to watch from the pier as dusk settles around the volcano and happy village boys dive into the surf for an evening swim ...

But complaining is a popular British sport, and these athletes are aiming for Olympic gold. They appear to feel relief by blaming someone, and do so without a thought for the bigger picture. Offended by this ungrateful attitude, I wonder how staff and crew must feel when confronted with such a large crowd of angry people.

Once all passengers are safely back onboard and having a belated dinner, the captain gives a report of today's mishaps. He apologizes repeatedly, even though none of it was his or the cruise line's fault, and when he announces that everyone is awarded fifty pounds of onboard credit in compensation, this gesture of goodwill elicits applause and cheering from many formerly grumpy tables.

Day 55 ~ Tuesday, 28th February 2012 ~ sunrise: 6.31am ~ sunset: 6.54pm ~ sea state: slight ~ wind: NW 3, gentle breeze ~ weather: sunny ~ temperature: 30°C

Changing Tables

We have three sea days ahead of us, and to me this is a very welcome spell of rest. I resume my earlier routine and head to the gym first thing in the morning. The benefits of regular exercise are really noticeable now and the scales report that five kilos were shed so far, even though I eat rather well. In this setting it is easy to avoid cakes and ice cream, opting for fresh fruit salad instead, to take the stairs rather than the lift, and to exercise lightly during those days at sea. Is this really all it takes to reverse the dreaded midlife midriff-expansion?

The day passes agreeably with writing on deck and drawing in the library, and then I get ready to meet my new dinner companions. The restaurant manager directs a headwaiter to escort me past my former dinner companions to another large table by the windowfront. Mercifully this table is out of their sight, at the far side of the Medina, and for a while I sit there by myself, studying the day's menu as well as my new surroundings.

The table waiter is all friendliness and smiles; in fact, he beams as if he had won the lottery. Can he really be *this* pleased to have me at his table? Now an Australian (from Brisbane) joins me. We introduce ourselves, exchange some basic information, and it turns out that his youngest grandchild is the same age as my son. Then another Australian (from Sydney) arrives and brings our number to a total of three, for his wife never eats dinner. The other seven places remain empty tonight, but each course is passed pleasantly in increasingly lively conversation.

Day 56 ~ Wednesday, 29*th* February 2012 ~ sunrise: 6.55am ~ sunset: 7.01pm ~ sea state: slight ~ wind: NE 4, moderate breeze ~ weather: sunny ~ temperature: 29°C

Waste Management

This leap year day is going to be interesting: We are entering the South China Sea, the popular presentation called 'Aurora Uncovered' will take place in the Atrium, and towards noon we shall be crossing the equator once more. In the evening there will be a Round the World Cruise Party, to be followed by a concert with New Zealand's leading tenor. – All in all, not a bad programme for the 29th of February!

This presentation of the ship's departments and their work reminds me of Open Days at school. Brochures and graphs are laid out on desks manned by officers, cadets, engineers and other crew members, pictures of the engine room cover display boards, and a professional PowerPoint presentation illustrates much technical information.

All of this is fascinating, but even more interesting is meeting some of the men and women in charge of running such a complex operation. I am a little bit disappointed that we cannot visit the actual engine room. This part of the ship would interest me the most; apart from the bridge, of course, which is also out of bounds. I suppose it is the idea of being in the presence of those great engines that appeals to me; of getting a first-hand impression of the technology that makes this incredible voyage around the world possible.

In my journal, I should like to include the numbers of nautical miles travelled from port to port, but they cannot be worked out from the cruise log we receive at the end of each leg. And so I take this opportunity to ask the bridge team for a list of these distances, half expecting to be told that they have more important things to do ... but no, they are ready and willing to answer questions such as these, and the first officer himself responds to my request.

He offers assistance in a strong Mediterranean accent and, in a charming little mime, pretends to be embarrassed by his Italian nationality, on account of the recent accident of the Costa Concordia cruise ship. (This dreadful event is still much on people's mind.) Yes, he says, the list of port-to-port distances shall be delivered to my cabin *pronto*, once he has had time to compile it.

The coxswain demonstrates Aurora's emergency and firefighting equipment, one of the deck cadets shows the use of a sextant. Quite an art, and a mathematical one at that! In answer to my question, the chief engineer confides that the fuel bill for our circumnavigation of the globe will be close to ten million US dollars, and the environmental officer and her waste disposal supervisors capture my interest with a description of what happens to the rubbish we produce:

Cans are crushed and compacted into neat blocks for recycling at a later date, glass bottles are ground to become asphalt underlay in road construction, all plastic is shredded for processing, paper and card are incinerated at sea, and the three cubic metres of waste food left in the kitchens per day are donated to the food chain of the sea. (I imagine that large numbers of gourmet fish must be following our ship around the world.) In sixteen days, thirty cubic metres of recyclable solid waste have accumulated, securely stored onboard until they are received in major ports by approved contractors. In fact, nothing but waste food and water is returned to the sea. In any larger port, a special boat comes alongside to collect the human waste for proper disposal. – I am impressed, and glad to see that P&O are taking the ecological impact of their cruise ships so seriously.

During this hour, the captain is available for photos and the signing of ship's merchandise, but I ask him to sign my journal instead. Though surprised by this novel request, he complies willingly, and it sparks the idea to collect more signatures from all the friendly crew and staff members who make my cruise so pleasant. All of them are thrilled when I present my big black notebook (by now a familiar sight), and soon their autographs cover a double page.

Then I retire to my cabin-hut for a peaceful nap, not inclined to repeat the earlier disappointment of an equatorial crossing. Yes, the ceremony might admittedly be more to the point this time, though I doubt it. Anyhow, a spell of rest in preparation for this evening is much more appealing.

The evening's party for world cruisers is in the Crow's Nest, and once again the captain makes us laugh with his speech. He lists the foreign nationalities amongst us, represented by large (Australian/Dutch) or small (Norwegian/American) groups of people, and I bring up the rear as the only Swiss national aboard. The people seated around me cheer when I raise my hand to be identified. Erin and Paul had invited me to sit at their table and introduced me to their friends, and as a result I feel very much included. From a table not far away,

Amanda and the others are watching, gimlet-eyed, waiting for something that will feed their need for malicious gossip. Martha stops by to introduce a Dutch couple she met. They lived in Switzerland for years, the husband is a teacher too, and we begin a conversation in Swiss German. But it is time for dinner, and so we shall meet again another time.

At dinner, the nice gentleman from Sydney and I are the only people at our large table, which allows conversation to become more suited to our particular interests. In the course of another delicious meal we range effortlessly over topics as diverse as British gardening, the history of the Philippines and certain spiritual aspects of Christianity. How pleasant it is to have a proper conversation once in a while!

And there is more to come. After the concert by the young tenor (*much* too loud; Opera singers really don't need sound amplification in small spaces), Martha's Dutch friend invites me to Anderson's bar, and tonight his manner is not at all boastful and irritating. It turns out that he worked as a Protestant pastor for most of his life, and this naturally leads us to talk about questions of faith and life and death, about God and the world – in fact, all my favourite topics. We also find out that we both like to watch films, and that our very favourites are those that deal with the mentioned topics in a wonderful way; most especially 'The Bucket List' and the delightful Japanese film 'Departures'.

And so it comes that I return to my cabin well after midnight, having actually enjoyed a social evening for once. It all felt so right, so effortless … How did that come about? Could it be that the dismal low point is now past? The cruise experience is certainly redeeming itself!

Day 57 ~ Thursday, 1st March 2012 ~ sunrise: 5.57am ~ sunset: 5.54pm ~ sea state: calm ~ wind: N 4, moderate breeze ~ weather: sunny ~ temperature: 29°C ~ time zone: GMT+7

Finding a Friend

I take my journal to the spa to collect more autographs, this time from its staff. The girls are especially interested and leaf through the whole book to see the illustrations. Sandie, the senior beautician, even asks if I would let her have a copy of this journal. It is her first cruise as well, and she would love to have such a record of it. – How touching!

In the steamroom, I try to subdue the beginnings of another cold, brought on by blasts of air conditioning on the recent coach trip. And on to the sauna, which harbours an as yet unfamiliar Australian. We chat, and upon learning that I am not British, he vents his annoyance with "the whingeing Poms" because, waiting in that queue on the pier in Bali, his feelings had been just like mine. But unlike me, he was bold and forthright enough to point out their unreasonableness to angry members of the crowd. As a big, bearded and burly Aussie he got away with it, but I shudder to imagine the social repercussions had I voiced my opinion likewise!

"Why do you think we Australians call the British the whingeing Poms?" he asks. Well – for obvious reasons, surely.

Returning to my cabin, I find Sandie in the corridor. She is looking for me and brings a big bar of chocolate as a gift, in return for the promised copy of my journal. This record of our cruise is special to her, she says, "truly amazing" and "precious as gold". I am touched that my work should mean so much and am surprised, moved and delighted by this unexpected appearance of a potential friend. All of a sudden, life seems brighter.

Day 58 ~ Friday, 2nd March 2012 ~ sunrise: 5.58am ~ sunset: 5.52pm ~ wind: 2, light breeze ~ weather: sunny ~ temperature: 32°C ~ distance travelled since Bali: 1,584 nautical miles ~ in total: 21,558 nautical miles

Vietnam

Our next port is hailed by the captain (who has been waiting and wanting to say this for a long time, as he tells us) with a cheerful "Good morning, Vietnam!"

The delicate line of cable cars that cuts across the bay prevents big ships from reaching the harbour, but the tender operation is swift today and brings us ashore half an hour ahead of schedule.

We set out on our excursion 'Nha Trang Highlights' in a coach that is pleasantly cool in the tropical heat. The tour desk manager, good as his word, has personally shown me to a front seat. (Simon, taking part in the same excursion, will report this new development to my former dinner table tonight. Watching my every move and gossiping about me has become their new favourite pastime, as it will soon turn out, but in the meantime I remain blissfully ignorant of these circumstances.)

We cross the Cai River on the Xom Bong bridge and visit the Po Nagar Cham temple, built in the eighth century from baked mud bricks. It was razed repeatedly by invaders, and the current version dates from the tenth century.

This temple complex in the Hindu style is unique in that it is devoted to *a woman*. She lived among the earliest villagers and was later elevated to the state of goddess. Yan Po Nagar is called 'Divine Lady' and 'Mother of the Country' because she had, once upon a time, taught men to fish and women to weave, determined the right time to plant and harvest crops, and knew how best to feed the children and heal the sick. (If I understood our guide correctly, then *large, important* and *female* are synonymous in Vietnamese culture.) At the side of this important female teacher's large temple, a small shrine is dedicated to her husband.

The temple houses a statue of this revered woman, dressed in finely embroidered silk and hung with strings of pearl and jade. Her altar is heaped with offerings, decorated with fresh flowers and sheltered by vermilion baldachins that are lined with many-coloured silken tassels into which smoky tendrils of incense rise. Local people come to worship here in a steady trickle and take no notice of us tourists, even though we get in their way in the limited space.

In the peaceful grounds, unsmiling pink-robed girls are showing a traditional dance in which pots of fired clay feature prominently. The dance is performed with hands, arms and shoulders in rhythmical, wave-like movements. Heads and feet remain still as these youthful dancers carry out a stylized version of that traditional, ancient task of girls everywhere: fetching water from the well.

Groups of locals pass the time of day in the pleasant shade of trees at this sacred site, talking or reading, but we head back across the river into the city. Motorbikes scoot in dense crowds, and we watch in amazement as these bikes execute daring manoeuvres that would certainly be frowned upon by our police.

"Did you *see* that?" – "Unbe*liev*able!"

If we were catholic, we might make the sign of the cross to ward off misfortune; but Vietnam is predominantly Buddhist, and now we are taken to the Long Son pagoda. Instructed to leave shoes at the door, we enter the sanctuary and are handed incense sticks as offerings to a gilded statue of Buddha, together with our prayers.

But our next stop is devoted to the great god Dollar. Dam market, the central covered market of Nha Trang, is a warren of stalls selling a dizzying array of goods. Here I find lovely shawls and a pair of comfortable flip-flops with thick soles to wear on future excursions. But, best of all, for all of four dollars I can get the dead battery of my watch replaced. For unfathomable reasons, this small but essential service is not available aboard our ship.

(*Cruiser's tip: Have watch batteries renewed before a long cruise, or take replacement batteries and tools with you. Otherwise you may have to find a jeweller's shop or a market stall. Although not really necessary on the ship, a watch is absolutely vital on shore excursions. You don't want to miss the boat, as they say.)

Because it is lunchtime, nearly all the stallholders are eating healthy-looking homemade soup and vegetables from china bowls, set out on footstools or counters. The fastfood culture has not gained a foothold here yet, and nobody is obese.

Our next visit is to an embroidery workshop, where we see young girls being trained in this traditional craft. Groups of girls and women are busy at long tables, stitching intricate designs with care and skill and fine silken thread. Every two hours they take a mandatory break to rest their eyes, but I suspect that this occupation will ruin their sight eventually, just like lace-making used to do in European countries.

Finished pieces are exhibited in the adjacent gallery. Embroideries with motifs of flowers, landscapes, fishes and tigers are displayed in large frames with price tags attached. Other items, such as gorgeously embroidered silky gowns, scarves, purses and more can be bought at the gift shop, and of course we are given ample time to browse.

Finally we visit the Oceanographic Institute to view specimens of local marine life, displayed in tanks that exude a certain communist drabness. Also on display is a dugong in formaldehyde and a whale skeleton, ploughed up on land in its enormous entirety by a surprised farmer.

A charming scene is played out at the reception desk. As these young girls complete the paperwork for our tour, they flirt modestly with our guide to assess his qualities as a potential husband. He does seem like a good catch.

Day 59 ~ Saturday, 3rd March 2012 ~ sunrise: 6.05am ~ sunset: 6.02pm ~ wind: 2 ~ weather: sunny ~ temperature: 33°C ~ distance travelled since Nha Trang: 207 nautical miles ~ in total: 21,765 nautical miles

Mekong River

This morning, Aurora docks in Phu My. The air is already at twenty-nine degrees Celsius before eight o'clock, and it will soon get even hotter. Today's excursion, called the 'Mekong River Experience', is an exclusive tour for two small groups, each one no more than six passengers.

This is going to be a three-hour drive of 180 kilometres each way, and therefore it is a relief to get seated right at the front of the minibus. In this group, no one seems to mind.

We are taken through Ho Chi Minh ('He who brings enlightenment') City with its adventurous traffic, and then across the vast Mekong Delta with its green tapestry of rice paddies that is dotted with family tombs, and farmsteads where dogs play and little boys run with kites. The buildings of town and countryside are thrown together in a variety of styles, and in a cheerful ramshackly manner that narrowly avoids squalor.

By the time we arrive at the river port of My Tho, our limbs are numb. We take a brisk walk around the harbour building to stretch our legs, and then board a motorboat that takes us across the opaque brown waters of the Mekong River.

We pass beneath a Japanese suspension bridge (they seem to be everywhere) and alongside a fish farm, and then we dock at Thoi Son, the 'Unicorn Island', for a leisurely walking tour on shaded footpaths.

Our first stop is at a small honey farm. We are shown frames of honeycomb, swarming with a grey-striped variety of bees, and then the young lady invites us to sit down in an open space under a large, many-pillared roof. She prepares a delicious honey drink at our table and pours it into little cut-glass tumblers. Then, raising a glass, our guide demonstrates how to toast in Vietnamese:

"*Mo* (one), *hai* (two), *ba* (three) – *yo!*" ... and down it goes! We all practise our first words of Vietnamese eagerly. We sample propolis, several varieties of honey and very nice peanut brittle, and of course we buy some of these delicacies in support of the local economy.

A sun-dappled path takes us through gardenlike grounds to a place where benches and tables welcome us in the shade. Here, platters of locally grown fruit are served: pineapple, pomelo and mini-bananas, as well as the more exotic jackfruit, sapodillas and milk apples. It makes the intense heat bearable and we enjoy each treat in turn.

Musicians with traditional instruments arrive and accompany young women who sing folk songs – mostly sad ballads about the lover leaving to go to war. Having only ever employed a monochord for acoustic experiments, this is the very first time I see it used to make music. The twanging vibrato produced by a little lever is especially intriguing.

Our motorboat is waiting to take us further down the river, to a place where we change into small Sampan-style boats that are rowed on a narrow canal by women in conical hats. This lovely, secluded waterway is part of a maze of similar channels that line the river's banks. Here, the upright leaves of water-coconut shade us from the strong sunlight, and yet it drips through their tall fronds in patches and sprinkles the mudbrown water with gold.

It is wonderful to glide silently along these greenish tunnels, hidden from sight! I am soon imagining childhood adventures in this setting. How truly marvellous it would be to have a little rowboat and be able to explore such secret waterways from dawn to dusk, like Huckleberry Finn, like 'Swallows and Amazons' ... Much too soon for my liking we reach our destination and have to disembark. The eyes of a man, idling in a hammock by the jetty, light up expectantly when I draw my purse to give a couple of dollar bills to our nice boatwoman. Will she have to hand over this tip to him? I hope not!

Now we take another footpath past pineapple plants and a farmhouse of carved coconut wood. Scrawny black hens are scratching in the yard, and a rusty bicycle leans drunkenly. At a small family workshop, a hardworking team of mother and daughter produces delicious coconut candy. Without fear, the little son handles a captive python and poses for photographs, while the man of the house hangs about and watches over his family's enterprise.

Set in flowery grounds, a beautiful restaurant awaits at the end of our walk. It is intensely hot, humid and well into the thirties, but a cool breeze moves through the open hall where we are served an exceptional meal. An elephant-ear fish from the river, encrusted in fine herbs and almond flakes, is plucked apart at our table by expert fingers and served, rolled into rice paper with thin slices of cucumber. An array of spring rolls is pinned, hedgehog-like, to the skin of a sliced pineapple, and a large balloon of crisply fried rice paste is cut up and heaped on a plate, to be shared out. Its unfamiliar taste is divine, and so is the whole exotic meal. Generous helpings of steamed rice and seafood follow, and a plump king prawn is shelled by our waitress for each one of us. Everything is so delicious that we eat a good deal more than we normally would. What a treat!

After the ample meal, we find our motorboat waiting at the adjacent pier and clamber aboard to cross the river. In the heat of the afternoon, the Mekong looks as sluggish as we feel, its brown waters seemingly immobile. A high tide is pushing upstream, making the wavelets hover undecidedly, and it is impossible to tell which way the river flows.

On the very long return drive to Phu My, most members of our group lie down on the benches of the minivan for a nap.

But I – although feeling drowsy myself – am compelled to watch the scenery of this fascinating country that rolls by, as well as the Vietnamese on their motorbikes:

Here is a young couple with cute twins. Each toddler is strapped to an adult, and their tiny facemasks have a red heart handpainted on each cheek. (Even in intense heat, facemasks and gloves are worn to keep the skin from tanning.) Then there are the lovers, her head resting on his back, arms clasped about his chest, and a proud look on his face ... but acquaintances and business partners, sharing a bike, leave plenty of room between their bodies in formal uprightness. Unwashed young men in torn trousers and flip-flops zip along at a brisker pace than dolled-up teenage girls in high heels. The girls' long hair streams out from cute, fashionable helmets as they laugh at yet another BFF-joke. There is also a stout woman, with supplies for her village store strapped to body and bike; the boxes and bundles and bags trebling the bulk of her vehicle and hiding its wheels. And a sweet little girl, all in pink and transported in the protective enclosure of her father's arms, gives me a friendly smile as she waves in passing. – So many lives, travelling in brief impressions past my wondering eyes!

To visit all these countries in close succession heightens my awareness of the fact that the fundamental themes of human existence are played out all around the globe in colourful variety. Only the human spirit could invent so many ways of living Life! Man, woman and child between birth and death: eating and sleeping, learning and working, playing and loving, caring and healing, grieving and praying, laughing and celebrating – these are the common denominators of the world's cultures, but there is a wealth of variation in the way all of this is done. Each ethnic group evolved a special style in dealing with every aspect of life, and they express their identity in language and dialect, in cults, beliefs and legends, in customs and traditions, crafts and science, cuisine, music and dance, literature, art and architecture.

As travellers, it is this wonderful variety we come to see, appreciate and learn about. Of course this is stating the obvious, but it is one thing to *know* it in abstract theory, and another to *experience* this fact with powerful immediacy in the course of a few weeks of cruising: What a glorious place our world is!

Day 60 ~ Sunday, 4th March 2012 ~ sunrise: 6.11am ~ sunset: 6.14pm ~ sea state: calm ~ wind: E 3 ~ weather: sunny ~ temperature: 32°C

A Favourite Place

It continues to be very hot, so I stay in my pleasantly cool hut and write all day, pausing only for a quick buffet lunch. There is much to record, and as I write, the impressions of yesterday pass once again before my mind's eye.

Late in the evening, after her shift has ended, Sandie and I meet in Anderson's bar as arranged. Both of us are there on time, and over glasses of tonic water we begin the process of getting to know each other. This is a girl after my own heart! I learn that she does not like alcohol, is punctual and tidy, prefers to sleep in the top bunk and relishes the fact that she has got a cabin all to herself. Unlike me, she also slides down the central banister in the ship's stairwell when nobody is there to see it. Beneath her feminine and beauty-conscious exterior, there seems to hide a tomboyish side as well, and – if similarity is the soul of friendship, as Aristotle claimed – this is a promising start.

Together we take a turn around the top deck, which is always deserted at this hour, and I point out my favourite stack of sunloungers above the bridge of the ship. Despite wearing high heels and an elegant dress, Sandie climbs onto the neighbouring stack at once, stretches out and suggests that we stay a while. And this we do, side by side, chatting companionably in the darkness.

Day 61 ~ Monday, 5th March 2012 ~ sunrise: 6.18am ~ sunset: 6.16pm ~ wind: 2 ~ weather: sunny ~ temperature: 33°C ~ distance travelled since Phu My: 452 nautical miles ~ in total: 22,217 nautical miles

Cambodia

Early this morning we arrive in Sihanoukville, Cambodia – a country whose ancient culture and beauty, as well as over a million of innocent people, were brutally destroyed by the Khmer Rouge under Pol Pot. Like Stalin and Mao, Pot was a deluded mass murderer who wanted to establish a communist paradise. In this he failed, just as his role models did, and the country is only just beginning to recover from the horror and the devastation. Cambodia is very poor, though more cheerful than anticipated. A boom of development is expected in the immediate future, since rich oil and gas reserves have been discovered off the coast and are about to be exploited. Foreign investors are moving into position, particularly Russians. Russia has close ties with Cambodia for obvious reasons, and many signs and notices are written in Russian, with Cyrillic letters.

Our local guide has a great fondness for statistical facts and figures. He also explains that Sihanoukville is named after King Sihanouk, whose name means 'lion-jaw' (siha-nouk). After Pol Pot's death in 1998, Cambodia was turned into a constitutional monarchy.

Now the country's Buddhist religion is being revived and temples are built to replace those that were destroyed, but these new structures resemble the gaudy architecture of theme parks and their artistic value is nil. Only the ancient temple site of Angkor Wat remains as a reminder of the true beauty that was once possible.

We are taken on almost empty roads into the countryside, so that we may see the traditional way of Cambodian living. Built from wood and little more than huts, village dwellings are raised on stilts and provide a shaded space beneath their floor. Here, the whole family hangs out in the shade, often in hammocks; children play and domestic animals are penned, protected from the strong sunlight.

The floor slats are spaced like a grid and allow the air to circulate in a natural cooling system. There is hardly any furniture, but faded pages from magazines are pinned to the walls for decoration. Everything is neat and functional and a reminder of how little is needed in such a hot climate. But the television, being essential, has pride of place.

The lady of the house must have toiled through a lifetime of poverty, and yet she radiates grace and quiet dignity as she poses with amiable patience for our cameras.

We are shown the local primary school, where a mixed class of different age groups recites long passages of a traditional text by heart. The teacher stands by quietly and smiles with understandable pride as the children put their heart into it, speaking with energy and expressive gestures. And, as in Bali, their loveliness is touching.

On my way around the compound, I attracted a little girl who has shyly taken my hand. She stays with me until it is time to board the coach again. Her friend and a small, curly-haired boy join us in the playground and cling to my other hand, and we watch a group of older girls practise double-Dutch-skipping with astounding dexterity.

I get to exchange a few words with young teenagers waiting at their desks, calmly and without making noise, for their teacher to arrive and the next lesson to begin. They are friendly, interested and well-behaved, and this setting looks so familiar and feels so comfortable that I can easily picture myself as a teacher here. I would live in a little hut on stilts – and surely one gets used to the oppressive heat eventually?

Some people of our group begin to hand out cheap plastic toys, pencils and sweets they brought along. It is easy to understand their good intentions – but what will it teach children, living in poverty, about the exchange of money for products or services in society, if western people appear as a kind of Santa Claus, handing out gifts the children will learn to expect? Would it not have been much better to leave these presents with the teachers, who could then have distributed them according to their knowledge of each child's needs?

And as for the little girl attached to my hand: has she not already learnt that any foreign visitor might reward her pretended affection with a gift of money? This could be seen as the beginning of prostitution – and unfortunately it seems unavoidable in the circumstances.

At the contemporary Buddhist monastery we visit next, a new crowd of Balinese children surrounds us, but these have postcards and bracelets to sell. Many of them also have a good grasp of Basic English and are charming, despite their annoying tenacity. I buy a pack of postcards from a gangly boy who is either too shy or too laidback to pursue us and crouches instead in the shade of a sculpted horse. (Though this horse is part of a religious statue, it looks as if it escaped from the carrousel of a funfair.)

(*Cruiser's tip: Wherever pick-pocketing might be a problem, leave your wallet behind in the safety of the tour coach. Any vendor you would like to buy from will accompany you there.)

A young girl, selling colourful string bracelets, is keen to talk to me. Exceedingly bright and a gifted student of English, she would make a wonderful pupil in any school. We have a lovely chat, and then she knots a braided string around my wrist with the words, "I give you this for free … for being my friend!" – These children certainly know how to touch one's heart, and they remain cheerful despite their humble circumstances.

(*Cruiser's tip: It is often distressing to witness life's inequalities around the globe. Some advance research on how best to meet the needs of children who are living in poverty and have to help with

the family income can be helpful. Buying their wares saves them from begging, stealing or going hungry, so do consider spending a few coins on things you don't really need.)

But because there is a modern, luxurious side to Cambodia too, we are served a splendid lunch of grilled tuna steak, king prawns and cuttlefish at the idyllic five-star Sokha Beach Resort. A long row of solid wooden sunloungers with thick white mats and towels awaits us in the natural shade of trees along a pristine beach. The hot sunshine is tempered by a gentle breeze as transparent waves roll in from the sea.

How delightful! ... We get more than three hours to enjoy this lovely place. I go beachcombing, and then try the traditional Khmer massage that is offered by local women beside a panel with fixed prices in US dollars.

But all too soon it is time to return to the ship. Both sides of Cambodia have appealed to me very much and I am sorry to be leaving already, hoping that this interesting country will find ways of making its natural resources available to benefit the people, rather than a corrupt elite and foreign investors. Because, if wise and compassionate adults were in charge, all of Cambodia's children could have the bright future they surely deserve.

Returned to the ship, I arrange with Sandie to meet up in our new special place once more. She has to work until eight o'clock, and I settle down in the Crow's Nest bar to pass the time with my journal and my usual tipple of tonic water, laced with lemon and a chip of ice. Well, at least it *looks* like a grown-up drink.

I am keen to write an account of this day at once, for ahead lies a whole row of shore days with many more excursions – a real challenge! For how does one remember *what* one has seen, and *where*? ... It all merges so easily into a blur.

(*World cruiser's tip: If you don't want to write a journal yourself, caption your photographs with key words and brief notes instead. Don't tell yourself that you'll remember the details forever. With the accumulation of hundreds of photographs and the passing of time, you won't.)

Then Sandie arrives and we talk, stretched out comfortably atop those secluded stacks of sunloungers. As Aurora floats us through the tropical night towards Thailand, a sprinkle of lights traces the receding coastline of Cambodia and a small number of the brightest stars begin to twinkle through the moon's glimmering light. And now I feel truly happy and at home on this ship, for I found a friend to talk things over with, and that changed everything for the better.

Day 62 ~ Tuesday, 6*th* March 2012 ~ sunrise: 6.29am ~ sunset: 6.25pm ~ wind: 2 ~ weather: sunny ~ temperature: 33°C ~ distance travelled since Sihanoukville: 238 nautical miles ~ in total: 22,455 nautical miles

Thailand

Sandie invites me to share breakfast at the Orangery. She is going to accompany a tour group into Bangkok, but my own excursion does not begin until noon and leaves enough time to visit the gym first. That place is usually busy as a beehive from the moment it opens its doors at eight o'clock, but now I find myself the only one there.

(*Cruiser's tip: Should you ever want the gym to yourself, choose a day at a popular port.)

Britta, hoping to have the day off, writes down a sequence of stretching exercises for me and adds cute little stick people as illustration. After my solitary gym session, we meet at the pool and talk, as we bask on sunloungers, about the perks of living and, in her case, working on a cruise ship.

(*Cruiser's tip: At sea, any cruise ship's pools are sanitized and refilled with fresh seawater daily, usually early in the morning. But close to shore and in port, poolwater has to be recycled for a while, and then more chlorine is added to reduce natural pollution. If you are sensitive to such matters, you may prefer to avoid the ship's pools on port days.)

Britta's friend, who works at the casino, joins us. Our talk revolves around aspects of being a single woman pursuing a career while searching for the right man, and how having children fits into this quest. They are in their twenties and thirties respectively, so this is a burning question; but to me, much to my relief, it is a matter of 'been there, done that'.

From my table at lunch I overlook the busy port and am able to observe those fascinating dock cranes in action at last. Unloading cargo ships, they lift big shipping containers as if they were merely blocks of Lego. I am also intrigued by the omnipresent 'Maersk' logo. Its white, seven-pointed star on an ice-blue square gives no indication of its nationality, but it marks large portions of all stacks of containers we passed since Panama.

At noon my tour sets out to visit an Elephant Village near Pattaya, and to my delight Norah (whom I have not seen lately) has booked the same tour. As we board the bus, I mention my problem with car sickness and describe the ill will my need to sit in front arouses in other passengers. With an energetic yet elegant snort, Norah declares herself ready to be my champion, should the need arise. – It seems that I have been blessed with another friend!

Norah has a very dry sense of humour and her witty, mordant comments amuse me no end. Heaven be praised, I so enjoy having someone to laugh with! Now it matters not at all that Gilbert and Amanda are on this excursion as well. Watching me like hungry hawks, their behaviour is hard to overlook, and yet I do my best to take no notice.

This Elephant Village had been established in 1974 as a sanctuary for working elephants; but because only female elephants can be trained for work and enjoy retirement here, a couple of bull elephants were acquired for breeding. Their latest offspring is a cute but naughty little elephant girl that likes to kick its keepers playfully. Norah now buys a bunch of bananas to offer its delicately curling trunk, and then we snap pictures of each other as we are riding the elephants on a turn around the village.

Later, seated on a shaded tribune for the show, we are shown how the mahouts handle their animal. How the steep flanks are climbed, how an elephant can be made to sit or lie down, how they work, what they eat, and how much they enjoy a bath … These mahouts live atop their elephant's bulk much of the time and seem well attuned to their animal companion.

Leaving the elephant village, we are taken to an ostentatious shopping mall of costly luxury goods, designed to appeal to the tastes of Russian oligarchs and their third wives. First we file past row upon row of craftsmen, seated with bent backs at secured workplaces to cut, polish and set precious stones. Then we come to a darkened hall where rows of glass cases contain the fruits of their diligent work. Illumined tanks of tropical fish are placed throughout as decoration. They add an upright element to that vast plane of gleaming display cases, while tiny spotlights call a coruscating response from thousands of gems in the hushed darkness.

The next hall sports water features with bridges that lead the dazzled customer towards delicate silks, snakeskin handbags and ornamental jade carvings ... but who needs such an obscene shopping experience? I seek out the coffee shop instead and write another postcard to my son.

Day 63 ~ Wednesday, 7th March 2012 ~ sunrise: 6.33am ~ sunset: 6.33pm ~ wind: 2 ~ weather: sunny ~ temperature: 35°C ~ distance travelled since Laem Chabang: 218 nautical miles ~ in total: 22,673 nautical miles

Ko Samui

This has been a rather difficult day, as can be seen from the letter I wrote to the tour desk manager the next morning. He had left the ship to accompany Martha's group on their five-day trip to Angkor Wat, and his young female colleague was much less helpful.

"Dear Sir, I need to inform you of the unhappiness I am experiencing as a world cruiser who booked an excursion in every port but unfortunately suffers from car sickness. In Laem Chabang, when I asked your colleague for assistance, she was very reluctant to help. I went to see her after the tour, to speak to her about my problem and her negative attitude. Her response was that without a letter from my doctor she could not help me, because 'people want to sit in front for all sorts of reasons', and the best she could do was to offer me a refund for all the remaining tours, 'so at least you don't lose out financially'. I have to say that this seems to me more of a punishment than a solution, and also that I find her proposal unprofessional and rather offensive.

On the 'Round the Island' tour in Ko Samui, I sat near the back of the coach because all the front seats were taken, and when I felt sick, the coach had to be stopped to let me get out. It was a near miss and I felt miserable. However, both guide and driver were absolutely professional in their assistance and did not need a doctor's letter to show some basic human kindness. Our guide even offered his seat and advised, 'If you get car sick, you must always sit in front!'

Fellow passengers helped out with ginger sweets and expressed their sympathy, only the P&O tour escort ignored the whole episode and never showed concern. I am sorry to say that this experience has spoilt what is otherwise a lovely trip."

As for the excursion: First we are taken to Kunaram temple, where the mummy of a Buddhist monk is displayed in a glass case above the altar. He died during meditation in 1973 and is sitting in that same pose to this day, as a reminder of Buddha's teachings and mortality. Black sunglasses, placed on the monk's face to hide his sunken eyes, add a touch of rock'n'roll to this eerie spectacle. It attracts thousands of pilgrims, and all year round they come to pray at his feet in reverent worship. The remains of this holy man are seen as a great miracle and are guarded by monks and a cute mongrel puppy, asleep on a chair.

At Hua Thanon Village, our next stop, we are shown how trained monkeys harvest coconuts in the plantations of their owners by twirling the nut on its stalk until it comes off and falls to the ground. Such a monkey can work for up to fifteen years and thus repay the considerable sum invested in its training. But in contrast to the working elephants, only male monkeys are trained for work, because the females get pregnant and then need time out to raise their offspring ... Sounds awfully familiar, doesn't it?

On our way to the temple of the Big Buddha, car sickness strikes and, hand clasped to mouth, forces me to hurry to the front of the coach. The tour guide responds instantly and instructs the driver to stop at once. The coach is pulled over and everyone gapes as the guide accompanies me outside. He turns away discreetly until the retching stops, and then gives me time to recover.

In an interesting twist of fate, Gilbert and Amanda are once again on the same coach and seated only a couple of rows ahead, but I barely notice them in my misery.

Disembarking at our destination, faint and shaky, my interest in Buddha statues, whatever their size, hovers close to zero. Anyhow, Big Buddha turns out to be a specimen of the modern theme park variety, and so I wander along a line of market stalls beneath large trees instead, trying to recover my equilibrium in their pleasant shade.

The heat is fierce today! Tourists turn sweaty and red-faced while Thais continue to look cool as cucumber. Thankfully it is only a short drive to our next destination, and lunch. The Nora Hotel & Resort is a stunningly beautiful place, its view of the bay is a holidaymaker's dream and the food is divine. A couple of musicians sing songs by Harry Belafonte to the guitar. I had missed those in St Lucia!

Sharing a table with a well-travelled gentleman who knows car sickness from personal experience, his sympathy and understanding are very welcome after recent events. As it happens, I am unaware that I am even now being watched by Amanda and Gilbert who, probably thinking that motion sickness must be like gastric flu, see my enjoyment of lunch as proof of their theory that I never felt sick at all. I shall be informed of their deductions later, but right now I enjoy the immediate relief of nausea which comes with firm ground, fresh air and good food.

Then we get two hours to spend at Chaweng Beach, where the heat is intense, the sand is crowded and the water temperature touches thirty degrees. Much more appealing is a gentle stroll into town, for its air-conditioned shops offer some welcome cool. Breaking up tarmac, a pneumatic drill is hard at work and its noise and exhaust fumes are a bit of a trial, but the street is lined with shoe shops selling gorgeous footwear at impossibly low prices.

(*Cruiser's tip: Unlike most other places, some shops in Thailand will not accept US dollars and insist that you change them to the local currency at little counters around the corner.)*

The return journey passes without problems. Our tour guide insists that I must remain in his place at the very front of the coach, which causes grumbling among certain passengers. A nice couple across the aisle offers me special ginger travel sweets from their personal supply, and the driver presents me with a nasal inhaler stick from his glove compartment. It gives off a strong eucalyptus scent that proves very helpful, and he signals that I can keep it for future use. I am touched by his kindness. Certainly, our cruise line's excursions staff could learn from these people who are such unforgettable ambassadors of their country.

Back on board, I just want to lie down in the dark; but after a cool shower and a call from Sandie, I take an aspirin to ward off a headache, dress for a formal evening and go to dinner. Dear Martha, returned from her long excursion to Angkor Wat, apparently requested to change tables too, for I find her seated next to me. What a nice surprise! Each passing day, she now confides, increased her dislike for the malicious gossiping of Gilbert, Amanda and Beryl, until she could not bear to dine in their company any longer.

New people boarded our ship today. We are joined at our table by Bruce, an energetic Australian widower, and two merry British couples who are cruising to Dubai.

Later I meet Sandie in the Crow's Nest bar and we look at pictures of her family: two beautiful daughters and a nice, supportive husband. She is happily married, the lucky girl! We have a lovely time, but Sandie is outraged when she hears of my tour escort's behaviour. All the ship's staff must have special training before they can accompany tours, she says, and caring for the passengers' wellbeing is considered of the utmost importance. On her tour, for example, a lady injured herself slightly, and so Sandie provided plasters and comfort and made sure she felt well looked-after throughout the whole excursion.

Hmmm, well – the tour escort on *my* excursion was a young man, one of The Headliner's top dancers – and he had brought his girlfriend along for the day – so maybe he was "easily distracted" and "not up to the job" ... Laughing about it with a friend certainly helps!

Day 64 ~ Thursday, 8th March 2012 ~ sunrise: 7.20am ~ sunset: 7.14pm ~ sea state: slight ~ wind: 2, light breeze ~ weather: sunny ~ temperature: 31°C ~ time zone: GMT+8

Exchange of Views

Another day, another leak in the corridor ... We are heading south-east into the Gulf of Thailand, the clocks have been put *forward* for a change and I face a daunting amount of journal writing, but my unhappiness needs to be expressed in that letter to the tour desk manager first. Then I join an exercise class and also manage to secure a washing machine for my pile of laundry that grows quickly in this heat.

Norah invited me to the Café Bordeaux, where she usually lunches with her husband. It is so nice to see her again and catch up on events. Now I show her the letter describing my unpleasant brush with car sickness yesterday, and after she has read the account, her response is similar to Sandie's. Norah is angry and declares the tour attendant's attitude shocking. She approves of my letter, but states that her own wording would have been much less restrained.

It is very helpful to have a second opinion in the matter, and it makes me grateful to have found these friends just when I needed them most.

In the ship's Photo Gallery I see the nice couple who were so concerned and helpful when I felt sick on the coach. The husband assures me that they know what misery it is to suffer from car sickness, for his wife has the same problem. But she also has Ménière's syndrome, and therefore a letter from her doctor that grants her access to a front seat without any difficulties. – I really ought to have thought of bringing such a letter too!

While we are thus engaged in conversation, I become aware of Beryl, hovering nearby. She pretends to be looking at the photographs with interest, but is clearly waiting for the moment when she can assail me. And, as the nice couple moves on and I turn to leave, she follows me to the stairwell and calls out to me. "I hear that you won an award for your performance yesterday! An Oscar, was it?"

Oh, how I wish that I could have found the strength to walk away without a word! But unfortunately her verbal attack draws a reply, and in the following frank exchange of views I learn her opinion: Since I was having lunch almost straight afterwards, I obviously never felt sick at all ... *There!* Her glee at supposedly having caught me out is remarkable, and my heart sinks. Should I give her a lecture on the causes and cures of motion sickness here, in public? Would she even listen? Not likely, for she is far too pleased with herself: "You're in the wrong, and you know it!"

That *she* may be the one who is wrong is clearly quite inconceivable. Now she calls after me, "I know *exactly* what I think of you!" I retaliate that she is a mean old gossip who knows nothing about car sickness and less about how I was feeling. Then I walk away and leave her to share her opinion of me with anyone who will listen.

I am not proud of my outburst and resolve to keep silent if there should be a next time. Truly, there is nothing more effective or more difficult than turning the other cheek! But I am not used to dealing with adults who behave like playground bullies – well, anyway, not since I left teaching, it must be said. Facts and reason, so important to me, play no discernible part in some people's minds, other than to be twisted to suit their purpose.

At my cabin, a letter from the tour desk informs me that my outing to the children's home in Port Klang has been cancelled due to lack of bookings. How disappointing! I was keenly interested in this orphanage, but it was the cheapest excursion of them all and had nothing sensational to offer, and so it probably did not appeal as much to others.

Day 65 ~ Friday, 9th March 2012 ~ sunrise: 7.45am ~ sunset: 7.18pm ~ wind: 2 ~ weather: overcast ~ temperature: 33°C ~ distance travelled since Ko Samui: 625 nautical miles ~ in total: 23,298 nautical miles

Singapore

It is still dark as Aurora approaches the shores of this island republic. The coastline is sparkling with coloured lights, and scores of illuminated vessels of all sizes are scattered on the water. Given its ideal position at the very heart of the south-eastern trade routes, Singapore is one of the world's most important and busiest ports.

On the drive through the city, our guide tells us about this small and populous yet tidy country. In Singapore, fines are imposed for dropping litter, for spitting out chewing gum or neglecting to flush a public toilet, amongst other disgusting offences of a similar nature. This fact has earned Singapore the nickname 'A Fine Country'. Here the general standard of living is high, especially when compared to its neighbours. Singapore has sometimes been called the 'Switzerland of the Far East', but its actual name comes from the Sanskrit for 'Lion Island' – *Singha Pura*.

Our destination is Singapore Zoo, one of the world's finest. Our excursion, titled 'Breakfast in the Wild', is really brunch with a delightful group of orang-utans. They remain totally unimpressed by the admiring human crowd as they pick delicately through a heap of greens, and we sit in the shade, enjoying our own meal and the view.

An Indian girl (slender, beautiful, well-educated and polite) gives an interesting presentation on the apes. Because of the orang-utans' great strength and weight, she says, only men can be employed as their keepers – but also because the apes only accept males as dominant members in their social group. Gender equality is unthinkable in orang-utan land! But, not unlike humans, female orang-utans are possessive and jealous, and the girl tells us that they will spit at her if they catch her talking to their keeper.

It is not as hot as expected, for today a solid cover of clouds shields us from the sun's equatorial force. I enjoy a solitary, unguided walk around the shaded grounds of the zoo and admire the clever way in which animal enclosures have been designed to look completely natural and even idyllic. The animals, content and relaxed, go about their business, doing whatever they would be doing at noon in the wild, which is mostly eating or sleeping.

Three gorgeous white tigers are one of the zoo's main attractions. Under the canopy of a large tree, and veiled by a curtain of vines, they all enjoy a nap, stretched out on rocks overlooking a verdant moat. The information panel claims that white tigers are all descended from the same forefather. Captured in India, this rare beast had lived in a Maharajah's palace for twenty years, and numerous offspring passed his unique colouring down the generations.

Our guide tells us that these white tigers, the siblings Omar, Winnie and Jippie, as well as that unfortunate day's visitors, had been "traumatized by a dreadful experience" in 2008. A Malaysian cleaner, who had earlier been shouting and throwing things, climbed into the tigers' enclosure and approached them by wading through the moat. Unused to such close contact with a human, Omar and Jippie met the intruder with curiosity rather than aggression, while Winnie ignored the whole episode.

The tigers' keeper later described that the two animals approached the man like a new toy, and not as predators. The angry cleaner stretched his arms wide and pushed out his chest as he walked straight towards the tigers. Severely mauled by their investigative pawing and playful bites, he died from multiple injuries after his rescue and before he could be taken to hospital. All eyewitnesses testified that at no point did the man call out for help, or try to get away from the tigers to save himself, though he eventually put his cleaning bucket over his head for protection. And since the man entered the tigers' enclosure voluntarily and against all regulations, his death was ruled a suicide.

Omar and his sisters, innocent of wrongdoing, were allowed to live and have been handled ever since with special care. (A distressing video on YouTube shows the entire incident, filmed by a visitor who at first believed that this was a show. I could not bring myself to watch it to the end.)

Wandering on, I see giraffes, sleek and slender as fashion models, snacking on a selection of leaves tied to a tall pole. In another enclosure, a pride of lions is resting in the shade. The male seems comatose, but his wives share the pleasant task of grooming their pelt while surveying their kingdom. Watching them, I compare the words for lion recently learnt with those I already knew: siha, singha, simba – and lion, leone, Leu, Löwe.

Before our time at the zoo is up I write more postcards, aware that they must be in the ship's mailbox before I go on my second excursion at three o'clock.

Back on board, there is just enough time for recharging the camera's battery while having a light lunch and a brief rest. Then I set out once more, this time on the 'Nostalgic Night' tour around the city. That title is clearly a misnomer, for it is still afternoon and we shall return to our ship long before it gets dark, but no matter. We are taken to a place where large numbers of trishaws are stationed, and told to board them in groups of two. Most people come in couples anyway, but for the solo traveller this is a tense moment. Fortunately Pat, a nice lady I recently became acquainted with, joins me now. She too is without a companion, and she too has no wish to share a trishaw with the only other single person – that same female member of staff whose attitude had recently made me write to the tour desk manager.

As we compare our experiences, it turns out that Pat is also unhappy with the way this woman dealt with her, did not like her attitude and found her unpleasant and unhelpful. We see that no one else wants to share a ride with her either, and are not surprised.

The trishaw ride through Little India is enjoyable. We pass rows of small shops and stores, open to the street and displaying their colourful wares. Men are sitting by the kerb, hunched over old sewing machines or just passing the time of day. Many unusual sights, sounds and smells flash past as our group is taken in convoy through this lively quarter.

After this ride, we get twenty short minutes to explore Bugis Street Market independently. The pervading stink of durian fruit is much like rotting meat and has to be endured as one browses the stalls, but the items come at real bargain prices. A black stretch belt with a metal butterfly clasp seems a nice souvenir of Singapore, and I buy a lovely pair of sandals for just a few dollars more. But twenty minutes are not nearly enough time to enjoy this market! I find myself torn between the wish to explore it further, and the very real possibility of missing my group as they move on.

Our next stop is the prestigious Raffles Hotel. Of course we sip the famous Singapore Sling in the Long Bar and drop our peanut husks on the floor, according to tradition. This must be the only place in Singapore where one is allowed to drop anything at all, but it does go against the Swiss grain to litter such elegant surroundings.

I savour the unique atmosphere and my alcohol-free Virgin Sling, wondering at the newly whingeing Poms who now complain that their drinks are "not strong enough" or "too sweet" or "not what we expected" ... What would that bold, burly and bearded Aussie tell them?

Taking a stroll around the luxurious hotel and its appealing shops, I look for something I could exchange my remaining Singapore dollars for, and in the end I choose a fine, hand-printed cotton sarong in one of the elegant boutiques. And there by the till sits a large glass bowl, filled to the brim with eye-catching seeds the size of cherry stones, ruby-red and glossy as if lacquered. What are they? The young girl at the till (Indian, slender, beautiful, well-educated and polite) explains that they are saga seeds and asks if I would like to take some with me. Yes, please!

As our group is boarding the coach, I notice that one lady bought a poster of Raffles, an Art Deco illustration of the hotel in its prime. I could kick myself for having missed the opportunity to add such a lovely picture to the growing collection of images on my cabin wall. How I wish I could go back and get one too – apparently there were six different versions to choose from!

My spirits plummet further when I find two letters from the tour desk in my mail box. One is a brief message announcing the cancellation of my booked excursion to the beach resort in Colombo, and the other one is the tour desk manager's reply to my earlier letter. He remains silent on the unhelpful attitude of his female colleague and the male tour escort, and skirts the issues I raised by praising the professionalism of team members I had absolutely no contact with. How odd! This is the second time I wonder why P&O does not teach its managing staff how to handle complaints properly and well.

It is past midnight when noises of drilling and vacuuming outside my cabin door break the silence and wake me from sleep. At first I try to ignore them, but because they continue for a long time I get up to see what is going on. Right outside my cabin door, a supervisor (Indian, tall and handsome, well-educated and polite) is on standby, and two Pakistani crew members with an industrial machine are hoovering pools of water from the sodden Axminster.

I call out repeatedly, trying to make myself heard over the din. Once the machine has been temporarily silenced, I snarl that it is impossible to sleep. How long might this noise be expected to continue? The hassled supervisor apologizes, explains that there has been another leak in the corridor, and assures that the job ought to be done presently. Embarrassed by his friendly and patient manner, I return to bed.

(This young man has had the right training, for sure, though it was probably imparted by his parents and not the cruise line. My journey around the world is revealing to me that the Indian Middle Classes are doing an impressive job in raising and educating their children.)

By now the early hours of the morning have come and gone, I am crabby with overtiredness, and it is a good thing that no one is handing me a questionnaire about customer satisfaction at this point.

~ ~ ~

~ The Fourth Leg ~

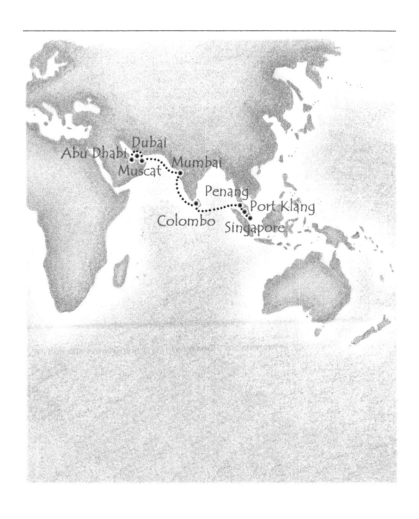

Day 66 ~ Saturday, 10th March 2012 ~ sunrise: 7.25am ~ sunset: 7.26pm ~ wind: 2 ~ weather: sunny ~ temperature: 32°C ~ distance travelled since Singapore: 177 nautical miles ~ in total: 23,475 nautical miles

Malaysia

It is all becoming a bit too much at the moment, and so I get up later than usual. I shall take this day off, rather than book a replacement tour for the cancelled outing to the children's home. After breakfast and a spell at the gym, I edit and label my photographs of the last three excursions and this helps to get things into a proper perspective, for I am cheered by the interesting places and the lovely things I have seen. But as the morning progresses, I am feeling increasingly unhappy about having blasted members of staff with my frustration last night. They were only doing their job, after all, possibly preventing us from being drowned in our beds – and so I go to Reception to find out to whom I should apologize.

    A member of the Angel Team (Indian, tall, beautiful, well-educated and polite) explains that the supervisors on nightshift are presently catching up on sleep, but she assures me with a smile that she will pass on my apology.

    Because it is a port day, lunch is a quiet affair in the Orangery. I look out at the terminal building in the bleak no-man's-land of Port Klang and watch a steady trail of rubbish as it floats downstream. It occurs to me that I could take my laptop ashore to check my emails without having to pay the ship's steep charges for access to the internet. This plan has its merits, and I set out to find the Wi-Fi area of the terminal. The designated lounge is closed, but many members of the ship's crew are netsurfing in a quiet corner of the hall, and there I join them now.

(*Cruiser's tip: If you find the ship's charges for internet access too pricey, consider taking your tablet or laptop ashore. The staff will have experience in these matters and be able to advise you on where to find the best internet cafés in various ports. There, rates and speeds will be much better. Setting up an especially complex password just for your journey is recommended.)

After answering some of the accumulated emails from home (Where am I? What am I doing? And when will I be back?) I google *saga seeds* and learn interesting facts. These seeds are dropped by the Red Sandalwood tree – the same tree whose bark yields a red dye, used by the Indian Brahmins to paint religious marks on their foreheads. These trees, originally native to India and South China, have spread throughout South-East Asia and across South America to the Caribbean. Their attractive seeds are extremely tough and must first be eaten and excreted by certain animals before they are able to germinate. Alternatively, if by-passing a digestive tract, they have to be scratched, or boiled, or dipped in sulphuric acid before planting.

Saga seeds are remarkably similar in size and weight, and that is why they were used as units of weight for fine measure throughout Asia and the Middle East. Four grains of wheat make up the weight of one saga seed, while four saga seeds weigh one gram. This was convenient for traders and craftsmen dealing in gold, silver and pearls in ancient times, and the Malay word *saga* can be traced back to the Arabic term for goldsmith. But saga seeds have other uses as well; they are given as love tokens, or are pierced as beads for jewellery, because of their scarlet heart-shape.

Next I look up *Maersk* and discover that this Danish enterprise is the largest container shipping company in the world, with a sideline in oilrigs and tankers, an annual turnover of many billions, and more than one hundred thousand employees worldwide. No wonder then that their containers are seen in every port and on any passing cargo ship!

Now I return to my nice air-conditioned hut for some serious travel-journal-writing. Tomorrow will bring another excursion, and so it is imperative to catch up and process the last outings. How I miss the days at sea! They separated our earlier ports cleanly and allowed us to digest all that we had seen and learnt.

The fourth leg of our world tour began in Singapore. Familiar members of staff and crew left and new passengers came aboard, and once again many friendly faces are missed as a fresh contingent of travellers wanders about the ship, looking lost and enquiring after the way to facilities which I could probably find blindfolded by now.

At dinner, Martha and I end up talking about religion. This is a subject about which she knows much from her personal life experience, and I relate in turn why I never doubted the existence of God, attempting to put into words what to my mind has no need for reasoning:

My childhood, spent largely outdoors and in creative play, taught me that nothing – *not one thing* – comes about without a creator. Dens built in the woods, animals formed from clay, tunes picked out on recorder or piano, a dolls' house made from card, candles dipped in beeswax, seasonal watercolour paintings, dresses and accessories sewn from scraps of fabric, strings of coloured beads, Christmas cookies decorated with icing, the script of a little puppet play – it was I who called them into being, shaping them according to the ideas in my mind.

At school, when learning about the cultural achievements of mankind, I saw that each clay pot and every sculpture, any building, bridge or ship bore the stamp of the mind that had created it as an expression of its own spiritual character, historic background and personal skill. It seemed quite clear to me that all form, content and function must therefore be a revelation of our human connectedness (or the lack thereof) to the primal creative spirit-background of the world: that to create is to *reconnect* with God – that it is indeed *religion*.

Sensing this, I never doubted that the whole universe in its miraculous complexity could be anything other than the expression of a creative spirit with the supreme power to give Life. Not as a bearded father with the ascribed function of a super-nanny or cosmic chief of police, but as an entity so vast and profound that it must needs permeate every atom, age and aspect of the universe – and since we ourselves are integral parts of this creation, it ought not to surprise us that we should be able to catch only an inkling of God's being in the clear but limited mirror of our minds; a dim reflection of His eternal love, splendour and glory.

Yes, it is our ability to love and create that makes us godlike in a humble yet crucial way, and whatever we do to learn about this beautiful world and love it as a precious gift, entrusted to our care, brings us closer to God.

Our creations, just like our handwriting, bear the seal of our true nature, but the magnificence of the natural world is God's signature and can reveal Him to the questing mind. Sacred texts and historic works of art bear witness to this truth from many angles, for the whole world speaks to us of God's existence. His handwriting is everywhere.

Day 67 ~ Sunday, 11th March 2012 ~ sunrise: 7.27am ~ sunset: 7.31pm ~ wind: 2 ~ weather: sunny ~ temperature: 32°C ~ distance travelled since Port Klang: 181 nautical miles ~ in total: 23,656 nautical miles

Penang

The sun is about to rise over Malaysia as I step out onto the top deck. Twinkling little lights along the shore are slowly fading while the skyscrapers of Penang begin to shimmer in shades of pink against the hazy grey hills.

My tour 'Around the Island' begins in Georgetown, where grand buildings remind us of its British colonial past. We learn that Captain Francis Light acquired Penang in 1786 from the local sultan and established a flourishing trade post in the name of King George III. (His son Colonel William Light, equally enterprising, later founded the Australian city of Adelaide and named it after the queen consort.)

Our guide spouts dry comments and grim humour. He tells us that the dense crowds of motorcyclists thronging the streets are known as 'temporary Malaysians' because so many of them die in road accidents every year.

We stop at a temple that houses a reclining Buddha, the fourth-largest in the world. Seemingly made of moulded concrete and gilded plaster, this statue is far too meretricious for my taste; but there are other fascinating aspects to this temple, for example lotus-patterned floor tiles or wall niches containing row upon row of ancestral urns, decorated with faded ribbons and photographs. Men and women come here to light bundles of incense in quiet prayer, and it is striking how many young people worship at these shrines.

Across the road is a Burmese temple with a gilded statue of Buddha, this one standing upright with his hands held out in a gesture of blessing. Meanwhile, at the souvenir stalls outside, battalions of little Buddhas in wood, brass and jade await the tourist's interest.

We continue with a short drive on a road that snakes into the hills and stop at a batik workshop. Here, craftsmen of all ages demonstrate the tie-dyeing process with skill, and also the painting of traditional motifs in wax and dye. At the shop, batik items of many colours, shapes and forms can be purchased. Tops, dresses, scarves and bags – thrilled ladies now crowd the changing rooms, and their husbands' scant reserves of patience are tried.

Our next stop is at Penang Butterfly Farm. Over a hundred different kinds of butterfly are hatched here! Other creatures are on display too, such as water dragons, carp, millipedes and giant scorpions, lizards, horned frogs and even snakes. Although it is very hot and humid inside the great dome, it is enchanting to wander around the beautifully landscaped interior with its cascading rill, its tranquil lotus pond and the dramatic tropical vegetation.

Butterflies flicker from fruit tray to leaf and from blossom to tree in a giddy dance as I try to get some good photos. This is not easy, for the butterfly model usually takes off at the crucial moment. Their exotic colours and patterns are exquisite, but I cannot bring myself to buy any of the dead specimens for sale at the gift shop. Pinned and framed, they come with a certificate that states their farm origins, but to see them lifeless takes away all the joy.

Bearing parcels of colourful batik items and framed butterflies, our group boards the coach once more. It follows the serpentine road into the hills, braking before each bend and accelerating towards the next one. The perfect recipe for car sickness! But after all the earlier unpleasantness I gave up trying to secure a front seat, and now, unable to see the road, accept that I may have to feel sick again. Regrettably, the tour desk manager went back on his word to help me out after Amanda sat him down for a talk. By chance I saw her seek this meeting, and by his altered manner I guessed what it had been about. As a seasoned cruiser, Amanda has longstanding connections to high-ranking staff and it seems that they do not want to cross her. Now that she has made my simple issue into a personal feud, I am at a loss to know how I should deal with it. But would this problem even exist if I were part of a couple and enjoyed the protection of a man? One is inclined to doubt it.

(*Cruiser's tip: On cruise ships, as elsewhere, some passengers will be more important than others, and those who are well-connected will usually get their way.)

(*Solo traveller's tip: As a single female traveller enjoying blissful independence, you may find that others resent your freedom and make you pay for it in some way. Try to be resilient, resourceful and relaxed, and keep practising these three Rs.)

Now we stop at a fruit and spice stall by the roadside and have gorgeous views of the valley. Our guide tells us about the spices for sale here. There is nutmeg and mace, pepper and cinnamon, cloves and saffron – all those treasures of the Spice Islands for which the Spanish, Portuguese and Dutch traders sailed around the world, exploring and mapping the globe in the process.

  We are shown how a rubber tree is tapped and watch as its white sap trickles slowly into a receptacle that is tied to the tree trunk. A dried length of this natural latex is passed around so that we may test its great elasticity.

Our final stop is at a Kampung, a traditional Malay village where rustic wooden huts, mostly on stilts, sit among fruit trees, herbs and flowers. But every year more villagers abandon the old way of life and move into modern houses that have air conditioning, a washing machine and a garage. These crude breeze-block buildings offer more comfort, but they destroy the appealing harmony that had long existed between the villages and the valleys. Our guide has strong feelings about the ugliness of progress, but he expresses his regret in diplomatic words.

On our return to the harbour we pass the jetties of powerful Chinese clans, the first immigrant families to settle here. Our guide talks about the political system of Malaysia and tells us that the name of its capital Kuala Lumpur means 'Mouth of the Muddy River'. Was this juxtaposition intended? There would be so much more to learn here – but we have reached the ship and must say goodbye.

In the mailbox I find a note from Sandie, inviting me to a mocktail. I freshen up quickly, slip on my new batik top that makes me feel like a Malay butterfly, and hurry to meet her. We sit in the Pennant bar, clutching tall glasses of iced pink Bananaberry Crush, and enjoy each other's company in the cool evening breeze. Sandie confides that the girls of the spa had been talking about my looks in relation to my age. If I were to dye my hair, they had said admiringly, I could easily pass for thirty-two. That is of course nice to hear, but I like my greying hair and do not see any point in pretending it doesn't exist, or that I am younger than my actual age.

Day 68 ~ Monday, 12*th* March 2012 ~ *sunrise: 6.45am* ~ *sunset: 7.06pm* ~ *sea state: slight* ~ *wind: N 2, light breeze* ~ *weather: sunny* ~ *temperature: 32°C* ~ *time zone: GMT+7*

Age & Health

With a start I awake from a dream in which a young hairdresser is trying to persuade me to dye my hair ... but even in a dream I resist this option. A woman once told me the sad story of her life. She had fallen in love with a younger man, and he with her. Because of her youthful looks (and dyed hair) she only admitted to being seven years his senior. He did not mind. Not living in the same part of the world, they met whenever possible and were always very happy together. But when he unexpectedly proposed one day, this put her in a difficult position. Getting married would force her to reveal her true age, but vanity would not allow her to confess that she was actually *fifteen* years older. She declined his offer. Her lover was in suicidal despair because he could not understand – and she could not explain – why she had refused him. His love turned to hatred and the ending was not a happy one. Her advice to me, and to everyone else, has since been this: "Never lie about your age!"

Another 'Hot Bamboo' massage is scheduled this morning. I am early for my appointment and find Manuel hungry for conversation and eager to talk. Working on a cruise ship, he tells me, reminds him of the dentist's aquarium in 'Finding Nemo' where the fish go quietly crazy in their glass tank, cut off from the real world. He also confesses himself amazed at "the cluelessness of the English" – mature passengers and young colleagues alike. Those years spent at school still left startling gaps in their general knowledge, and this surprises him. Educated in Argentina (a country that is not ranked anywhere near Britain on the scale of developed nations), Manuel repeatedly experiences disbelief at what passes for basic education in Britain. (In 'My Fair Lady', the musical for educators, Professor Higgins confirms Manuel's observation thus: "*This* is what the British population calls an elementary education ...")

Manuel is interested to hear my opinion on this state of things as someone who used to be a teacher in England, but I have to confess myself uninvolved because I taught in an educational system that is quite different from the mainstream. I explain that the Waldorf curriculum has a decided yet discreet spiritual background and places its focus on the developmental stages of the child, not on perpetual testing. The history of mankind with its successive achievements in the sciences and the arts, in music, movement, handcrafts, language, literature and drama plays a much bigger part in our education. Though there are several Waldorf aka Steiner Schools in Argentina too, Manuel has never heard of them before. They really seem to be education's best-kept secret, despite a history of a hundred years and worldwide success and popularity.

But now it is time to begin the treatment. I enjoy it fully, and this time with dry eyes. The hot bamboo is working its magic and I am at peace with the world, newly filled with memories of pleasant classroom experiences.

Afterwards I meet Norah and her husband for lunch once more. Bob's reduced sight and hearing mean that he cannot really take part in our conversation, and my heart goes out to him. It must be horrible to become so isolated from one's surroundings! But Norah looks after her husband with great patience and kindness, and an alertness to his needs that is testimony of many years spent together. This deep bond is touching to witness, yet it makes me acutely aware of my freedom, and grateful for it.

I booked a 'Body Composition Analysis' with Jovan to learn more about the interrelation of exercise, nutrition and detoxification, and their combined effects on the body. Jovan explains that the body's acidity levels increase through the intake of coffee, alcohol, junk food, sugar and medication, which may lead to all kinds of illnesses in the course of a lifetime, and even to cancer. The natural state of the body at birth is slightly alkaline, because this allows the immune system to protect our organism most efficiently. Studies have shown that cancer cells cannot develop in an alkaline environment but thrive in an acidic one. Therefore a healthy diet aims to restore and maintain the body's alkaline level at around 7.3 on the pH scale. The liver, being the organ which detoxifies the body, deals with the poisons our organism is subjected to. Surplus toxins are reabsorbed by lymph nodes and deposited in the body's fat cells, but the body attempts to protect itself from these stores of toxin by surrounding them with water. This process is known as water retention. Fat cells thus become much enlarged and form the lumpy tissue commonly known as cellulite.

Meanwhile, the liver is busy cleaning the organism by flushing out toxins with perspiration, urination, respiration and excretion (p,u,r,e for short). At the same time it also generates energy for muscle movement by turning fat into sugar. But the stored body fat, surrounded by its coating of water and toxins, is no longer soluble and available to the liver and cannot be converted to energy through exercise. That is why even skinny, athletic people may have cellulite, and why exercising alone is not enough to lose excess body weight. Exercise is in fact only *one* point in the triangle of a healthy lifestyle. The others are nutrition and detoxification.

It all makes good sense and I am resolved to take these things into consideration; because, as a German saying goes, "Health is not everything, but without health everything is as nothing." Or, as Britta quotes, "A healthy person has a thousand wishes – a sick person only one."

We are leaving the Malacca Strait to cut across the Indian Ocean below the Bay of Bengal on our course for Sri Lanka. After Colombo, Aurora shall be entering waters frequented by pirates and will be operating on a raised security level. The captain informs us by letter and via broadcast of safety measures that concern the passengers and requests that we all take part in a safety drill tomorrow. We learn that armed naval guards will be coming aboard, and also that the ship's external lighting will be reduced to a minimum at night. The Promenade Deck (near sea level) will be closed and remain out of bounds for passengers during the hours of darkness.

All of this makes for a bit of excitement, but I cannot imagine pirates daft or desperate enough to take on a ship of this size, with so many cumbersome souls aboard. Of course this eventuality now becomes topic number one amongst us passengers. Tom suggests that the Aurora Vocalists could assemble on deck to blast approaching pirates with 'Delilah' – a plan that certainly has its merits. We picture a group of nervous Somalis in the corridors of Deck 7, trying to figure out which way to go, and – in tune with the general levity and alluding to 'Pirates of the Caribbean' – our captain broadcasts a warning to the ladies that no pirate we might possibly encounter will look like Johnny Depp.

Tonight brings another 'Welcome Aboard' party, to receive new passengers in style and to celebrate the beginning of the fourth leg. I have once more been invited to join Erin, Paul and their friends and am welcomed in their amiable circle. Amanda, Gilbert and Beryl are seated a few tables ahead, directly in my sightline, and so I cannot help but notice that they are telling a new couple about my assumed misdeeds, for they keep looking over at me pointedly, with outraged expressions. Though tempted to give them a cheerful wave, I decide to take no notice of this egregious behaviour.

After the party I go to meet Norah and Sandie in the Playhouse cinema, as arranged, and introduce my friends to each other. The film 'Slumdog Millionaire' is being shown in preparation for our arrival in Mumbai and, needless to say, we enjoy it very much.

Day 69 ~ Tuesday, 13th March 2012 ~ sunrise: 6.21am ~ sunset: 6.41pm ~ sea state: slight ~ wind: SE 4, moderate breeze ~ weather: sunny ~ temperature: 32°C ~ time zone: GMT+6

Captain's Life

The captain has to make an unpopular announcement today: The unfortunate timing of the tide in Mumbai compels him to cut our stay in Colombo to half a day, and for that reason the all-day excursions to Kandy and the elephant sanctuary are cancelled. According to the harbour master in Mumbai, the only time slot available to us is early in the morning, or else in the evening. The morning slot is the only one possible for Aurora, but to arrive in time we have to leave Sri Lanka earlier than planned. Obviously, our day in Mumbai has top priority. The ship's staff and crew, mainly from Mumbai, have been looking forward to seeing their families for many months, and all passengers obtained expensive visas.

The captain also apologizes for the temporary closure of the Curzon theatre. A leak in the sprinkler system flooded the back rows, he tells us, and a piece of panelling fell from the ceiling in the downpour. – All of this happened before the show in the evening, few people were there and no one was hurt, but there are sure to be complaints.

In 'Hornblower' (my favourite films about ships and adventures at sea, starring the captivating Ioan Gruffudd in his most congenial role) Captain Pellew warns his protégée, the valiant young Horatio, with the words: "Now you have tasted the bitter brew that is a captain's life."

How would *our* captain describe it? He must make each unpleasant announcement in person, and then field the response of furious or upset passengers. He has to deal with stubborn harbour masters, suspicious immigration officials and stone-faced drug squads, not to mention the additional problems that come with being at the head of a large and mixed team – and all of this while casually doing his *real* job of taking sole responsibility for steering a very big ship with several thousands of souls safely around the world.

Clearly, a captain doesn't need any additional hassle as he deals with the multifaceted day-to-day operation of his ship. Not only does he manage the bridge team as it charts and steers the ship's course; he decides how best to enter tricky harbours in inclement weather, makes sure the time plan of a strict itinerary is adhered to, keeps an accurate log and oversees all legal and safety regulations. Being a cruise ship captain is a demanding job, and meeting the clientele ought to be an enjoyable aspect, not a nightmare.

(*Cruiser's tip: Leave the captain alone! Your life is in his hands.)

Day 70 ~ Wednesday, 14*th* March 2012 ~ sunrise: 6.18am ~ sunset: 6.22pm ~ wind: 2 ~ weather: sunny ~ temperature: 34°C ~ time zone: GMT+5.5 ~ distance travelled since Penang: 1,273 nautical miles ~ in total: 24,929 nautical miles

Sri Lanka

From the top deck, I watch as a sprinkle of lights turns into Colombo's dockyard at dawn. Today, our berth is beneath a row of enormous dock cranes, as if we too were a cargo ship. I am thrilled by the sight and glad of this rare opportunity to be right in the midst of a dockyard's security zone, but some passengers resent this berth and complain that the ships of *other* cruise companies get to dock at a *proper* cruise terminal. To me, a close-up view of how the stream of our goods flows around the world is fascinating.

Participating in Colombo's road traffic is another rare experience, for there are dense crowds of cars, lorries and buses, interspersed with auto-rickshaws (those motorized three-wheelers called *Tuk-Tuks*) and even the odd oxcart.

Our tour coaches get a police escort on motorbikes to ensure that we do not get stuck in traffic, for every minute is precious today. The tours depart as early as half-past seven, and all passengers have to be back on board by noon. Norah and I, looking forward to spending more time together, get on the same coach by exchanging the tour-bus sticker I had already collected earlier. This last-minute swap also means that I shall no longer be on the same coach as Amanda and Gilbert – Lord Krishna be praised!

Police presence in Colombo is impressive. Young, lean and smartly uniformed, police officers of both sexes can be seen everywhere as they guard buildings and direct traffic at every roundabout, even supervising pedestrian crossings in pairs, positioned at either end. The facades of buildings are almost obscured by colourful panels, and all the street signs come in the distinct alphabets of Sri Lanka's main languages: Singhalese, Tamil and English. I am annoyed with myself for not having spotted *singha*, the lion, in the word Singhalese, though it is perfectly obvious once our guide mentions it.

A good deal of structural damage is still in evidence, caused by bombings in the recent war with the Tamil Tigers. Some areas we pass through are squalid and swamped with rubbish, and therefore of great interest to crows. They perch in ominous numbers amongst the bustle of the street, eerily reminiscent of Hitchcock's famous film 'The Birds'.

This colonial island, once known as Ceylon, still shows historic substrata of Portuguese, Dutch and British influence everywhere. Its colonial past underpins the young nation of Sri Lanka that gained independence in 1948, like India. And, after her husband's assassination, Sirimavo Bandaranaike, as Chairwoman of the Freedom Party, was elected the world's first female Prime Minister in 1960.

Our guide recalls the terrible tsunami that devastated the coastal regions in 2004 on Boxing Day. It was a four-day holiday on the island and, in addition to tourists, more local people than usual had left their homes inland to enjoy the beaches. Unfamiliar with the dangers of tsunamis, they were intrigued when the waters began to retreat and exposed the seafloor. Many went to have a closer look instead of running for their lives, and so they were killed by the huge wave that rolled in at a speed of several hundred kilometres per hour. Those who survived and tried to save lives went under in the next wave, even more powerful than the first. That day, well over thirty thousand people lost their lives in Sri Lanka alone, and the survivors were traumatized.

Apparently, just a fraction of the huge sum of foreign aid monies raised actually found its way to the people and helped to rebuild their lives as intended; much disappeared into deep pockets and secret bank accounts. It has long been observed that "Foreign Aid is the poor of the rich countries giving money to the rich of the poor countries" and here this happened once again. Our guide reports seeing for himself how well-meaning foreigners, coming to help those who had lost everything, stayed in five-star hotels and enjoyed the high life, which naturally caused suspicion, bitterness and resentment among local people. – We become aware that the memory of these events has barely faded yet.

Our guide is a fount of facts and stories which he presents in a rapid stream with endearing enthusiasm, but after a while we need a break from the overpowering flow of information. It is not quite a tsunami, but almost. The Singhalese guide's English is fluent and he has an impressive vocabulary at his command, but one of his pronouncements has us shaking with supressed laughter. As we drive past a first-rate girls' school, he informs us that "the young ladies who come out of this college are bright, disciplined and well-moulded."

This ambiguous statement becomes our private joke and we shall be laughing about well-moulded ladies in the days to come.

Our first stop is at Colombo's impressive National Museum. No gaudy theme park sculptures here! At last we can view Buddha statues that are moving in their genuine beauty and grace. Of course these statues are centuries old, which must be the reason why they radiate such spiritual power and an impeccable taste that seems quite beyond the reach of more contemporary artists.

The Asokaramaya Temple is our next destination, but its Buddha statue (contemporary, sleek and yellow) and the cheesy murals in garish colours lack appeal, and so I wander the pleasant courtyard instead. It is shaded by an enormous Bodhi tree *(ficus religiosa)* whose impressive trunk is ringed with little shrines, each one containing a figurine of Buddha.

The oldest of currently living trees grows in Sri Lanka. In Anuradhapura – Ceylon's capital city in ancient times and one of the world's oldest continuously inhabited settlements – a sacred Bodhi tree has a documented history that reaches back to the year 245 BC, and it is said to be a direct offspring of the Bodhi tree under which Gautama Buddha attained enlightenment.

It is time for refreshments, served at a hotel near Mt Lavinia Beach. Seated in pleasantly cool shade, Norah and I watch a crow as it sips and samples the swimming pool's turquoise waters, and I use this moment of rest to write a postcard to my son. "My dear, this is a place you would love. I won't see much of it because we only have half a day here, but what I saw, I liked. Tomorrow our ship shall be entering waters with pirate activity, so if you do not get any more postcards, prepare to raise a ransom."

Learning from experience, I prepared my postcards in advance today, with stamps and address. This precaution proves valuable, for once again port officials are zipping up the ship's mailbag just as we return, and my postcards are slipped in at the very last moment. Apart from the ongoing problem with car sickness, the sending of postcards turns out to be the only stressful aspect of this cruise: either there are no suitable postcards to buy, or there are no local stamps available, or else there is no time to post them.

(*Cruiser's tip: The ship's shop stocks a good selection of postcards showing the ports you will visit. Often superior in quality to any you may find ashore, these cards usually sell out before you reach the place in question. If interested, buy them well ahead of time. On the other hand, stamps cannot be bought until you reach a port, and sometimes they will not be available onboard at all. You can then obtain them on your shore excursion, or your local guide may agree to do the posting for you.)

Now everyone is back on board and Aurora turns her bow away from Sri Lanka's shore, accompanied by grumbling about the lost half day from the usual suspects. (Complaints to the captain will follow.)

Sandie and I meet up to enjoy a companionable break at the Orangery. Sitting and chatting over a nice cup of tea by the windowfront, we are surprised to see a school of dolphins. They show their back fins as they break through the water, and some of the little ones even attempt playful jumps. What a lovely spectacle!

At dinner, Martha reports that her Dutch friends were on the coach with Amanda and Gilbert and overheard them talking about me in a way that was "really not very nice". In fact, her friends were upset by the meanness of comments which centred on wishful fantasies that an accident might befall my coach. – Well, I am no longer surprised or hurt and think that this matter is best left to karma.

(*Cruiser's tip: Should you be so unfortunate as to make enemies on a cruise, don't worry. The dimensions of a cruise ship will allow you to avoid them with ease. Your paths may cross once in a while, most likely while going ashore, but there is safety in numbers.)

A new version of 'Jane Eyre' is shown at the cinema tonight and portrays the chilly gloom of Dickensian England very credibly. Apart from that – and contrary to our hopes – the story illustrates the point that finding your soulmate does not mean your troubles are over.

Day 71 ~ Thursday, 15th March 2012 ~ sunrise: 6.33am ~ sunset: 6.43pm ~ sea state: calm ~ wind: 2 ~ weather: sunny ~ temperature: 32°C

Pirate Watch

Awaking shortly after four o'clock, my thoughts are drawn to the future, for our return to Southampton is moving into sight and as yet I have no idea what will happen then.

There is another leak in the corridor, but I pass the plumber and his stepladder, his buckets and sodden towels without batting an eyelid. It is such a common occurrence that everyone has become quite used to it. Not in the mood for exercise this morning, I change my routine and have breakfast at the Medina. There I write and edit my journal entries, surrounded by the amiable and attentive care of the waiters who are familiar with my preferences by now. They know of my notebook and my desire for solitude at a little table by the windowfront, and they obligingly ensure that such a table is available to me.

Norah likes the Zumba class and has invited me to join her this morning, but the Indian immigration formalities with face-to-face interviews are taking place throughout the day and I don't want to be caught mid-Zumba, as it were. Instead, I take my journal to the shady Promenade Deck and continue to write. The sun is hot, the sea calm, the horizon hazy, and the busy shipping lane along the continental shelf of India marked by cargo vessels, large and small.

A security officer with a pair of binoculars has taken up position by the railing and is watching out for pirates. He tells me that although there is no real threat yet, everyone is getting used to operating at 'Level Two'.

I am intrigued by the installation next to him, which appeared overnight and looks like the case of an old cinema reel; but it has instruction labels, knobs, curly cables and ear protection attached and is in fact an amplifier. Reluctant to distract an officer on watch, I cannot resist asking what the device is for. He, however, is happy to chat and explains that it is a Long Range Acoustic Device or LRAD, a sound system so powerful that its two-tone alarm would hurt any pirate's skull with its piercing sound. It also emits a warning to any approaching vessel, recorded in twenty-two languages:

"You have now entered the Aurora safety zone – please turn away!"

English and Arabic are the main languages, he says, and I am surprised to learn that although this message is available in German, it is not recorded in Somali, an Arabic dialect. Really? Even though most pirates are Somalian and without formal education? The officer agrees it makes little sense. He has never heard the device in action yet and admits that it might be quite exciting to try it out. But when I ask if pirate vessels show up on radar, he signals in mime that he has not heard my question. This means, of course, that he is not at liberty to talk about this aspect of the topic.

Well, these anti-pirate measures certainly add a new and interesting dimension to our journey!

Meanwhile, the Indian immigration process has been ticking along in the background. Repeated calls for the next hundred passengers punctuate all our activities today, and my turn comes shortly after three o'clock. Queuing outside Vanderbilt's with my sheaf of papers, I witness exasperated complaints of fellow passengers who seem to think that the whole procedure has been set up expressly to annoy them. There is no thought for what the situation demands, and no effort to comply graciously.

"And all this for five hours in India!" hisses the lady in front of me. The man at my back, standing much too close and invading my personal space, exclaims "Jesus Christ!" at intervals, puffing bad breath in my direction. Now, if I were that big, bearded Aussie, I would tell him boldly that I find his behaviour offensive on three levels (social, religious and hygienic). Instead, I manage a fixed smile as I turn my head aside, hold my breath and keep my thoughts to myself.

India acquired a taste for administrative paperwork during the British Raj and is now making the most of it. In preparation for this cruise, obtaining the mandatory visa for

India was a stressful and costly procedure for some of us, but no problem for others. Yet, in every case, the required photographs *must* have a particular format that is unlike any other, and instructions on how your face *must* and *must not* look cover more than one page. The nationality, as well as possible changes of nationality, have to be declared of both your parents – and if one of them should hail from Pakistan, you're in trouble.

But now the Indian visa in my passport receives the necessary stamp of approval and I am free to go to my next appointment at the gym. Today, Jovan shall be carrying out the heart rate test that is part of his Body Composition plan. Right now he is occupied with a client's foot analysis, and so I take a seat and watch the procedure.

At its end, Jovan invites me to stamp my footprints on paper too and the result is astonishing: Both arches are so high that the heels leave round, isolated marks that stand alone, separated like islands by a gulf of blank paper from 'the mainland' with its toes. Jovan, expressing his surprise, exclaims that he has never seen such footprints before. Then he places the print in a display case, next to another set that shows completely flat feet and illustrates the opposite end of the range of possibilities.

Jovan hands me a heart rate monitor to tie around my chest and I walk on the treadmill for several minutes to warm up. Its level of resistance is increased every two minutes until I reach 'Level Ten' and am reminded of what it felt like to hike in the Scottish Highlands during my road trip earlier. I keep going, my heart pounding at a rate of 152. Now Jovan lowers the resistance level progressively, but to his obvious puzzlement my heart rate refuses to drop accordingly and remains stubbornly high.

Telling me to relax produces no relaxing effect whatsoever. He repeats the process until he has me walking at maximum speed, and again the pattern is the same: The rate of increase is totally normal, and even Jovan, who is not given to easy or excessive praise, declares it *"verrry* good" ... but the rate in the resting phase remains so high that he checks my pulse to see if the monitor is working correctly.

I joke that my heart rate seems to match my unusual footprint, or that his close proximity might be responsible.

"Oh, come on – you're not sixteen anymore!" Jovan snorts. A fair point; though it could be argued that at heart we remain sixteen in all the later ages of our life ...

Anyhow, Jovan, though perplexed by the unexpected result, tells me not to worry. As a next step he is going to work out my personal exercise plan, which we shall discuss after Mumbai.

I don't feel like dressing up for a Black Tie dinner and ring both Martha and Norah to let them know that I shall not be coming to the Medina tonight. Slipping on some comfortable leisurewear instead, I go up on deck to watch the sunset. Tonight the sun flames in fiery orange-red, surrounded by a haze of dove-grey that fades to a range of iridescent pastel colours high above. The calm sea below complements this stunning picture with a matching slate-grey that is unbroken by any reflection of colour or light.

"The sun with one eye vieweth all the world" wrote Shakespeare; and there it floats, this fiery eye, suspended in splendid uniqueness, and looks back at me.

Sandie and I will meet up later in our favourite place on the top deck. Meanwhile, my notebook and I have dinner at the

Orangery. The waiters beam their friendly smiles at me and the Dutch ex-pastor stops by for a chat. It makes me realize how very much at home I feel on the ship these days, having perfected the kind of cruise routine that suits me.

(*Cruiser's tip: Long cruises lend themselves more than short ones to individual tailoring. There are so many ways in which you can spend your days, evenings and nights, that even on the same ship no two cruise experiences may be exactly the same in the end. Be bold and do your own thing.)

Day 72 ~ Friday, 16th March 2012 ~ sunrise: 6.47am ~ sunset: 6.47pm ~ wind: 2 ~ weather: sunny ~ temperature: 36°C ~ distance travelled since Colombo: 908 nautical miles ~ in total: 25,837 nautical miles

Mumbai

Before the sun rises, I am up on deck where crew members with mobile phones arrange to meet their families, some of them travelling all the way from Goa. Martha is about to go on another special excursion, this time to the Taj Mahal, and will be absent from the ship and our dinner table for a few days. I shall miss her; but Norah manages at the last minute to hop on my 'Mumbai Highlights' tour. She secures seats at the front of the coach (helping out with my problem) and we enjoy the day in each other's company.

Our local tour guide is a quietly dignified and lovely older woman whom Norah and I like instantly. (Others will complain about her later – no idea why!) She is a member of the Zoroastrians whose ancestors settled in Mumbai after fleeing Persia and the Muslim Conquest in the tenth century. Farsi is no longer widely spoken, but there are still temples where the four elements are worshipped according to the ancient tradition. Earth, water, air and fire are revered as expressions of the supreme deity Ahura Mazda. His sacred flame at Udwada has been kept burning continuously for a thousand years and is even now a pilgrimage site.

We shall pass the Zoroastrian 'Towers of Silence' later. They are closed to the public, because here the Parsees expose the bodies of their dead to the sky so that vultures may dispose of them. Zoroastrian religion forbids pollution of the sacred elements Earth and Fire with cremation or burial, but in our days the rapidly dwindling numbers of vultures in and around Mumbai make this ancient burial rite a bit of a problem.

With its wings spread wide like those of a guardian angel, the Zoroastrian symbol of the Faravahar is printed on the windscreen of our tour coach for protection. Three rows of feathers on each wing represent the good thoughts, good words and good deeds every Zoroastrian strives for, thus rising above the bad thoughts, words and deeds denoted by three rows of tail feathers. Two streamers on either side of the central ring stand for the forces of good and evil between which a soul must choose at every moment, like the human figure shown inside the ring. In this Circle of Life, it faces the one and turns its back on the other.

Driving through the city, we see splendid colonial buildings from the British Raj mixed with sights of a totally different way of life. Our first stop is at the famous Gateway of India, an imposing archway by the sea that was hastily erected in

1911 when King George V and Queen Mary stepped ashore. It then took another sixteen years to complete the landmark with rounded turrets, pointed arches and trellis stonework in an appealing Indo-Saracen style. The Taj Mahal Palace Hotel has an interesting story: Jamsetji Tata, a citizen of Mumbai, made his fortune in the steel industry but was refused entry at a British grand hotel on account of being Indian. Tata decided to build a hotel of his own, in prime location opposite the Gateway of India, and designed the splendid Taj Mahal Palace Hotel to surpass all colonial hotels in every conceivable way. Then, instead of refusing access, he invited the British in to enjoy his hotel's magnificence. – What a truly stylish revenge!

Our tour coach is not lacking in modern comforts, contrary to concerned warnings in the excursions brochure. The air conditioning is pleasant to return to after each walkabout, but the heat is not nearly as fierce as expected. Those areas we are shown are not the overwhelming, dense and noisy chaos we anticipated after watching films of India. There are many people, to be sure, but not bewildering or oppressive crowds. It is not quiet, for cars honk their horns as freely as they do in Rome, but no noisier than in other big cities. All places we visit are calm, safe and pleasantly shaded, for big trees line most streets. We are approached by vendors and beggars, but not hassled. They are easy to ward off and will take no for a no. The people we see living in slums and on pavements seem to accept their situation in life calmly and cheerfully, which must surely be the result of Hinduism and its caste system. People go about their business as oxcart handlers, sweepers, roadworkers, stallholders, taxi drivers, police officers, vendors and housewives in a kaleidoscope of attractive moments too numerous to capture on camera, and almost impossible from a moving coach.

Our next destination is Mani Bhavan House on Laburnum Road, where Mahatma Gandhi stayed when in Mumbai. It contains a library of over fifty thousand books on this great man's life and work. Although faced with initial resistance, Gandhi's ideals of truth and non-violence influenced and reformed India and inspired devoted followers worldwide. He corresponded with Leo Tolstoy, who also endeavoured to change society for the better, at the same time as Rudolf Steiner worked tirelessly towards similar goals in Europe. It was an age when men of high spiritual intelligence and deep human compassion strove against truly overwhelming odds to bring about a better world for all, guided by their insight. Where are such men today?

These are my thoughts, face to face with Gandhi's portrait and his simple room with a row of spinning wheels. Lovingly created miniature scenes around the house show twenty-eight important moments of Gandhi's life, leading to his assassination in January 1948, just after India gained independence from its colonial masters. – There is certainly much food for thought here!

We drive on to the Hanging Gardens that straddle the hill above Mumbai's water reservoir. From here one has a good view of the immense city that stretches out to the horizon. In these pleasant grounds, ownerless but well-fed dogs snooze peacefully in the shade. One of them has draped himself on a sunny park bench and seems to like having his picture taken, for he smiles and stretches his paws when I point my camera at him. Wandering on, I am thrilled to find twelve glossy scarlet saga seeds among the dusty leaf mulch on the ground. Had I not learnt about them earlier, I would hardly have noticed them.

Young women on an outing with a class of primary school children are playing Blind Man's Buff in the shade of trees, and a group of smiling teenagers poses for pictures on a boot structure, built to illustrate the English nursery rhyme *'There was an old woman who lived in a shoe'*.

Does the essence of a healthy childhood of outdoor play and fun, largely lost to teenage pop culture in the West, live on in India? I am impressed by the happy and peaceful scenes we witness here.

The marble Jain Temple on our tour has been replaced with a visit to the temple of the International Society for Krishna Consciousness, ISKON – better known as the Hare Krishnas. Their house of worship is adorned with much plaster stucco, high-tech security cameras and a profusion of chandeliers. Monks in saffron robes with clay marks on their foreheads, prayer beads in one hand and a mobile phone in the other, loiter in passages and on balconies. Women, bent over a low table in dim light, string flower garlands for a celebration.

On our way to the museum we pass a vast roadside slum, huddled beneath huge trees that spread their branches over the dense collection of huts. These makeshift dwellings look like something that children might build if they had enough cheap materials at their disposal.

On the pavement alongside the dusty multilane road, a child-sized woman is doing laundry. She spreads washed clothes over the metal roadside railing while her husband, on blankets in the shade nearby and resting his back against a wall, watches over wife and son. This little boy bounces his bare-bottomed baby brother as he marches along the lines of stationary traffic, begging. Full of irrepressible good spirits, he flashes sunlit smiles and waves to us as our coach moves on. To him, being coated in grime and dressed in rags is no impediment to being happy, and his smiling face makes me realize that on my way around the world I have not yet seen another that radiated such joy and contentment.

We make a brief stop at the Dhobi Ghats, that great open-air laundry where hundreds of workers divide the steps of the washing process between them, and row upon row of shirts, towels and sheets offer up the moisture in their fibres to the blazing midday sun.

Vendors crowd around our coach, now stationary in dense traffic, to hold up embroidered cloth in all colours of the rainbow, peacock feather fans and carved wooden boxes, in the vain hope of earning a few small coins. In the midst of the unpleasantness of their situation – the heat, the noise, the exhaust fumes, the tourists unwilling to buy their wares – they still smile at us with genuine friendliness.

A man is sleeping on the pavement beside the busy road. A layer of newspaper, neatly spread out, and a skinny arm flung over the eyes are his only protection. Why *here*? What made him choose this of all possible places? It seems like a silent invitation to the heavens to better his lot in life.

We have reached the former Prince of Wales Museum, now renamed the *Chhatrapati Shivaji Maharaj Vastu Sangrahalaya*. Now *that* is not an assemblage of syllables the British visitor will learn to pronounce in a hurry, and it may have been chosen for this very reason. More than a name, it is a proud and defiant statement of cultural identity.

Inside, a truly splendid collection of ancient artwork speaks eloquently of the spirit-awareness of former times, and the beauty of these items is delightful. Sculptures of stone and brass show Krishna, voluptuous goddesses and pensive Buddhas; graceful elephants are carved from wood, a terracotta model depicts three musicians and, amongst a great variety of other interesting exhibits, exquisite drawings by a master of his art outline scenes from ancient legends. All too soon our tour is over, and it leaves me with the keen wish to see more of this fascinating country one day.

Day 73 ~ Saturday, 17*th* March 2012 ~ sunrise: 6.34am ~ sunset: 6.52pm ~ sea state: calm ~ wind: 2, light breeze ~ weather: sunny ~ temperature: 29°C ~ time zone: GMT+5

Piracy Facts

After the morning's usual gym session, I enjoy a swim in the deserted pool while a shoal of fish breaks the ocean's surface repeatedly. They seem quite large and are probably hunting. Then I dry off in the sun that is blazing less fiercely today. The vitamin D deficiency we set out with in wintry Britain must surely be cured by all this sunshine on tap.

Aurora has now entered the Arabian Sea and is gliding smoothly across its tranquil waters. Today's highlight is a talk on piracy by a commander of the Royal Navy. He came aboard in Mumbai to advise the captain on our journey through dangerous seas, and I take copious notes of all that he tells us: Over the past few years, the worldwide shipping trade has quadrupled in volume. Almost all the goods we buy come from overseas, most of them from China. Cargo ships have to pass through a number of 'choke points', of which the canals of Panama and Suez are the main ones. About twenty-three thousand ships a year, carrying the majority of the world's container goods, pass through the Gulf of Aden alone and make it one of the busiest shipping lanes. At its southern edge sits Somalia, a failed state that harbours Muslim extremists, and their activities exacerbate an already desperate situation. Piracy, much more profitable than traditional farming or fishing, quickly evolved into a system of organized crime that has no difficulties finding willing recruits among the men of Somalia. At the date of writing, the highest ransom ever achieved was in the region of twelve million dollars. A very impressive sum in such a poor part of the world!

Pirate activity is seasonal because the monsoon causes extremely rough and dangerous seas in the Indian Ocean. The pirates live in hidden, moveable camps along deserted stretches of coast, and these camps grow in size as boats, weapons and other paraphernalia are gathered. Sometimes they are spotted from the air and this may lead to a raid.

Having learnt from the experience of others, countries began to work together in policing sea lanes, and the crews of ships took pains to be prepared. As a result, successful attacks dropped close to zero in 2011 and forced the pirates to adapt to the new situation. Now they venture out farther than ever before and, in doing so, take considerable risks. The pirates are mostly Somalis, some are Yemenis and a few are Indian. Malnourished and uneducated, they are easily persuaded to lay their lives on the line for the slim chance of a better future, but quite a few of these young men in little skiffs will be lost at sea.

Lookouts on the bridge of commercial and passenger ships find it difficult to distinguish between innocent fishermen, human traffickers and pirates. They all use the same type of boat, but tell-tale signs are hooked ladders and automatic weapons, Russian AK-47s being the weapon of choice. These are pointed at the bridge in an attempt to intimidate the crew and force them to slow down.

Easy targets for pirates (the so-called high-risk vessels) are those with a maximum speed of less than fifteen knots, a freeboard lower than six metres, no defence measures, and in daytime transit with "a complacent and compliant crew". None of this applies to cruise ships, obviously, and now the commander confirms my hunch that pirates would be daft to target a ship of Aurora's size; for if she should swing her stern towards them, pirates would have a hard time keeping upright on the powerful wake she generates, and no skiff can keep up with her maximum speed.

Other than that, razor wire and downward spikes are used to prevent pirates from boarding, though these are not employed on cruise ships. To repel boarders, cruise ships rely on firehoses, additional fencing, dummy lookouts and LRADs, as well as special security personnel. Armed guards, waving their automatic weapons at an approaching skiff, are known to make pirates turn away. But although cruise ships are low-risk vessels, it is their high level of preparedness that ensures their safety.

Military units of the EU, NATO and CTF 151 are now patrolling pirate territory, but their limited resources have to cover an area the size of Europe (its lands *and* seas) and so they focus on the International Transit Corridor that leads to the Red Sea and the Suez Canal. Navy vessels are positioned there in a strategic line, along which we shall safely travel.

The fact that so many nations take part successfully in the fight against piracy has forced the pirates to change tactics. Recently they began to make forays into territorial waters, exploiting the fact that international military ships cannot operate there. They crept into harbours and took vessels at berth, once the ship's crew felt safe and relaxed their guard. It is like a game of cat-and-mouse, the commander says, and he sounds sympathetic to the plight of these people.

"A stable Somalia is of course the best solution," he concludes, "for if these men had proper education, jobs and a future, they would not become pirates."

Unfortunately I will have to miss the afternoon showing of 'Gandhi' at the cinema, for now it is time for my follow-up session with Jovan. This film interests me particularly since I visited Gandhi's memorial museum yesterday, but I also enjoy the sessions with Jovan, our knowledgeable trainer. Now he explains the first part of the exercise programme he has put together in response to the earlier heart rate test. Jovan is a nice person with whom I feel at ease. I learn new things from our talks, and in his general attitude as fitness coach I recognize an affinity of style, for he uses the same kind of amiable no-nonsense approach which I had favoured as a teacher.

All day I looked forward to meeting Sandie after dinner. We plan to attend the late second showing of 'Gandhi' and now pass the hours in the Pennant bar, trying to keep awake and reasonably alert after a long day. And the film is indeed well worth staying up for! Gandhi's life story with its struggles, his increasing influence and his courageous concept of non-violent resistance are well told and profoundly inspiring.

Day 74 ~ Sunday, 18th March 2012 ~ sunrise: 6.12am ~ sunset: 6.15pm ~ wind: NW 3 ~ weather: sunny ~ temperature: 34°C ~ time zone: GMT+4 ~ distance travelled since Mumbai: 848 NM ~ in total: 26,685 nautical miles

Oman

For the first time on this journey the sea appears shrouded in mist. The haze is so dense one can barely make out the sea's surface, but the captain informs us that this haze is actually sand dust, misting the air in the aftermath of a great storm. I witness our arrival in Muscat from the Crow's Nest.

"We have dolphins at eleven o'clock!"

Everyone present rushes to the windowfront and looks on, entranced, as these lovely animals gambol ahead of our bow, breaching and diving like a joyful welcome committee. And now the haze lifts to reveal the stark desert coastline of Oman – a country of which I know nothing.

Today's guide is a charming young Arab who radiates cheerful friendliness and amiable generosity of spirit. With quiet pride he tells us about his young nation and its ruler. Initially Oman was a barren region, inhabited by nomadic tribes who migrated, mostly from Yemen, to scrape a living from their animals in the desert, and from fishery along the coast. Influenced by the Persian dynasties who successively ruled the region around the Persian Gulf and controlled its important trade routes to the Far East, the people of Oman were among the first to meet and accept the new religion of Mohammed the Prophet in the 7th century.

But by the late 1400s, the fiercely catholic Portuguese arrived in the wake of Vasco da Gama, wrested the port of Muscat from the Muslims and established a trading post of their own *en route* to India. For 143 years, Muscat remained occupied by the Portuguese, and they made their mark with an impressive fort that protected the harbour.

Then, in the mid-1500s, the ascending Ottoman Empire desired control of the all-important trade routes. These new invaders captured Muscat twice in thirty years and ousted the Portuguese with the active help of rebellious local tribes, but they were themselves deposed by the Omanis about a hundred years later.

Thus began, in 1741, the rule of a long line of Sultans, and Oman was never again taken over by a foreign power. The importance of the old trade routes declined in modern times, but by the 1960s deposits of natural gas and crude oil were discovered. Today's ruler, His Highness Sultan Qaboos bin Said Al Said began his reign by deposing his father in a bloodless coup in 1970, and then he went about modernizing the country. The sultan set Oman on a new path and opened it up to the world, reformed education and economy and the healthcare and welfare system. Grand buildings and superb roads were speedily built with western engineering, mainly along Oman's coast that extends over a thousand kilometres. New job opportunities continue to be created, and tourism too is on the rise.

And yet Oman remains a sultanate, which is the same as an absolute monarchy. The Sultan is also Prime Minister, Minister of Defence, Chief of the Armed Forces, Minister of Foreign Affairs and Chairman of the Central Bank – in brief, the country's 'father' in the traditional tribal sense. The lack of political diversity is balanced by the fact that everything we see seems very well taken care of.

Of course our guide cannot and would not tell us anything about the hidden darker side that is later revealed by a scan of Wikipedia, such as the violation of civil rights, strict censure of expression, disappearances, torture, slavery, and a high suicide rate amongst the poor and exploited Indian labourers. In Oman, as everywhere, the creation of a society that is liberal and humane and fair to all participants has not been accomplished yet.

From our coach we spot an intriguing building in the shape of an eggcup. It sits in a raised location, overlooking the harbour, and is built in the shape of an Arab incense burner. What could it be? Our guide tells us that it is the landmark of a popular amusement park.

Well-kept flowerbeds border the main road with their colours and beautify the centres of roundabouts. Quite an achievement in the desert! Decorative streetlights and pretty domed bus shelters add to the appeal of the scenery, and to express the cherishing reverence which desert dwellers have for the element of water, a fountain of dancing jets enlivens a public space below a sun-baked cliff.

My group is driven through the city of Muscat to the Oman Dive Centre to enjoy a 'Beach Break'. Dense traffic makes the coach advance in a stop-and-go motion that instantly causes nausea, and so I move to an unclaimed front seat where I can stare at the road and pretend to be driving myself. It is the only way to prevent the queasiness from developing into an unpleasant accident; but it gets me in trouble once again, for now two elderly women in the seats of the next row are annoyed. At first there are only hushed mutterings about my perceived insolence, but then one of them pushes my head aside with some force when it gets in the way of her camera. *Ouch!* Upset at being treated in this brutish manner, I try to breathe calmly and reflect on the Mahatma. What would *his* response have been? Gandhi, being Indian and thus a person of colour, had once been pushed off a train in South Africa. This must have been much more hurtful, and yet it put him on his path of non-retaliation. Attentive to such experiences, Gandhi soon became convinced that violence always hurts the perpetrator if there is no response in kind.

I decide to embrace this principle, and to my surprise the brutish woman approaches me once we are on the beach and offers a sincere apology, saying that she is not normally like this and doesn't know what came over her.

Wow! Non-violence really works! Even if you are not the Mahatma.

Keen to put this distressing incident behind and ready to enjoy the day, I fetch a sunlounger and drag it to a shady place under the broad awning that stretches along the beach. But an Italian *signora* (from the Costa cruise ship berthed next to us) claims the empty space for herself, signalling that her own lounger is only temporarily placed in the sun. With a smile I point out the obvious: There is surely enough space for both our loungers! She turns to her friend, exclaiming in peeved Italian that she does not know what I am saying; and her friend, turning to me, tells me to drop dead – in the way in which people pick up rude phrases in a foreign language without actually speaking it.

Well, I am truly grateful that an awareness of Gandhi's attitude and guiding principle was brought to me in a timely manner! Determined to leave all this unpleasantness behind, I walk away to explore the wide strip of sunny sand, and to swim in the warm shallows. The water is so crystal-clear that shoals of fish can be seen, flitting about. It is not necessary to snorkel, for their marks and shapes can be studied perfectly well from the air.

We have three hours to enjoy sun, sea and sand, and a nice complimentary fruit drink. A backdrop of desert hills shows impressive erosion patterns, carved into tilted layers of pale sedimentary rock, and from a beach bar ahead, Bob Marley's familiar songs accompany my wanderings along the beach: "No, woman, no cry ..."

I had not expected to hear reggae in an Arab land and notice that this music is an instant link to global culture. Is it for the benefit of foreign visitors alone, or do the people of Oman like Bob Marley too?

Returning to the pier, we stop at the sultan's main palace. It has a peculiar shape, almost like a kiosk, and appears much less ostentatious (at least from the outside) than the avenue that ends at its wrought-iron gate, lined with neo-medieval architecture and polished marble pavements.

All around, new buildings are sprouting from the hot desert sand and convey the sultan's ambition to develop a cultured, clean and contented nation. There is absolutely no squalor anywhere – not a scrap of rubbish on the ground nor splashes of graffiti on bare walls and pillars. Nearly all the members of our group comment on this fact after mentally comparing what we are used to with what we see here. And if the amiable character of our guide is at all representative of Arab men, I shall have to revise my mental image of this part of the world entirely.

But unfortunately the cliché of the ignorant, insensitive tourist is confirmed yet again, for two women in our group are wearing nothing but a sarong over their swimsuit. They had left the ship in this outfit, ignoring our port talks and the printed guide that emphasized the importance of dressing respectfully in Muslim countries. Now one of these women asks the guide to let her leave the coach early for a private look around the souk. – But why would she want to go out, dressed like this? The entire top half of her torso is exposed flesh, for her sarong is tied across breasts that rest low on her belly. It seems inappropriate even to our eyes, and I shudder to think what the people of Oman will make of it. Cringing with the shame she is not feeling, I should like to remind her to get suitably dressed before going out, but the unpleasant earlier experiences with other people make me remain silent, even though I find this situation the most upsetting of all.

And sadly this is not the last example of questionable behaviour today. Our chauffeur, who had driven faultlessly before, has a little difficulty at a busy intersection.

"Is a driving test not required in your country?" asks a woman loudly and with fake innocence.

Really, it does make one cringe! Do these people study rudeness and insolence, or is it a natural talent?

(*Cruiser's tip: Every traveller ought to behave in a way that is respectful to others and commands respect in turn.)

This day has taken its toll. Saddened and tired, I return on board for a short meal and a long rest, but then, as evening falls, I gaze at the coastline of this fascinating country and watch as little lights begin to glimmer in the dusk. I would love to go ashore once again, wander around Muscat's souk and harbour, collect more impressions ... but I realize that I am not up to it. Today's experiences with fellow humans left me feeling bruised, dejected and vulnerable, so I just take a few turns around the top deck, with a heavy heart, and then retire to the shelter of my homely hut – acutely conscious of a missed chance.

Day 75 ~ Monday, 19*th* March 2012 ~ *sunrise: 6.12am* ~ *sunset: 6.15pm* ~ *sea state: lively* ~ *wind: NW 3, gentle breeze* ~ *weather: sunny* ~ *temperature: 23°C*

Gulf of Dismay

This morning, still affected by the disappointing examples of human behaviour witnessed yesterday, my mood is down in the dumps. But, by contrast, Jovan is in exuberant spirits and sparkles like fireworks as he drives the exercise class with energy and humour. He likes his musical backdrop loud and gives the volume control an extra twist today, but loud rap music is more than I can cope with right now. I wonder if it would not be better to retire to a quiet spot until the pain is properly processed – but then, after a glance at my probably miserable expression, Jovan readjusts the volume to a more manageable level in a touching gesture of consideration that makes it impossible to leave.

I struggle to focus on the physical exercises. They fail to distract me from the annoyance, the hurt and dismay that are churning in my mind. Longing to be with my journal, I expect that it will ease my mind to get down to the process of writing that proved so helpful in every difficult situation. And at last the time comes when I can settle down with my notebook at a quiet table on the Promenade Deck.

When a break is needed, I go to the railing for a look at the horizon and a chat with the Indian security officer on watch. This one is especially easy to talk to, and his amiable manner does much to calm my spiky soul state.

In the Gulf of Oman, the sea is rougher than it has been for weeks and the temperature dropped by nearly ten degrees. I learn from the officer that the heat, rising from the desert lands on either side along the gulf, generates cooling winds that come whistling down over the sea and churn up the waves. From these prevailing wind conditions and the topic of pirates we drift to the subject of arranged marriages, for his own marriage is much on his mind. This modern, well-educated and scientifically trained young Indian now tells me that he trusts his parents to find him a good wife. Reading disbelief on my face, he hastens to explain why he thinks it right that his parents should choose a suitable girl for their daughter-in-law, and why he happily accepts such an ancient custom. Listening to his reasoning, I am almost persuaded that it might indeed be a good solution.

When Norah rings my cabin, we agree to have lunch together; and, comparing notes on our different excursions yesterday, it turns out that she experienced a day of trials as well. Bob's health had improved sufficiently to make a brief excursion possible, but then a shuttlebus suddenly whisked him away without his wife and his scooter. Norah had to do a lot of running to reunite the three of them, she saw next to nothing of Muscat and was left dismayed and exhausted.

This evening, I am in no mood to dress up for a Black Tie dinner and make my way upstairs to the Orangery instead. Dinner at this self-service restaurant is becoming ever more popular among the passengers, because they too are tired of the frequent formal nights. A nice lady from Norway states that she finds it pointless to put on a glamorous gown in the evening, for now, after weeks at sea, the general ambience of life on board has begun to resemble that of a youth hostel. Indeed! One bulky senior passenger wore nothing but a very small towel wrapped around his loins as he waited for the elevator – a sight never seen in any cruise ad!

Day 76 ~ Tuesday, 20*th* March 2012 ~ sunrise: 6.17am ~ sunset: 6.27pm ~ wind: NE 3, gentle breeze ~ weather: sunny ~ temperature: 33°C ~ distance travelled since Muscat: 390 NM ~ in total: 27,075 nautical miles

Abu Dhabi

This morning, the dusty remains of another sandstorm are veiling the sky. It is possible to look directly at the pale disc of the sun overhead, but hard to make out details of the port. Abu Dhabi means 'Father of the Gazelle' and is the capital of the United Arab Emirates. Once renowned for its thriving pearl industry, the whole region declined once the Japanese invented the cultured pearl. But since the discovery of oil in the late Fifties, prosperity on a truly magnificent scale reigns this former desert wasteland.

Our tour guide is a young man from Sri Lanka who came to work here "because of the money". As one of the exploited class of foreign workers, he is nevertheless full of praise for the way in which things are done in Abu Dhabi and speaks of the ruling family with awed affection. He tells us that the country sees four to five days of rainfall per year on average, though last year there was no rain at all. About 80% of the land was desert until Sheik Zayed, becoming ruler of the emirate in 1966, worked successfully to change that percentage: "They used to say agriculture has no future, but with God's blessing and our determination, we have succeeded in transforming the desert into a green land."

Billions of oil revenue were invested under his rule to set up farms that were then given to farmers for free. Machinery, irrigation, training and greenhouses – all was paid for. Such generous subsidies made farming attractive and the desert emirate almost self-sustainable in its food production. Water, not money, is the greatest problem here. "When we dig, we find oil, not water," our guide states with a grin. Water comes from huge desalination systems along the coast, but the wastewater of cities is treated and reused on a large scale in the fields, while condensation from the air conditioning of skyscrapers irrigates the parks.

And so, within the short span of three decades and almost unbeknownst to the world, Sheik Zayed achieved an environmental miracle by "transforming swathes of desert into green land, setting up greenbelts around farms and forests around cities". He was not only a keen and practical, but also a wealthy and powerful environmentalist, and so the list of his successful ventures is long and impressive. Roughly 130 million trees – yes, that's right, *one hundred and thirty million* – have been planted to date. This number increases every year and effectively reduces the emirate's carbon footprint to nil. Sheik Zayed, "the man who tamed the desert", banned fishing in Abu Dhabi as early as 1977 to protect the exploited marine life, set up diverse conservation programmes for endangered native animals and personally financed a pet project of five artificial lakes. These lakes have become a sanctuary for migrating birds and are stocked with fish that multiply like the children of Abraham.

Other projects of no direct economic profit were also close to the wise sheik's heart, for example the reforestation of about two hundred natural islands in the Persian Gulf. These newly planted mangrove forests attract much wildlife and greatly increase biodiversity along the coast.

In 1997, Prince Philip of Britain, as president of the World Wide Fund for Nature, presented Sheik Zayed with the organization's highest award in recognition of many such magnificent achievements.

At the time of writing, Abu Dhabi is the wealthiest capital in the world, because its abundance of crude oil translates to an astonishing sum *per capita*. Only a fifth of its population are Emirati and eighty percent are foreign workers, both white-collar and blue-collar. Like all other Gulf States, Abu Dhabi operates a strict class system. Born as a citizen of this small emirate, one is automatically entitled to incredibly generous benefits such as free healthcare, free education including studies at a university abroad, a substantial grant (doubling as an incentive) upon marriage with another Emirati rather than a foreigner, financial help with the first family home ... but if one happens to be a foreign labourer who is working to build this nation's wondrous infrastructure, one just gets to admire and envy its uniquely citizen-friendly system from a close distance.

On our way to the Grand Mosque, the fourth-largest in the world, our guide tells us more about Abu Dhabi's late ruler, Sheik Zayed bin Sultan Al Nahyan. He became the revered father of the nation and united the seven emirates as their first president in 1970. We learn that *sheik* means 'he who was chosen to rule because of his wisdom'. It explains how the title was initially conferred and seems entirely appropriate in this case. Although without formal education himself, Sheik Zayed made free education available to all his people, particularly to girls. An inscription at the museum quotes his words: "A woman constitutes half the society and keeps the house. A country aspiring to build itself should not keep a woman in the darkness of illiteracy and prisoner to the shackles of oppression."

Sheik Zayed shared the oil-fuelled wealth with his subjects through a system of very generous benefits, but also with the other, less affluent because oil-less emirates.

Much beloved throughout the land, he died in 2004 and was succeeded by his son Sheik Khalifa bin Zayed Al Nahyan, the eldest of his nineteen sons by four wives.

The Grand Mosque, built in his honour and dedicated to his memory, was completed in 2009 and is a superlative marvel. Acres of carved white marble are reflected in blue pools, and over a thousand pillars are inlaid with flower garlands of shimmering gemstones and mother-of-pearl. It houses one of the world's largest chandeliers, made by Swarovski and weighing over nine tons, and also the world's largest carpet, handknotted in Iran from finest wool and silk. It covers over seven thousand square metres and weighs almost forty tons.

Nobody can say exactly how much all this splendour cost, though the question arises in all our minds. Money was clearly not an issue here, and one imagines how delighted marble quarries, carpet weavers, crystal jewellers and others must have been when their craftsmanship was honoured with commissions of this magnitude, and the corresponding payments made work profitable.

Accustomed to capitalism's imperative that buildings have to be erected quickly and cheaply, most societies have come to accept the resulting ugliness as a matter of course, but this Grand Mosque is a reminder of the way in which magnificent building projects by wealthy rulers of past ages once sustained the arts and crafts. It is unexpected, and the scale almost unbelievable.

But before we can go inside, we women are taken to a changing room and handed a black *abaya*, and a matching *shayla* to cover our hair. Norah and I have a great time as we put on these unfamiliar garments and try to keep them in place. We take pictures of each other and note that a floor-length black robe is optically slimming. Unexpectedly, it also makes one feel modest and protected, and I suppose that in time one learns not to get tangled in the slipping headscarf or to trip over the gown's hem. We also receive a plain white plastic bag to carry our shoes in, and then we are ready to enter the inner hall to gape at the fairytale splendour.

The great hall is ornamented with intricate geometric patterns that are based on the number five, in accordance with the 'Five Pillars of Islam'. These are: 1) the testimony of faith, 2) regular prayer, 3) giving alms to the needy, 4) fasting in the month of Ramadan, and 5) a pilgrimage to Mecca. The number five is repeated in flower-petal stars that are engraved in the glass panels of windows and doors, and also in the gilded palm fronds that top marble pillars.

It makes me think that the faithful who worship here must be inured to such opulence, for it is difficult to devote one's soul to prayer when there is so much to see ...

Our next stop is the Sultan's Old Palace, now turned into a museum. Here we can see for ourselves how nomads of the desert lived, once they left their traditional tents for a settled lifestyle. I should have preferred the tents myself, but these dim rooms enclosed by thick walls were undoubtedly very good for keeping cool in the intense heat, and they provided better, because more secure, shelter in sandstorms.

We drive on to Al Ain near the border of Oman, where an oasis of 160,000 date palms stretches out, interspersed with banana and mango trees. We learn that *Al Ain* means 'oasis', and that the proximity of Oman's mountains generates a bit more rainfall in this region. It is my first visit to an oasis and strikes me as quite wonderful.

Nearby is the Al Ain Museum, whose archaeological section displays finds from the prehistoric Hili Tombs. Evidence of human industry, such as fragments of clay pots and beads of carnelian, speak to us across more than four thousand years of a thriving culture in this region.

Quite hungry by now, we appreciate the wonderful buffet lunch set up at the Hilton Hotel. For once I too have dessert and enjoy delicious honey-and-nut-filled mini pastries with strawberry mousse.

A bit sleepy from the meal and the heat we arrive at our last destination, the Camel Market, where dromedaries are sold under shading roofs. But pens and roofs are not of metal fencing and corrugated iron, as one would expect. No, they are solidly built and tastefully decorated. – How nice even the simplest and most mundane buildings can be made to look when the budget is generous!

One of the baby camels is just a few days old. Lying by its mother's side, its impossibly long, stick-like legs are stretched out in the sand. Our guide explains that all camel herders and traders come over from Pakistan to work for the Emirati owners of camel farms. Standing or sitting in little groups, these herders chat while scrutinizing coachloads of foreign visitors who descend amongst them to *ooh!* and *aah!* at their animals. But none of them try to sell us their wares, which is quite a novel experience by now.

Indeed, Arab camels are lovely creatures with blond, shaggy pelt, long legs and limpid eyes. After watching them for a while, I begin to see how individual they are – not just in their looks, but also in the way they behave. What might it be like to live day by day alongside these animals? I imagine that one gets quite attached to one's camels.

On the way back to the harbour, our coach flies at well over 120km per hour along a wide-laned, immaculate motorway. Apparently there is a speed limit, but at 140km/h it seems a restriction only where Porsches, Ferraris and Lamborghinis (so beloved of Arabs) are concerned.

During the drive we hear about falconry, a sport of the elite since ancient times. There are still around nineteen thousand falcons kept throughout the Emirates and, though mainly used to hunt rabbits and bustards, they also take part in annual shows and competitions. The award-winning Abu Dhabi Falcon Hospital treats injured birds and carries out annual check-ups. A falcon is regarded as a member of the family and is allowed to travel *inside* the cabin of airplanes, provided it has a valid passport and a prebooked seat next to its owner – though I imagine that the best of them travel by private jet.

By the time we return onboard after this tour of nine hours, I am too exhausted to change and go out for dinner, even to the Orangery. But a roastbeef baguette, ordered from Room Service, helps me to recover enough energy to deal with the day's crop of interesting photographs, for I am most keen to see how the snapshots of the camel market turned out.

And then a sudden impulse leads to an impromptu haircutting session. I have always enjoyed cutting hair and am used to trimming my own, rarely happy with the work of hairdressers; but I learnt their techniques by observation and usually travel with a pair of hair scissors. Propped open with rolled-up towels, the angled mirrors in the bathroom afford a good view of side and rear, and after much careful snipping I am pleased with the result and go to bed, very happy with this day.

Day 77 ~ Wednesday, 21st March 2012 ~ sunrise: 6.25am ~ sunset: 6.33pm ~ wind: 1, light airs ~ weather: sunny ~ temperature: 33°C ~ distance travelled since Abu Dhabi: 73 nautical miles ~ in total: 27,148 nautical miles

Dubai

Port Rashid is the local deepwater harbour for cruise ships, and two Costa liners will be joining us here this morning. Nearby lies the famous QE2 in retirement, looking sadly insignificant and forlorn in the dusty wasteland of this port. While awaiting her uncertain fate, she seems to be dreaming of the days when she was Queen of the Oceans.

Fine sand dust continues to cloud the skies as we go ashore "with the speed of a thousand gazelles," according to our captain's catchphrase which he varies from port to port. In Sri Lanka, for example, it had been "with the speed of a thousand Tuk-Tuks".

After my positive first impressions of Oman and Abu Dhabi, I cannot warm to Dubai. At first sight, a cold soullessness, enhanced by the money-manic materialism of its superlative shopping malls and luxury hotels, strikes me as repellent. Admittedly, I am tired and would prefer a day of rest to yet another sightseeing tour, and that is probably why nothing appeals to me. This city's hyperbole and its obsession with "the world's biggest" and "the world's best" come across as off-putting. Is it the Arab passion for racing camels, horses and cars that excites such fiercely ambitious competition? This attitude reminds the teacher of boastful little boys in the sandpit – and Dubai is arguably a very big sandpit, though hardly "the world's biggest".

Today's tour guide also comes from Sri Lanka, and the coach driver is Indian. Both of them seem to feel proud of their new homeland, and this pride rings through the words of our guide as he explains the meaning of the elements that constitute the flag of the United Arab Emirates: a green stripe for the parched land, a white stripe for hard-won peace, a black one for the precious crude oil, and a crossbar of red for the strength and the will to defend them all.

At the Bastakiya Quarter we are shown the typical architecture of those early Persian settlers who established the simple little fishing village that mushroomed into Dubai. Some of these buildings have square towers called *barajeels*, open on two sides and screened with latticework. These windtowers act as a natural cooling system by catching any breeze and drawing it into the dwelling below. Nowadays, several cultural offices and the philately society are housed in these venerable and immaculately restored buildings.

Dubai Museum, our next destination, gives a picture of life around the Gulf in former times. Unfortunately, the lighting is so low and the limited space so oppressive that I soon flee to the museum's gift shop. Here I can buy stamps for my postcards, and these stamps unsurprisingly feature a falcon, for this noble and popular bird has been chosen as a symbol of the United Arab Emirates.

After the visit, we stand around in the sizzling heat and the exhaust fumes from several coaches and wait for our frantic guide to round up a member of the group who has gone missing. It seems to take forever, but eventually the man is found, sitting in blissful ignorance on the coach of another tour. – What a dreadful numbskull! ... Everyone is seething with annoyance, but nobody says a word.

(*Cruiser's tip: Don't do this to your tour group! Be alert and aware and don't wander off without knowing exactly when and where to meet again. Comparing your own tour number with that of the coach also helps to avoid errors.)

On foot we go on to explore the alleyways of the Old Souk, pleasantly shaded by attractively designed wooden roofing. Sumptuous textiles are displayed in artful arrays that catch the eye, shimmering and glittering in all the colours of the rainbow. But because we spent half an hour waiting for the lost sheep, we have no time to stop, browse or shop. What a pity! Our guide is herding us along with an anxious eye on the clock, worried that he might lose another member of his flock if he allowed us to wander.

We reach the creek that divides the city and board a water taxi called an *abra*. It takes us to the Spice Market on the other side, where stalls display large bags filled with all kinds of interesting wares. There are desiccated limes, curly seedpods, dried rose petals and amber-coloured lumps of frankincense, to mention but a few. Shelves bear row on row of delicate iridescent glass bottles that contain perfumes, and piles of wine-red carpets are stacked by the roadside. It all reminds me of the poem 'The Golden Road to Samarkand' (by James Elroy Flecker) with its vivid descriptions of old Middle Eastern splendour and merchandise: "We have rose-candy, we have spikenard, mastic and terebinth and oils and spice, and such sweet jams, meticulously jarred, as God's own Prophet eats in Paradise ..."

At the end of the tour we get time to wander through the Gold Souk by ourselves. Dense rows of jeweller's stores catch the eye with opulent displays of treasures that could have come straight from Aladdin's cave.

Tucked into the side alleys are yet more textile shops and, not being in need of gold jewellery at the moment, I take a closer look at the displays of gorgeous and colourful shawls. Various salesmen do their best to convince me of the merit of their pashminas and the extra special price they will offer me, and I notice that they think nothing of grabbing my arm to drag me across to their stall ... This is rather disagreeable and never happened in any of the Asian countries.

But there are so many interesting and unusual sights! Soon I have snapped all the pictures my camera's limited memory can hold and spend the remaining time wandering around contentedly. And it is just as well to be selective, for who wants to sift through thousands of photographs later?

(*Cruiser's tip: Look through your harvest of images at the end of each daytrip, keep only the really good ones and label each picture with the help of the excursions brochure at the earliest possible moment.)

Back on board I write more postcards to my son, from Abu Dhabi and Dubai respectively, and mail them in an envelope with the card from Mumbai, which is still waiting around because it was not possible to get hold of stamps at the time. I do hope he appreciates these troublesome greetings from around the world!

It is time to get ready for dinner, and as I turn on the shower to rinse the day's patina of sand dust from hair and skin, a sudden flash of comprehension reveals that *this* must be the reason why women cover themselves from head to toe in desert countries where water is so scarce that daily showers and frequent laundry are out of the question ... Of course! The traditional abaya is a *dustsheet!* All at once I see that this covering is eminently practical, for it shields clothes and hair from the fine sand that is always blowing in the wind, and it protects the skin from the fierce sunlight at the same time. This fashion really does make good sense here, and I wonder if the oppressive religious dimension was not added later. For even Berber nomads, charging through the desert on horseback, usually wear protective pieces of cloth wrapped around head and face, and only their eyes remain visible, squinting in the glare of the sun.

Day 78 ~ Thursday, 22nd March 2012 ~ sunrise: 6.20am ~ sunset: 6.30pm ~ wind: 1, light airs ~ weather: sunny ~ temperature: 35°C

More of Dubai

Today's excursion is called 'A Walk in the Clouds' since it includes a view of Dubai from above, as seen from the top of the *Burj Khalifa* – presently "the world's tallest". What might Dubai do to preserve this hard-won claim once the Chinese, or any other nation, set out to build the next tallest building? Maybe some kind of telescopic extension could be hidden in the tower, to be deployed when the time came to trump rival claims? ... Ah, in this competitive climate I am beginning to think like an Arab, I notice.

On boarding the coach, the local tour manager kindly gives me permission to take a front seat. He seems familiar with the problem of car sickness and does not doubt my word, and his helpful attitude makes me immensely relieved and grateful. When the coach is almost full, Beryl comes along with Simon in tow, casts a baleful look in my direction and plonks herself squarely in a seat across the aisle. Simon (recently promoted to Best Friend) hesitates to occupy one of the reserved seats, but she announces that "if it's all right for *somebody*, it's all right for us." – Great! Another opportunity to practise non-retaliation, Gandhi-style. I resolve to take no notice and keep my eyes right of centre.

An amiable coach driver from India is called Krishna, and our tour guide introduces himself as Mohammed, an immigrant of Persian descent. But his nickname, he confides, is King of Bling, because he likes his watch, mobile phone and all other accessories encrusted with rhinestones.

Mohammed and Krishna! With a team like that, what could possibly go wrong? It promises to be a very good day, despite those malevolent vibes emanating from Beryl across the aisle. Our guide is a flirtatious young man who smiles at me winningly at every opportunity. I sense that this enrages Beryl further, but there is nothing I can do about it.

Mohammed delivers his speech in praise of Dubai and its ruler with enthusiasm, even though he is not entitled (as the grandson of immigrants) to the generous benefits that are granted to all native Emirati. Yet he tells us about these abundant grants with the intention to impress us. And we are impressed, no doubt about it ... for it is such an unusual concept that the governing clan should not just look after themselves, their families, friends and secret bank accounts, but actually share the country's wealth with the rest of the population.

Mohammed also tells us about arranged marriages, customary in this part of the world and not to be confused with forced matches. Marriage is much on his mind, because his own parents, and particularly his mother, are occupied with searching and finding a suitable wife for their dear son. Mohammed has no objections, because he knows that the parents have his best interests at heart and will choose well. Whereas he himself might fall for a pretty face, he says, his mother will make sure she learns the girl's mind, knowing from experience what is important for a successful marriage. Her son will meet the chosen candidates and their relatives to form his own opinion, and eventually select his preferred girl from five options.

"But if I should choose ... well, option six," he laughs merrily as he slices a finger across his throat, "that would mean instant death!"

Mohammed's attitude towards his marriage reminds me of my talk with the Indian security officer who presented the case of his arranged nuptials in very similar terms, and it makes me wonder if these traditional eastern societies might not have found a solution to the thorny dating problem ages ago. Divorce rates are certainly much lower, though there are various reasons for this.

What kinds of possible husbands would *my* parents have presented me with, I wonder? I can't claim that I did a great job of it myself. Father was always willing to embrace any man of my choosing, though he must have been secretly disappointed. But Mother's main criterion seemed to be that she ought to want to marry the guy herself.

"If you don't like any of the men we choose, why don't you introduce us to some you *would* like?" Sister once asked her, referring to the old tradition. Is it so unreasonable to suppose that my parents would have presented me with better options than those losers I found by myself, following my heart? – Oh, the heart! Such a fallible organ, with such a faulty sense of direction ...!

We arrive at Dubai Mall, "the world's largest" with twelve hundred shops featuring the top brands of New York, Paris, London, Milan and Tokyo, and one of the world's largest dancing fountains, among other attractions. Above the mall rises the world's tallest building: the gleaming, elegant spire of the Burj Khalifa, looking as insubstantial as a mirage in the strong sunlight.

Before our prebooked trip to its top we have half an hour for a look around the mall. Curious what it might taste like, I purchase camel-milk chocolate from a quaint stall. The precious little chocolate bar costs all of seven dollars.

Then it is time to join long queues for the high-speed lifts that whisk visitors to the 124th floor of the tower. These elevators ascend at ten whole metres per second – a speed that affects the eardrums somewhat. I am amused to hear from our guide that there is indeed a telescopic extension of unknown length hidden at the core of the tower, ready to defend Dubai's world record against future competition.

We learn that the Khalifa tower is named after the ruler of Abu Dhabi (son and successor of Sheikh Zayed) who gave the money required to build it. Needless to say, it was a very, *very* large sum. And this tower was not built in his *own* emirate, you understand, but in that of a neighbouring ruler, since Dubai is expected to run out of oil in the foreseeable future and will need a more reliable income from its tourist attractions. – Well, viewed from the outside, it would seem that these emirates are truly united.

Today the view from '*The Top*' is clouded by the haze of sand that lingers in the air and gives Dubai a dusty look. Ocean and desert views are veiled, but it is also impressive to look down on this grandiose city that was stamped from the hostile sands of Arabia.

Tall buildings of imaginative design are grouped around sparkling pools, like slim Bedouins chatting by a well. A network of motorways accommodates Dubai's three million cars (at an average of two per inhabitant) without getting gridlocked. And yet it is the public transport system that impresses me the most, for alongside the main roads run elevated tracks of driverless speed-trains, sleek as modern works of art. No rubbish is strewn around their clean-cut and graffiti-free pillars, and the elegant aspect of the whole structure is a pleasure to the eye and an invitation to leave the car at home. Though petrol is cheap in Dubai, the air-conditioned metro is cheaper still and arrives at four-minute intervals. – Switzerland, eat your heart out!

On the groundfloor of the Burj Khalifa, Dubai's ruler His Highness Sheik Mohammed bin Rashid Al Maktoum is quoted: "The word impossible is not in leaders' dictionaries. No matter how big the challenges, faith, determination and resolve will overcome them."

Not to mention a boundless stream of dirhams and petrodollars! Wikipedia: "His family wealth is estimated to be in excess of US$48.5 billion." – With this kind of bank balance, one may well be tempted to feel invincible!

Oil is the sap that makes this wondrous city thrive amongst the dunes, and Dubai is an impressive illustration of what can be achieved if money is not an issue. The Burj Al Arab, the Palm Jumeirah, the Atlantis Hotel and the real-snow skiing park at the Mall of the Emirates are yet more striking examples. Indeed, it is the world's demand for oil that lies at the heart of it all, and if that demand – or the oil – should run dry, the pitiless desert might well reclaim all that was built here with such pride. The United Arab Emirates are aware of this peril, and they seek to break free from their dependence on crude oil by creating business opportunities for foreign investors on a large and tax-free scale, as well as developing tourism through their superlative attractions.

This day, feeling less exhausted, I am better able to appreciate the unique character of this impressive city, and to respect its efforts to create something truly outstanding. Tourism, though often deplored and maligned, has become a driving force for peace and prosperity in a contemporary, practical manner. In former times, explorers, travellers and traders had set out to conquer, plunder and destroy other cultures, but we who travel today usually open our hearts and minds to foreign lands and customs. We learn to respect people who are different, and find in the end that they are not so different after all.

But the most impressive thing I saw in Dubai was not in the nature of the world's biggest, grandest or best. No, it was a little scene that happened before my eyes as I waited for my group to reassemble in the street outside the mall.

A tall Emirati, easily recognisable in his traditional long white gown, called a *kandura*, came walking along the pavement. His wife, covered head-to-toe in her black *abaya*, followed several paces behind. A cheerful nanny in a plain brown robe and a colourful embroidered headscarf brought up the rear, pushing their daughter in a buggy. The little girl alone wore western clothes. The road was empty of people or traffic apart from this family group, and so they naturally caught my eye. And suddenly, as they came towards me, the man stopped, turned to his wife and held out his hand in a tender gesture that required no words. His loving sentiment was just as easy to understand in English as in Arabic, and it moved my heart. The wife, probably smiling behind her veil, put her hand in his, and hand in hand they passed me and continued on their way.

Though touched by the sight, I was also puzzled, for this piece of evidence did not match what we had been told in our port talks, regarding public displays of affection. Couples had been strongly advised not to touch at all, and particularly not to hold hands, to avoid giving offence in Muslim countries. I must have looked visibly astonished, for the nanny with the buggy gave me a wide smile as if to say, "There goes another prejudice!"

This lovely impression showed how effective and in keeping with the Prophet's intentions it would be if Muslims could teach western minds the true meaning of their religion and their culture, their views and their habits, and in such a humane way. My concept of the Arab world, unavoidably stereotyped, certainly shifted to a more positive view over the last few days. It really does not do to see other cultures through the lens of the media alone, and I liked what Sam, a retired teacher from Canada, had said to me earlier on our excursion: "You don't return from a journey like this as the same person you were when you set out."

Returned to the quayside, I have one final question for our guide. It concerns my new sideline in comparative language studies, currently limited to the word lion; and because he speaks both languages, Mohammed can tell me that lion in Arabic is *asad* and in Persian *shir*. I also take a picture of his incredible watch, sparkling with a profusion of rhinestones, and wish him all the best for his forthcoming marriage. May his parents choose wisely!

~ ~ ~

~ The Last Leg ~

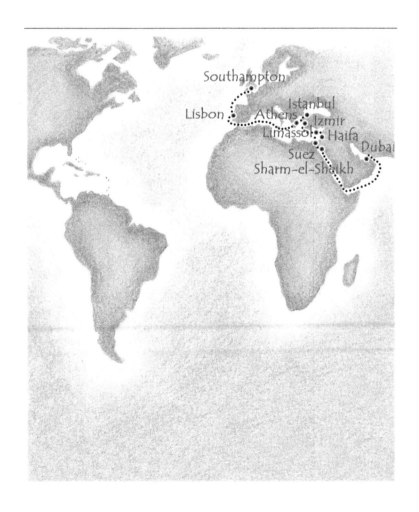

Day 79 ~ Friday, 23rd March 2012 ~ sunrise: 6.11am ~ sunset: 6.11pm ~ sea state: calm ~ wind: SE 2 ~ weather: sunny ~ temperature: 30°C

Litter Indicator Scale

At last we have a sea day again, with another four to follow; much-needed time to write, to reflect and process all that I have seen, heard and learnt. I enjoyed Dubai more on the second day and feel sure that there would be a lot more to appreciate. Some dark spots, problems and difficulties must surely be part of the shining city I have seen so briefly, yet there is much to admire in Dubai, in Abu Dhabi and Oman. I had not expected such a palpable ambition to build better versions of a modern civilization, and my own impressions made me realize how skewed my picture of the Arab world was, influenced as it is by news of the sinister and repressive system that operates in Saudi Arabia.

Visiting so many countries in a row, what struck me particularly were observations relating to rubbish. The lack or presence of litter in cities and landscapes seems a reliable indicator of how healthy and well-functioning a nation is. Now I am tempted to compile a 'Litter Indicator of Nations' that assigns each country a place on its scale, according to the amount of litter within its borders.

On my litter indicator scale, Oman and the Emirates, Switzerland and Scandinavia, Singapore and Japan would occupy the top spots, but I am not convinced that fines for dropping litter are the reason for their general cleanliness. There are other forces at work here, and though I cannot be certain what they are, my guess is that they include a stable political situation, a dependable infrastructure, a responsible governing body, lower levels of corruption, good education and job opportunities, beautiful and well-kept surroundings, and the people's resulting pride in their homeland. The fact that moral attitudes of humans are linked to the condition of their environment seems quite indisputable.

Day 80 ~ Saturday, 24th March 2012 ~ sunrise: 6.10am ~ sunset: 6.31pm ~ sea state: slight ~ wind: S 2, light breeze ~ weather: sunny ~ temperature: 31°C

No Man in My Life

We cleared the Strait of Hormuz around two o'clock this morning and are back in the Gulf of Oman, heading once more into pirate territory and the tropics. I awake late and well rested, ready for my follow-up session with Jovan.

Today we go through the second part of my personal exercise programme, so that I may learn to carry out those resistance training sequences correctly. He set them out on a sheet of A4 paper and hands me the neatly printed page in a clear plastic pocket. I am quietly delighted that here is someone who does things the way I like to do them. Though such care is sometimes lampooned as perfectionism, I could not agree more with Jovan's succinct summary: "Do it well, or what's the point?"

Lunch at the Café Bordeaux with Norah and Bob has now become a pleasant daily event because we enjoy each other's company, and the age gap of one and two generations is no obstacle in this case.

Today's main topic is Bob's anguished concern that there is no man in my life. I assure him that past experiences with men made me realize that I prefer to live alone, independent and free; that travelling solo is delightful, and that I am not looking for a mate. But this is not something Bob can understand or accept, and he attempts to change my mind. Today he is on good form and throughout the meal proposes single friends and wealthy cousins of his own age, whom Norah in turn declares unfit for the purpose. It is an amusing game and I laughingly play along, for Bob, regardless of his great age and frailty, is witty and very likeable.

After the meal I go to write some more at my usual table on Deck 7. Suddenly the bridge announces "Dolphins to port!" and everyone to starboard leaves their sunlounger to hurry to the other side. But upon arrival, the voice emanating from the public address system informs us that the dolphins have now dived under the keel to the starboard side, and so we all turn around to rush back to our erstwhile positions. The situation is comic and strongly reminiscent of the scene at the station in 'Les Vacances de Monsieur Hulot', but we are rewarded with the sight of dolphins, surfacing repeatedly and gladdening our hearts.

Norah invites me to walk laps around the Promenade Deck with her while Bob is resting, and as we amble along, I tell her my favourite joke:
    A husband and wife, married at the age of twenty, are now seventy and celebrating their golden anniversary. At the family feast, a fairy appears. "To reward your happy and enduring marriage, I shall grant you one wish each."
    She turns to the wife. "What would you like?"

"Oh, I've dreamed of the perfect kitchen for years," gushes the woman and describes her ideas in great detail.

"Very well!"

The fairy waves her wand, and behold – the old kitchen is renewed, exactly as described.

"And what is your wish?" The fairy now turns to the husband, who confides in a lowered voice, "I should like a wife who is twenty years younger than I am."

"Very well!"

The fairy waves her wand, and behold – he is ninety!

Norah laughs out loud and plans at once to recount the joke to Bob, who is twenty-five years her senior, though we share the feeling that he won't find the joke quite as funny as we do. In fact, he will protest repeatedly, arguing that the fairy *misunderstood* and that this was *not fair* ...! Norah finds this even funnier and shakes with suppressed laughter when she tells me of Bob's reaction later.

On our leisurely laps around the deck we pass Beryl and Simon repeatedly. They are cosied up, side by side, on adjoining sunloungers. A little farther ahead sits the woman who pushed my head aside on the coach in Oman, and near the end of the row is the old lady who had pocketed Norah's mobile phone in an unguarded moment. Norah had put it beside the washbasin on a trip to the toilets, and then it was gone ... Now she tells me about this incident and describes what trouble she had to get her phone back, even though it kept ringing inside the old lady's handbag in the presence of witnesses when Norah had Reception call her own number to prove the theft.

And so this promenade is a tiny bit like running the gauntlet, though we all do a good job ignoring each other.

But, side by side with a friend, this uneasy situation gains a humorous quality it would lack if I were all by myself.

(*Cruiser's tip: Be very careful whom you trust, even in the safe environment of a cruise ship. Check out handy travel safes such as the classy little Safego, "a lightweight, portable safe, designed for safeguarding valuables in the most populated areas: beaches, pools, hotels, cruises, parks, and more. With its heavy-duty lock and unique flexible steel cable, Safego can attach to almost any secure fixture. Lock away your phone, keys, wallet, camera, sunglasses, jewellery, and other personal belongings.")

To celebrate the beginning of the final leg of our journey, we have another formal night with a Welcome Aboard party for the five hundred passengers who joined our ship in Dubai. We old hands know the captain's speech by heart, and yet he always finds new and amusing bits to add. I am sitting with Erin, Paul and friends again, my face turned towards the setting sun and my back on the hostile group of Beryl, Amanda and Gilbert at a table nearby.

Erin's nice friend remarks on my "lovely eyes" and expresses surprise that "no man has snapped you up yet." Her genuine admiration is like "balm for an aching heart" – as a teacher at art college was fond of declaring dramatically whenever he was offered a compliment. (It was something I hardly understood at the time, though it did make a lasting impression.) This teacher set us a project titled *The World and I*; truly a great topic with endless possibilities but doomed to failure, because we were just a bunch of kids who hardly knew the world, much less ourselves ...

It occurs to me that I am now working on this project in my notebook as I trace the interrelationship of the world and my own view of it – twenty-eight years later! Proof that as teachers we work for the future, and the things we do and say in the classroom may not bear fruit until decades have gone by.

Erin asks if I would accept a copy of her little book of poems for and about children, a collection she published some time ago. On our tour in Cambodia she observed with a professed touch of envy how well I get on with children, and it made her think that I might enjoy her verses too. Of course I accept her offer and am quite bowled over by the warmhearted and generous attitude of these women.

What did I do to deserve their kindness? As little as I did to deserve the unpleasantness of other people, I'm sure.

Day 81 ~ Sunday, 25th March 2012 ~ sunrise: 6.36am ~ sunset: 7.00pm ~ sea state: slight ~ wind: N 3, gentle breeze ~ weather: sunny ~ temperature: 31°C

Proving Wilde Wrong

At one o'clock in the morning, I am woken by the sound of people returning to their cabin next door. After slamming drawers and talking loudly, they eventually quieten down and go to sleep while I remain awake for hours.

(*Cruiser's tip: You may be lucky or unlucky with your neighbours in adjacent cabins. Turn a blind eye and a deaf ear to the occasional disturbance, but have a polite word if they continue. After a late night and various bars, people tend to forget your need

for quiet sleep. Only complain to the management as a last resort, and avoid making noise yourself.)

I pass the night writing about my impressions of Dubai until my eyelids grow heavy. Consequently I get up late, feeling rather hung over, but there is another pleasant massage to look forward to, this time with 'Hot Stones'.

Manuel and I begin a conversation that takes on a life of its own, leaves the ground of polite chit-chat and does not touch down until much later. For once I do more listening than talking and find myself in agreement with what he shares of his views. Eventually he refers to a good friend of his, a woman about my own age. I am intrigued, for I have never yet encountered a man of any age who was prepared to be just a friend and not a lover. Despite all initial promises it always turned out to be all or nothing in the end, and the platonic, friendly interest in the other as a person, separate from one's own life, remained elusive … I found a quote by Oscar Wilde instead, stating that men and women can love, hate or remain indifferent to each other, but can never be friends. I would have loved to prove him wrong and spent much of my twenties trying, but his observation remained painfully true. (The young man who most earnestly declared that we would prove Wilde wrong eventually became my husband.) Yet here I am, talking to someone who maintains that it is indeed possible, and seems to have proof.

We agree to pursue this interesting topic another time and get down to the treatment. Large Balinese lava pebbles, ground flat and smooth by the sea, are heated in simmering water. Then they are applied to the chakra points and drawn over the skin in flowing movements, with repeated rubbings of the fragrant oil that is such a treat for the skin.

Although seemingly comatose with bliss, my mind is alert. I follow each movement and heat source with total awareness, wondering all the while how someone so young can already be so good at his profession. At his age, I was still clueless – or so it seems to me now.

Again I enjoy the wonderful sense of completeness which any good massage therapy session brings. Developed and perfected over long ages, all of these treatments provide a fascinating glimpse into the wealth of ancient knowledge about the human body. We ought to make more use of them in our busy and often stressful lives! It is not easy to find the time, and a therapist whom one trusts, but on this ship it all comes together fortuitously.

Day 82 ~ Monday, 26th March 2012 ~ sunrise: 6.06am ~ sunset: 6.25pm ~ sea state: calm ~ wind: 1, light ~ weather: sunny ~ temperature: 29°C

Red Sea

Unsurprisingly, the Red Sea is not red at all – much to Bob's disappointment. The air is muggy and the sea throws up waves that seem to hover on the spot. Patches of seaweed float past, seabirds fly low over the water, and large vessels can be seen at intervals along this busy shipping lane.

Our security officers continue their watch and keep scanning the distant horizon with binoculars and patience ... It must be one of the most boring jobs on the planet! Surely they cannot help hoping that a little skiff of dubious aspect would make an appearance once in a while?

I am at the gym as soon as it opens, to secure a treadmill – preferably the one in the quiet corner – to begin my personal exercise programme. I vary my speed of walking and keep track of the minutes according to Jovan's instructions before me. The effect such a list of times and numbers has on the mind is remarkable, because without it I would not have been able to keep going for anywhere near the fifty-five minutes of exercising I manage today without a break.

At some point, about halfway through, I do consider stopping early, for isn't it quite all right to start slowly? But I keep going regardless and realize (with Jovan in mind) that the best teachers are those whose approval or disappointment matters.

When using gym equipment so far, I always felt that I had reached my limit once I had burnt about a hundred calories. But today, and after following the personal training plan persistently, the machine computes that three hundred and fifty-eight calories went up in smoke. I am impressed – and shattered.

Then I enjoy a cool shower on deck and dry off in the warm sunshine, but when it gets uncomfortably hot I retire to my cool cabin-hut. Yesterday there had been a little card to fill in, and today the carpet has been shampooed in my absence at the desired hour. The room smells fresh, looks clean and feels nice. Worn out by the unaccustomed physical exertion at the gym, I lie down for a while and promptly nod off, but a phone call from Norah reminds me that the time has come for another companionable lunch.

After Abu Dhabi, Norah (among other people) had admired my homemade haircut and then mentioned that Bob's hair needed a trim too. Her husband was beginning to look like a mad conductor, she said, but he remained firmly opposed to a visit at the ship's hairdressing salon. Could I possibly take care of the problem?

Bob had enough faith in my skill to accept Norah's proposition, and so, after our shared lunch, I visit their suite with my special hair scissors. Norah has already prepared the scene by wrapping Bob in her clear plastic rain poncho, which is admirably suited to the task. I set to work, snipping away at the wisps of his lovely silver mane. It doesn't take long to get rid of the mad conductor and all are pleased with the result. As Bob plants a light kiss on my cheek to express his gratitude, he remarks roguishly, "I am ninety-four years old, but this is the first time I've kissed my barber!"

Well, as for that: It is the first time I ever trimmed the hair of someone who went to school with JFK.

I would like to lie down, exhausted from the intense exercise session earlier, but drag myself to the launderette instead, to iron the lovely shawl Norah has given me for Bob's haircut. There, two ladies report that they just attended the enjoyable 'World Cruisers' Lunch' … and wasn't I supposed to have been at this event too?

Oh *no!* I cannot believe that I forgot about it, having made arrangements to join Erin and Paul at their table. This is the problem with living in a timeless universe!

I hurry to my hut, call Erin and Paul's number and leave a message of remorseful apology. Then I lie down in the dark and wonder how people can possibly get addicted to the gym in general and exercise in particular. It certainly does nothing to improve *my* wellbeing!

The phone rings, and it is Paul. He merrily informs me that our group's lunch will be on the first of April, that

I have not missed it, and that he had made a similar mistake earlier. Bless him for trying to make me feel better! Relieved, I wander the borderlands of sleep until it is time to dress for dinner. I drape Norah's shawl over a simple black outfit, and we all agree that it looks good when I visit her table for a brief interval between main course and dessert – something else that has become a pleasant little ritual.

Later, Sandie and I meet under stars that seem more brilliant since the outside lights have been turned off as an antipiracy measure. It is pitch dark on deck. Advancing very slowly, I take care not to bump into things as I follow her voice that guides me towards our stacks of sunloungers. I clamber up as if blind, but gradually my eyes adjust and, by the time I have given her an account of my challenging day in Oman, I am able to see all the familiar details of the ship. Above us twinkle a myriad stars, and the low sickle moon hangs beneath Venus like a cradle.

Day 83 ~ Tuesday, 27th March 2012 ~ sunrise: 6.21am ~ sunset: 6.43pm ~ sea state: slight ~ wind: NW 4 ~ weather: sunny ~ temperature: 29°C

Process of Revolution

By the time I leave my cabin it is half-past eight – unusually late, as a kindly cabin steward remarks when I pass him on my way to breakfast. He works halfway down the corridor and our paths seldom cross, therefore I am touched that he should be aware of the pattern of my day.

Affectionate greetings from various members of staff and acquaintances accompany me on my way around the buffet, and I become aware that soon I shall miss these nice people, this pleasant lifestyle, and the contemplation of one ocean or another from the breakfast table.

In the early hours of the morning, Aurora crossed the latitude of 20 degrees north and left the piracy zone behind. Security is operating once more on 'Level One', all hosepipes and LRADs have disappeared, the deck lighting is back on at night, and the Promenade Deck no longer out of bounds after dark. If pirates had been spotted at any point, we did not hear about it – but I think we were never in any danger.

I attend a lecture on dictators: how they gain power, how they hold on to it, and how they eventually lose it … all very interesting, but one statement stands out and resonates most strongly in this teacher's mind: "Education is the most revolutionary process we know." – And tomorrow we shall arrive in Egypt, where a revolutionary process is ongoing.

Day 84 ~ Wednesday, 28th March 2012 ~ sunrise: 5.36am ~ sunset: 5.59pm ~ wind: 1, light airs ~ weather: sunny ~ temperature: 28°C ~ distance travelled since Dubai: 2,719 nautical miles ~ in total: 29,867 nautical miles

Egypt

Our tour guide is a lovely Egyptian lady. She takes us to Na'ama Bay in Sharm-el-Sheikh where we shall be spending the day. On the way we learn that *sharm* means bay, 'Bay of the Sheik', and that the town is known as 'City of Peace', on account of numerous international peace conferences that took place here. Our destination is the beach of the Marriott Hotel, where attractive umbrellas of solid wood spread their shade mushroom-like over rows of comfortable sunloungers that line a crescent of golden sand. There is plenty of space for all, and not a trace of the unpleasantness that affected my day in Oman.

At ten o'clock we board glass-bottomed boats that take us to the coral reefs for a session of fish-spotting. Blue flying fish swarm around bizarre, bulky shapes of corals while yellow butterfly fish flutter by in lemon-shaped cuteness. Two large iridescent parrot fish nibble fearlessly at the thin coating of algae on the underside of the boat, giving us a close-up view of their colourful scales.

Identification charts also feature an Arabian Picasso fish. Possibly from his abstract phase? I should love to see it, but today it is not on show, alas. But we are drifting over the largest brain coral in the Red Sea, a giant bulkhead that is estimated to be some five hundred years of age, and is still going strong. Ringing this ancient coral are tiny fishes, their dark shapes speckling the turquoise haze of seawater like a halo. How absorbing it is to look into this hidden world and witness the fluid movement of a shoal of fish as they change direction in perfect unison!

Then we relax in the shade of an awning on the top deck and admire the view of the sheik's bay while sipping a complimentary soft drink. The sea is calm and the floating pontoon wobbles only slightly as we return to the beach, balancing precariously. Lunch is to be served in less than an hour, so there is little point in settling down at the beach. I tour the hotel shops in the foyer to pass the time. In the gift shop, a young Egyptian with velvety eyes sells me postcards of the pyramids at an exceptionally good price. I also take a look at papyrus pictures, but decorated with glitter they are of no interest to me. The young sales assistant, eager to show this collection, soon understands that I cannot warm to such kitschy reproductions of Ancient Egyptian art.

All at once he remarks, "You have beautiful eyes." Surprised, I reply that this has not been mentioned for a long time – well, not by a man anyway – upon which he tilts his beaming face. "Maybe no one see you properly."

Wow – he is good, this youngster! One straight to the heart! As I strive to recover from my astonishment, he leans forward to dab a spot of suntan oil from my collarbone with considerable tenderness. Hobbled by disbelief, I aim to stop him in his tracks. I have a son in his twenties, I say; he himself cannot be much older, I could be his mother …

Without missing a beat, he replies with a charming smile, "Maybe – but you could also be my wife."

He wastes no time, that's for sure! I avoid the arm he is about to drape around my shoulder, wave goodbye and make a quick exit. – What an accomplished flirt! Quite the expert … but what is his motivation? I made it plain that I was not going to buy anything other than postcards, and he must surely know that I cannot smuggle him to a better life on my cruise ship. Are Egyptian men really that desperate?

Our tour guide is reading a newspaper in the lobby, and I join her for a chat about the political situation in Egypt. Her hopeful opinion is that no one, not even a Salafist, wants the country to suffer any more economic damage, and that tourists should therefore have nothing to fear in the present uncertain situation. "Really, one year without tourists was bad enough!" she states with a shudder.

I learn that she studied archaeology and Egyptology and has worked as a tour guide for many years. The upheaval of the revolution in Egypt affected her and her colleagues directly. When tourists stayed away, the guides found themselves out of work and without much-needed income.

Now it is time to go to lunch. The buffet of appetizing dishes is a splendid affair and is presented by the cooks themselves. They stand to attendance with beaming smiles: nice-looking Egyptian men with impeccable manners who are ready to interact with their guests in a restrained and courteous way. They seem pleased when I return to the buffet later with my personal thanks for a really excellent meal.

Then I wander the golden sands with my feet in the clear shallows, enjoying my first day in Egypt and feeling quite safe. My sunhungry friend likes to spend her holidays in Egypt whenever possible, and now I feel that I would not mind returning one day ... and no, it has nothing to do with the winning ways of the young shop assistant.

At the end of the excursion I take a picture of our especially nice tour guide. She gives me an affectionate hug.

"Now you have a sister in Egypt," she says.

On the gangway I turn to look back once more, wave goodbye and hope for her sake that many foreign visitors will continue to enjoy the positive side of Egypt, with all the splendid sites and sights it has to offer.

This day has left a glow in my soul that matches the sunset which now deploys its radiant colours over the Sinai Desert. And, as Aurora sails away, a farewell committee of dolphins jumps and dives alongside, playfully enjoying the waves our ship heaps up as she heads for the Gulf of Suez.

Day 85 ~ Thursday, 29th March 2012 ~ sunrise: 5.42am ~ sunset: 6.06pm ~ sea state: slight ~ wind: 1, light airs ~ weather: sunny ~ temperature: 26°C ~ distance travelled since Sharm el Sheikh: 177 nautical miles ~ in total: 30,044 nautical miles

Meeting the Pyramids

Our excursion to the pyramids will take many hours, which is why we have to assemble in the Curzon theatre at half-past three in the morning. But this seems quite a reasonable sacrifice to make for a visit to the last Wonder of the Ancient World. Sleepy-eyed we board the tenders. They are obliged to travel in convoy for security reasons, and transfer to port takes the better part of two hours after an engine on our boat fails and slows us down.

My gaze is drawn by flickers of light, dancing on the dark water. Their scattered numbers are reflections of a large and solitary light in the distance and strike me as a beautiful metaphor for the myriads of human souls in relation to the divine spirit: Created by the same source and cast upon the waves of the world for a brief duration, our transient souls are forever reflecting the glory of the One Light through our existence – mirroring it from countless angles.

After disembarking at the port, we are sorted into nine large coaches. Smartly uniformed port officials come to check our passports, and an unnecessary delay occurs because a lady with dual nationality has brought her *other* passport along – the one *without* the immigration stamp. She is not returned to the ship, as the less charitable among us hope. No, we all have to wait while her passport is taken away to be stamped at a distant office.

At the Port Tawfik terminal we are all required to leave the coach and take our bags through a security check inside the building. It is a fairly swift procedure and nothing untoward is discovered, but by the time we actually leave the port it is getting light. Like our tenders, the coaches have to travel in convoy too, escorted by police in black cars. We are told that, although there is no danger of attack, this procedure is "the rule".

Like myself, our local tour guide likes her mornings quiet and does not immediately launch into a lecture on the long and eventful history of Egypt. For the next couple of hours we are driven through the desert over which the sun rises steadily. Approaching Cairo, we pass construction sites of high-class satellite towns, built for Egyptians who can afford to live outside the overcrowded metropolis. Our guide tells us that these days of revolution slowed such developments. At the moment, she says, all are waiting to see who the next president will be, and what government is going to steer the country towards the better future everyone is hoping for.

Breakfast is served at a hotel near Giza, and for the first time on this world tour its quality is disappointing. But who is to complain when they are about to see *The Pyramids?* Behind shambolic buildings, reams of cables, traffic lights and road signs, they appear out of the haze: otherworldly apparitions, seemingly weightless in a misty hue of dove-grey. But as we get closer, their triangular shapes assume a golden-coloured weightiness, and to see them in three dimensions for the first time is awe-inspiring and a moving moment.

    First we are driven to a place some distance away, so that we may get the best view and a good photo opportunity without the city in the background. And here we also meet vendors of cheap, ugly trinkets and owners of dear, lovely camels – all of them scraping a living by pestering tourists for money. The Bedouins offer camel rides, and having one's picture taken whilst sitting astride the animal.

Regarding these offers: Experienced travellers say that, on occasion, tourists have been taken on rides into the desert and kept there until they had forked out a lot more than the agreed price; and cameras were at times not returned unless a hefty ransom was paid. Our guide warns us emphatically not to get involved with *anyone* offering us *anything,* saying that vendors and Bedouins had become rude, aggressive and insolent since the revolution, and that it is difficult to keep them in check.

After all those dire warnings it surprises me how easy it is to keep these men at a distance. As a solitary female I am an easy target, but shaking my head without making eye contact is all it takes to send them looking for other potential customers. Eventually, and feeling quite safe, I stop to take a look when an old man offers me small reproductions of the pyramids in some kind of murky-coloured clay, of incorrect proportions and most likely Chinese origins (around 2010?), claiming that they are genuine stone and *very* beautiful – but seeing my critical expression makes him change their price from ten to two dollars. I assure him that I do not think them worth *any* dollars at all, and that I would not want them even as a present. To my surprise, this makes him laugh. His dark eyes twinkle, a moment of wordless complicity ensues, and his cheerful shouts of "Welcome, welcome!" accompany my steps as I wander on.

We drive past the smallest of the three great pyramids, with an ugly gash in its side, and stop at the middle one that appears to be the tallest, though only because it was built on higher ground. Here, camels and coaches mingle in the car park. We are able to go exploring by ourselves for a while and I head directly for the base of this manmade mountain. No one else is there at that moment and, grateful for the unexpected solitude, I lay both of my palms against the sun-warmed yellow limestone and feel it radiating soft heat, like the skin of a living creature. Looking up the ragged slope to the towering top makes me feel very small, but moved by the presence of something so ancient and so outstanding, so imposing and so durable, even in its decay ... And decay is the overriding impression here, for these magnificent blocks of stone are being eaten away like the features of lepers, and their stacked layers crumble and lapse from the geometrical lines that once fixed them cleanly in space.

Wandering among eroded stone blocks that line the remains of an ancient paved road, I try to picture the scene as it was when all was new – a nearly impossible task, to be sure, but nonetheless thrilling – when, suddenly, the sound of cantering hooves at my back alerts me to the fact that I am no longer alone. A Bedouin in traditional dress approaches on horseback and calls out to me.

It is an archetypal joy, I discover, to be hailed as "My Queen!" by a man on an Arab horse, and though it seems prudent not to take notice (after all, we *have* been warned), those words reverberate in the background of my mind for the rest of the day and make me walk more upright. Oh, the power of that which is spoken! The Egyptian priest-kings certainly knew the magic of words and had them preserved in sacred writing ...

Our next stop is Khufu's (or Cheops) Great Pyramid. A museum was recently built at its side, right over the burial pit of the royal funereal barque, but first we get a chance to climb into one of the lesser tombs. It is like going down into a cave system or mine shaft. We have to stoop low and hold on to the handrails on either side of a narrow tunnel that descends and turns until it reaches the chamber at the heart of the monument – an empty, broken space that echoes with our voices. More and more people are coming down after us. It takes a while until they figure out that they will have to let us come up and squeeze past them before they can continue, and no, it is not a pleasant feeling to be stuck down here …! What strategy did the tourism police officer who is guarding the entrance have in mind? Is it not his task to prevent such congestion?

But it seems that the mind of Egyptian tourism police works in mysterious ways. When I place a tentative palm on the Great Pyramid's pitted stone blocks, two policemen yell at me and wave their arms in indignation. It is hard to grasp what damage my innocent greeting could possibly do to this huge mountain of stone that survived so much pillage and looting. I am prepared to pose this question, but is it wise to argue with irascible representatives of the law, now running towards me at a gallop?

Fortunately, our tour guide now comes to my aid. She berates the officers in a torrent of furious Arabic and tells me in a forceful aside, "Please, touch *all* the stones you want!"

How foolish of me! I had supposed that the purpose of police officers in jeeps, on camel and on foot was to protect foreign visitors from violent attacks and other mishaps, but the officers see it as their job to protect the pyramids from us tourists. How odd then that their aggressive surveillance is so erratic! For, crossing over to the museum, I see a group of schoolchildren scaling the Great Pyramid's forbidden slope undisturbed, because no police officer is watching that side.

It does not make a good impression and leaves the foreign visitor with bad feelings. Our tour guide is very aware of it, though the police officers are not.

Inside the brand-new museum, visitors are required to slip dirty white cotton covers over their footwear to protect the gleaming floor from the sand dust on their soles. A dour individual at the counter is in charge of handing out covers, according to the size of each visitors' feet. Or at least that is what one *imagines* he would be looking for. But as it turns out, he is not interested in such details. And when I ask him to exchange my covers because their torn soles render them pointless, he just waves me away in an irritated manner. On our journey around the whole world, this is the first time we are not treated as welcome guests, but as a nuisance.

Waddling like ducks in our oversized flippers, we now study the exhibits in their glass cases. There is a heap of the original grass rope, found with the ship in tight coils; also a large, intricate knot tied with similar rope, and a scale model of the pharaoh's solar barque. We gaze into that pit, beside the pyramid, above which this museum was constructed. Lined with massive slabs of granite, it is where the funereal barque was discovered, in layers of loose pieces that took a team of Egyptian experts about twenty years to excavate and reassemble meticulously. *Hmmm* ... but would it not have taken a taskforce of Emirati a mere fraction of the time? By now I am inclined to think so.

The solar barque is displayed on a platform above our heads, suspended in streaming light, and, climbing flights of stairs, we are able to admire it from all angles. Thick honey-coloured planks of cedarwood form the vessel's sleek curves and a cabin with a simple awning. All these components are joined with artful knots of tough, tightly-wound grass rope.

(And this cabin really *does* look like a hut! I *must* tell Martha about it ...!) Two rows of oars with long shafts and pointed knife-like blades resemble spears, and the whole design is of a splendid, simple elegance that derives its aesthetic strength from the majestic purpose for which it was built: to bear the mighty pharaoh into the land of *Ra*.

But present-day Egypt hardly lives up to the appeal of its glorious past! We find the museum's toilets guarded by a large, unpleasant woman whose bulk fills the entrance space and who expects payment before she will let any visitor use the facilities. Waving our tickets at her, we protest that we are not willing to pay again for what ought to be included. But there is no room to push past her, and so we turn to our guide for help. That well-meaning woman is upset because her attempt to present her country in the best light has been foiled again, and she begins to argue with the woman. This 'Gorgon of the Toilets' now mimes that she needs to make a living, but none of us consider her presence worth any money. Our guide, dismayed, turns to the museum's staff. They refuse to get involved, and so we decide to boycott the facilities and await our imminent return to the hotel.

But what is happening here? It is not at all easy to understand why this stylish and modern museum does not employ the woman to clean the toilets out of hours, covering her undoubtedly meagre wage with the entrance fee. Why is she allowed to offend the museum's visitors and thus give Egypt's tourism a bad reputation? For it is undeniable that this experience leaves yet another unfavourable impression. Surely the people of Egypt ought to know better? After all, they alone among nations were able to accumulate several thousand years of experience in the sightseeing business ...!

Our rest stop at the hotel's gleaming toilets is followed by an unremarkable lunch, and then we are taken to a shop where papermaking from papyrus reeds is demonstrated. Ancient Egyptian tomb art, painted on such papyrus, is displayed in a gallery where one can buy whatever appeals.

Driving on through Cairo, it becomes clear that Egypt would occupy the very bottom on the scale of my recently conceived 'Litter Indicator of Nations', for never have I seen more rubbish anywhere. It is by far the worst of all countries we visited! Indeed, the state of Egypt's environment makes a powerful case for declaring the public use of plastic illegal at once. (At dinner, returned from an excursion that featured camel rides with Bedouins, Norah reports that plastic scraps blown into the desert cause the death of wild camels, since they mistake them for food.)

Why, I ask myself; why is it taking so long to address the problem? Surely anyone can see that it will not go away by itself? But there is so much amiss in Egypt that the factors suspected of placing a country high on the 'Litter Indicator of Nations' may have to be addressed first.

My impression is that the fabric of Egypt's society has been badly damaged and appears to be in shreds. And, as we drive through the chaotic rubbish-ridden desolation that is Cairo, we get an eerie glimpse into an apocalyptic future where cities turn into a particular kind of hell as buildings crumble and decay alongside the rules and laws that make for an ordered and responsible society. In this context, the link between the environment and human morality becomes visible yet again. What will happen when the ray of hope, inspired by last year's revolution, is disappointed and turns to disillusionment? The writer Rohinton Mistry observed in a brilliant study of his native India that "it is a fine balance between hope and despair" ... and indeed, in Cairo there is a sense that this exploited country is teetering between the two, on a knife's edge.

We have reached the Nile and board a large boat, decorated to resemble the pleasure-craft of a pharaoh. Inside, tables are set with cakes and biscuits, to be enjoyed as we cruise slowly along the banks of this venerable waterway.

A band tunes up and a gorgeous young belly dancer performs this Arab form of seduction for our entertainment. Her well-moulded body (on the voluptuous side) is clad in satin, tightly pink, and tiny tassels are dancing up and down the high slit of her skirt. Yes, she is very good. A look at the men's faces around the room confirms it, and the frontman of the band has his eyes riveted on the girl with the dreamy smile of the cat that got the cream.

Next on the programme is a timid young man who performs a whirling Dervish dance of great length, wearing an enormous hoop skirt. I have never seen such a dance before and am unable to watch it now, for such spinning makes me feel instantly dizzy and nauseous. Instead, I go upstairs to enjoy the view of the river and its urban banks from the top deck, noticing that the waves that float our boat shimmer in the original shade of *Eau de Nil* – a colour that was made fashionable by the Art Nouveau movement in the late 19th century and remained wildly popular throughout the Thirties.

All too soon this restful part of the day's programme comes to an end and it is time to board our coaches once more for the long return to our ship. Aurora traversed the Suez Canal in our absence and is waiting for us in Port Said. Our arrival is expected there at around half-past five, but in the end we shall be two hours late – to the dismay of our captain and his officers, concerned about their schedule.

It is a drive of a good three hours through city and desert. As evening falls, wobbling along the motorway at 100km/h feels unsafe in the extreme, for the road surface is not suited to the speed. People walk along the multilane motorway as if it were an ordinary city street, crossing over occasionally. In any case, motorway lanes are a meaningless concept here. Anyone will drive anywhere on this wide strip of uneven tarmac. Coaches and lorries straddle two lanes, overtaking manoeuvres are carried out left and right, and even through the middle if there happens to be a convenient gap. Horns are honked freely, but to little effect.

The common rules, laws and regulations that govern our daily life, and which we accept and obey for the benefit of all, have been dangerously eroded here.

Soon my fingers hurt from being clenched tightly as I try to make up my mind: Should I shut my eyes and pretend to be elsewhere, or stare doom squarely in the face?

Finally arrived in Port Said, a sudden and heavy downpour of rare rain floods the roads and makes a detour necessary. Resulting traffic jams delay our coaches further. But then, exceedingly glad to have made it back alive, we hurry past a long line of souvenir stalls (with initially hopeful, but soon sorely disappointed vendors) towards our ship, straining at her anchor and impatient to leave.

Hurried security checks, terse announcements from the captain, a cool shower, a hot meal ... and then a welcome spell of sleep after this long and interesting day.

Day 86 ~ Friday, 30th March 2012 ~ sunrise: 6.37am ~ sunset: 7.07pm ~ wind: SW 4 ~ weather: sunny ~ temperature: 15°C ~ time zone: GMT+3 ~ distance travelled since Suez: 208 NM ~ in total: 30,334 nautical miles

Cyprus

It is not easy to get excited about a tour to 'Larnaka and Lefkara' after the Great Pyramids and the Nile. But Cyprus is a beautiful island and, for a traveller returning from the East, also the first place that seems more familiar than exotic in its vaguely European way. The temperature of just fifteen degrees reminds us of home too.

We set out in a coach steered by a young Cypriot unlike the usually large and placid coach drivers, for he is lively and of slight build. It takes him some time to work out how to silence the screeching overtones of the microphone that torture our ears, to the comically mimed dismay of our tour guide Maria. She is a charming older lady, and she knows how to make us laugh with witty remarks and funny jokes as she imparts political and historical information.

Our first stop, at the village of Kiti, is the Byzantine church *Angeloktisti*, rumoured to have been made by angels because of perfect proportions and a heavenly aspect. The wall behind the iconostasis has a mosaic of Virgin and Child from the 6th century and, as all religious art of former times, its simplicity radiates great spiritual power.

The row of icons on the screen brings back memories of painting similar images with my pupils in an enjoyable art project. Here, the bottom half of each icon is covered with a panel of Perspex, so that worshippers may kiss the feet of these saints without soiling the paint, and a sign requests that lipstick should not be worn.

The mosque we visit next is unusual because it is dedicated to *a woman*. But then Umm Haram was the paternal aunt of Prophet Mohammed himself, and she travelled to Cyprus in the Arab raid of AD 649. At her advanced age this may have been too much of an adventure, for she fell from her mule and died during the siege of Larnaka. In the 18th century, the Hala Sultan Tekke Mosque was built over her tomb.

Although it is of modest size, situated in Greece and open to all faiths, some Muslims consider it the fourth most important holy place after 1) the Grand Mosque in Mecca, 2) the Prophet's Mosque in Medina, and 3) Jerusalem's Al Aqsa Mosque. Ottoman ships customarily lowered their flag in passing, and some saluted Umm Haram's resting place with cannon shots – intending to frighten the Greeks at the same time, I should think.

This pleasing building has attractive grounds too that invite visitors to linger and study the narrow Islamic grave markers. A large and gorgeous rose adds its perfume to the sweet scent of mimosas, unfamiliar seedpods catch my eye, shed by conifer trees, and a couple of dear little cats jump on the wall to have their heads scratched.

Moving on, we pass a salt lake nearby that once produced a salt known as 'The Queen' for its superior quality, but these days the lake is no longer used and dries out in summer.

Soon we come to Larnaka with its Church of Agios Lazarus. The story goes that, after his resurrection by Christ in Bethany, Lazarus came to Cyprus and was made its first bishop. In the crypt we see his (second) tomb, empty since his remains were removed to Constantinople in AD 898. But the reliquary houses a piece of his skull, seen shimmering through a circular pane of glass.

Now we sit in the carved wooden pews, listening to Maria's presentation and observing Cypriots at their worship. They approach the reliquary, kiss the glass pane of the holy relic, cross themselves and pray; a smartly suited businessman, a housewife, and a young woman with a headscarf who seems particularly troubled – all perform their daily worship in an introspective and unselfconscious manner.

On this journey around the world, I have witnessed the prayers of people in many countries; have seen the same touching sincerity in temples of Hindus and Buddhists, in mosques and in churches; the same devotion everywhere to the Spirit of the Universe, perceived in different guises. Those who have lost faith in the divine seem the poorer for it. Then a celebrity cult rushes in to fill the vacuum, for the human soul has a great need for reverence and will not be without. And those who claimed that religion is nothing but opiate for the masses were also the greatest mass murderers in history ... "Wherefore by their fruits ye shall know them." (Gospel of St Matthew 7:20)

The Church of St Lazarus is solidly built in beautiful stonework and richly ornamented with gilded carvings. A row of precious icons lines the screen, and their faces, their symbols and gestures tell the story of Christ's life, death and resurrection. Glowing candlelight glints on gold leaf, traces of frankincense linger ... it is all very old, very beautiful and still very much alive; not just a relic, but the beating heart of a large community.

As we drive up into the mountains to the village of Lefkara, we are reminded of such long-forgotten items as socks and coats. Lacking these, we shiver in the chill of the mountain air. A snack at a local taverna is most welcome at this point.

Pitta bread with halloumi cheese, tomato and cucumber soon revives our flagging spirits, and then we get to wander by ourselves around the idyllic village to browse its shops. These specialize mainly in Lefkaritika lace, embroidery and delicate gold jewellery.

(*World cruiser's tip: Pack a large, light, foldable holdall in your cruise luggage to accommodate your purchases on the way home. Alternatively, buy a nice travel bag at one of the many markets you will be visiting.)

An amiable shopkeeper welcomes me. Business is slow and he is eager to chat, asks where I am from and what I have seen on my journey around the world. And although I do not buy anything, he will not let me go without pressing me with gifts from his shop. I am very reluctant to accept them, but he insists that I must have a bar of vanilla-scented olive oil soap and a fine sea sponge. Ignoring my protests, he puts them in a bag and reaches for a large, iridescent shell to add for good measure ... but a little tussle results, for now I grab the bag and clamp it firmly shut. Amused by such practical resistance, he relents and points out the way to the village church instead. This church is really worth a visit, and as yet I have no symptoms of what Maria called 'Traveller's ABC': "Another Bloody Church, Another Bloody Castle ...!"

We return to Limassol along the coast. Amongst its seaside resorts and international five-star hotels, beautiful boutiques and cool cafés, it is amusing to see typical Greek enterprises: 'St Cristoforo Driving School', 'St George Car Hire', and a building firm, ominously called 'Nemesis Construction' ... Really, who would risk contracting *them?*

Arrived at the port, I take a picture of our charming tour guide and the driver. Maria gives me her envelope of fresh lemon blossoms, picked in the garden this very morning and brought along so that we might enjoy their heavenly scent. Now they sweeten the air in my cabin, and my memories of Cyprus. Contrary to expectations, the excursion has not been a let-down after the pyramids and the Nile. Indeed, it has been a very enjoyable day!

After dinner, increasingly worried about my as yet uncertain future, I send an email to my friend Helena, concerning the date of my return and the possibility of a stay at her house. This takes eleven minutes and costs eight pounds, including the initial sign-up charge of £2.50.

Is this reasonable, I ask myself, and then the assistant at the Cyb@study. Apologetic, he replies that the cruise line has to pay roughly sixty thousand US dollars per month for its internet and mobile phone satellite services. – Well, they certainly want that money back from us!

(*World cruiser's tip: Prepare your folks at home that they will not be hearing from you much, and then switch off your phone for the duration of your trip around the globe. While at sea, your cell phone's access to the world must rely on superb technology known as phone-to-satellite transponders. And yes, it works – but at much higher per-minute rates than those you are used to, and so a roaming 'cellular at sea' can rack up an iceberg of costs.

The offered ship-to-shore phone service will also come at considerable expense, and anyone who contacts you by phone from home will be hit with extra charges. And so, unless you have earth-shaking news to transmit, you may prefer to remain unavailable.)

Day 87 ~ Saturday, 31st March 2012 ~ sunrise: 6.29am ~ sunset: 6.59pm ~ wind: 1 ~ weather: sunny ~ temperature: 23°C ~ distance travelled since Limassol: 159 nautical miles ~ in total: 30,493 nautical miles

Israel

A new dawn brings another arrival at yet another port in yet another country, and we are about to meet another land and its culture, another religion and more history, but I am not in the right frame of mind to absorb more information today. Those recent excursions were intense and a couple of days at sea would be very welcome now, but such restful intervals are becoming increasingly scarce, now that we are returned to our old continent with numerous pearls of ancient culture scattered liberally around the rim of the Mediterranean.

As Aurora glides into the harbour of Haifa, the grand Baha'i Temple gleams in the morning light, perched on the slope amidst elaborately landscaped gardens. It will be the first stop on today's tour – not the temple itself, but a look down over its site from Mount Carmel near the Stella Maris monastery, our next stop. There, a magnificent nineteenth-century church is built over what is said to be Elijah's Cave. According to legend, Elijah hid in a cave on the slope of this ridge when he had fought the priests of Baal. Much later, the Carmelite order quarried an additional cave at this location, sanctified and crowned it with an altar and a large statue of the Holy Virgin, known here as 'Our Lady, Star of the Sea'. And at the apex of the cupola above her head, a star, painted around a circular aperture, lets in a beam of light that connects heaven and earth.

It is the Sabbath today, so the town is deserted and everything is shut. Some of the streets are even barricaded.

Our driver is a handsome grey-eyed Arab, our tour guide a lovely Jewish woman, and they are clearly great friends, in spite of their nations' archaic enmity. And, after Gwen, this guide is only the second person I met on this journey who is familiar with Waldorf education, for some of her friends are teachers at the local Steiner school, open to Jews *and* Arabs.

We drive along the waterfront towards Acre, the site where a crusader citadel once overlooked an important port known as Akko. The dilapidation of contemporary buildings clashes with the beautiful ruins of a medieval city, rising in graceful arches amongst rubble and rubbish. The excavation of this 'City beneath the City' is ongoing, and its restored spaces are used for cultural events.

Medieval stonework has an appeal, even in its stark bareness, which present-day architecture just cannot hope to match. The purity of its natural stone, dressed and shaped to planes and curves, conveys power and devotion at the same time. We pass through these vast courts and pillared halls of the Knights Templar and learn that the Gothic arch and the Bourbon Lily were inspired by what crusaders found in the Holy Land: Arab architecture with pointed arches, and the wild lilies that are growing abundantly along this coast. The bas-relief of a heraldic lily at the base of the stone vault's ribs illustrates the point. And all of this solidly crafted masonry speaks of its architects' earnest belief that they were building for eternity. They had no inkling how brief their presence in this land, and indeed in history, would be.

It makes me think of Dubai and its valiant building projects. What timespan will be allotted to them? And what thoughts and feelings will the ruins of our world inspire in travellers of a future age? What might they wish to preserve, and what will they learn about our ambitions?

We wander on through the maze of little lanes in the Arab quarter around the area of the excavation site. The stalls of the bazaar are doing a brisk and profitable trade despite the Sabbath – or because of it. To our eyes, this way of shopping seems exotic and quaint, but it is just normal everyday life in a large part of the world. Little stalls with colourful heaps of fruit and juicing equipment provide a healthy and refreshing drink for the thirsty shopper. A spice store is decorated with gourds and antiques, with pictures of Arab horses and faded Hollywood film stars. A young vendor sells assorted sweets, protected from dust and flies by clear plastic domes. Bowls of glossy olives whet the appetite – and everywhere, groups of Arab men pass the time of day, sitting by the wayside, networking and gossiping.

A walk along the top of the old city wall by the seaside brings back memories of Dubrovnik, for it too gives one a good view of the picturesque assembly of buildings and courtyards, with interesting glimpses of the life they contain.

On the return journey, our guide sings Hebrew songs with us. *Shalom, chaverim* – peace, friends, till we meet again!

This tour only took half a day but was all I could cope with. Most people have gone on the long excursions to Jerusalem and Bethlehem, braving coach drives of several hours each way, but I look forward to an extended nap this afternoon. Yesterday, a notice had informed us that there would be no water on C Deck this morning, and now a team of plumbers is deployed in a major operation, seemingly set to fix those leaking water pipes once and for all. The corridor's carpet is protected by layers of plastic that crackle like bubblewrap under my feet. Ceiling panels are removed and stepladders placed at strategic intervals. One of these ladders, blocking my cabin door, is whisked away at my approach with a "So sorry, madam!"

Looking forward to a peaceful siesta, I lie down and close my eyes, but sounds of dripping water come from the direction of my bathroom. I check the taps and find them all turned off, but the dripping persists, sounding like an old toilet cistern that fills up slowly and noisily. I return to bed, hoping that whatever is filling up here will soon be done.

At first I am not concerned, for surely everything is properly fixed by now. But the drip-drip-dripping continues like the Chinese water torture, and in the end I can stand it no longer. Going outside to investigate, I find the corridor restored to its customary state. The ceiling panels are back in place and the plumbers have disappeared, taking their stepladders and acres of plastic with them.

However, *one* problem must remain unsolved, for the sound of dripping water is heard even more clearly out here. Looking around, I notice a firehose compartment next to my cabin door and open it – to find a jet of water spurting from a pipe join and into a pool at the bottom of the cupboard, already several inches deep ...

Well, better not wait until *this* fills up!

I report my discovery to Reception, and minutes later the supervisor arrives, a plumber with an industrial-sized water-hoover in tow. I leave them to it and lie down once more, even though restful sleep seems less and less likely.

(*Cruiser's tip: Should you notice anything suspicious, report it to a member of staff or to Reception at once. They will investigate the matter and sort it out. Don't ignore your instincts if they tell you that something is wrong.)

Of course the water pooled inside the cupboard seeps under the adjacent bathroom floor and from there into my cabin, partially soaking the carpet. Returning from supper, I find a large dryer inside the door, making a racket and whirling loose pieces of paper about. One of these is a note from the supervisor, requesting me to contact her. Overtired by now, I shove the dryer into the corridor and call the supervisor to say that I cannot cope with *any* more right now. All I want is a good night's sleep – and never mind if the carpet is wet! She apologizes repeatedly. "So sorry, madam!"

Day 88 ~ Sunday, 1st April 2012 ~ sunrise: 6.40am ~ sunset: 7.31pm ~ sea state: slight ~ wind: E 3 ~ weather: showers ~ temperature: 24°C

Flooded Cabin Floor

Today I am offered the use of a spare cabin, because there is work to be done on my soaked carpet. What a bother! I had so been looking forward to a quiet day in my homely hut. But a massage appointment is scheduled this morning and the 'Thai Herbal Poultice' treatment proves calming and relaxing. Manuel tells me about the tour he accompanied to Jerusalem. It was long, intense and exhausting, but of course very interesting.

In the nick of time I make it to the World Cruisers' Lunch and share a table with Erin, Paul, and the same deck cadet who explained the use of the sextant earlier. Over another splendid meal our conversation revolves around ships and the city of Portsmouth, for it is home to all three of them.

Erin had longed to hear details about my excursion to the pyramids, but that tale will have to wait for another time. She is only just recovering from viral pneumonia and still feels and looks frail. Nonetheless we all have a lovely lunch. I enjoy the occasion even more than the first time – and how long ago that seems!

Day 89 ~ Monday, 2nd April 2012 ~ sunrise: 6.54am ~ sunset: 7.35pm ~ wind: NW 4 ~ weather: cloudy ~ temperature: 15°C ~ distance travelled since Haifa: 674 nautical miles ~ in total: 31,167 nautical miles

Turkey

Our captain recognizes the value of catchphrases and likes to make use of them. Today, as he announces our imminent arrival at a new port, he jokes that we shall be going ashore "with the speed of a thousand turkeys ..." and, although predictable, it does make me smile.

Weather is more British now – cool, grey and cloudy, with showers of rain thrown in for good measure – but the local guide who takes us to the ruins of Ephesus is fiercely proud of his native country, just like any Turk I ever met. He relates that Izmir was once a Greek city called Smyrna, but this name did not trip off Turkish tongues and was changed to something more comfortable. He also tells us that Smyrna is the very place where, once upon a time, the great (though regrettably Greek) poet Homer was born.

After Istanbul and Ankara, Izmir is Turkey's third-largest city. The country is largely agricultural, and we pass peach orchards that are just beginning to unfold magenta-coloured blossoms. Spring is all around. Birdsong and tender green of fresh leaves welcome us into the zone of changing seasons. After Egypt and Israel, the total absence of rubbish along the roadside is remarkable. The countryside is clean, tidy and well cared-for, which puts Turkey on an unexpectedly high level of my recently invented 'Litter Indicator of Nations'. Well, I have never heard of anyone else using such a scale.

Soon our destination is reached. The ancient city of Ephesus is linked by name to *Apasas* ('honey bee'), an even older Hittite settlement. Here we walk on excavated roads, paved with thick marble slabs and lined by rows of broken columns. I delight in running my fingertips along swirling Ionian stone spirals, curling leaves of acanthus and chiselled Greek inscriptions ... and through the fur of the friendly cats that tip-toe over broken pieces of masonry.

Our guide describes the historic importance of the site and conjures a lively picture of this cosmopolitan town in Antiquity, thought to have counted a quarter of a million inhabitants in its prime. But then Ephesus, a junction of the trade routes that linked three continents, fell into decline, for its harbour silted up and choked the lifeblood of commerce from its vessels. The city's former importance was lost and the people moved on, leaving its splendour to decay.

My group is followed by a local photographer who makes a living by snapping portraits of foreign visitors. It has taken him no time at all to work out that I am camera-shy, and now he seems determined to outsmart my evasive tactics. Soon we have a wordless game going between us. He pretends to be occupied with other subjects, but whenever I look up, I find his lens aimed at me above a wide grin that says, "Ha, gotcha!" This makes me laugh, and I retaliate by aiming my camera in his direction, making him laugh too. He turns away and ambles along, pretending to give up, but all the while planning his next ambush.

By the time we return to the coach, our pictures are ready and waiting at only three Euros each. To my surprise, this charming professional's persistence resulted in not only one, but *two* portraits I actually like and am happy to buy. A colleague is in charge of the sale. The photographer, whose name is Aslan, is not to be seen. I cannot thank him, though I should like to do so. But I did get a nice snapshot of him too, giving me the thumbs-up.

On the return drive, our tour guide hands out sachets of hand-sanitizing gel that bear our cruise line's logo. Seeing it, a fellow passenger quips, "Watch out – they're probably leaking!" – It makes me laugh out loud, and I chuckle all the way back to the harbour.

Day 90 ~ Tuesday, 3rd April 2012 ~ sunrise: 6.45am ~ sunset: 7.29pm ~ wind: 1, light airs ~ weather: sunny ~ temperature: 13°C ~ distance travelled since Izmir: 288 nautical miles ~ in total: 31,455 nautical miles

Istanbul

At sunrise we reach the port of the city that famously sits on the edge of two continents. It is cold this morning, only six degrees as yet. Socks and a coat are definitely back on the list of life's necessities! ... Aurora passes a row of impressive buildings in the dawn's rosy haze. I am not able to identify them, but today's tour around 'Imperial Istanbul' is sure to change that. It is just a short coach drive to the centre of the city, sitting on raised ground and overlooking the bay. We begin by walking along Hippodrome Square in the morning sun and our guide describes the immense popularity of the horse-and-chariot races that once took place on this stretch. These racing events were more to the taste of the Eastern Empire than the gory gladiator games of Rome, and records of former champions, along with the names of their horses, survive to this day.

We approach the tall and gleaming spire that is the obelisk of Pharaoh Thutmosis III of Egypt. It had been quarried and polished at Karnak around 1600 BC, but was later set up in this place by the Emperor Theodosius. How to get this big needle of stone into a vertical position posed a considerable technical problem at the time, and a record of the solution is carved into the marble pedestal. This pedestal is now much eroded, but the obelisk of granite, although very much older, still looks as new in its clean-cut neatness. In fact, it could be mistaken for a modern replica.

Close by, we gather around the tightly coiled strands of the Serpentine Column that rises from its circular pit like a thick rope of Verdigris. Our guide explains that each one of the strands once had a serpent's head, and these heads bore a golden bowl. The bowl was stolen and the serpents' heads knocked off long ago, though fragments survive in the Istanbul Archaeological Museum. This tripod, known to the Greeks as 'Tripod of Plataea', was kept in Apollo's temple at Delphi. It was made from metal gleaned from the weapons and shields of the defeated Persian army, and dedicated to the gods in gratitude for yet another Greek victory against overwhelming Persian odds. But in AD 324, the passionate and imperial collector Constantine added this tripod to the growing compilation of foreign treasures he amassed in his own city of Byzantium – aptly renamed Constantinopolis.

I am diverted from this open-air history lesson by the sight of a Turk, striding along the road with a tall tower of layered bread balanced on a platter atop his head, seemingly unaware of the load he is carrying. I hasten to capture this unusual sight on camera, and soon the man is surrounded by customers wanting to buy a snack; mainly locals, but also a few adventurous tourists.

The walk has brought us to Sultan Ahmet's Blue Mosque. With our shoes carried in bags provided by the efficient local tour operator, we enter the mosque at the side reserved for visitors. Signs in several languages state that female visitors are to wear long skirts and to cover their hair, but I see no attempts by supervising staff to reinforce this rule. They just check that we removed our dusty shoes before stepping onto the carpet which the faithful touch with their foreheads.

Inside, colourful tiles gleam in the soft light cast by windows and chandeliers. These tiles are more varied in hue than expected and by no means just blue, and they represent Islam's symbolic motifs in intricate patterns.

Decorative calligraphy embellishes the interior space, in keeping with Islamic tradition that holds the word sacred and celebrates its written form. Surahs from the Koran, as well as the names of the Prophet and his successors, take the place of the pictures and sculptures that are commonly seen in temples and churches of other faiths. In our lessons last year, my pupils were astonished to hear that Islam considers representation of the natural world, and the human figure in particular, a sacrilege, and they were intrigued to discover the high level of beauty expressed in geometric patterns and calligraphy.

This lovely space, with its main cupola fanning out in semi- and quarter-domes, was built to the plan of the Hagia Sophia nearby. *That* building is about seven times larger, we now learn, but *this* mosque is the only one outside Mecca to have six minarets – an extravagance permitted to the sultan alone. He also had a private balcony to the left of the *mihrab*, shielded from view by lattice screens.

In the reserved area, men are performing their ritual prayers side by side. Watching these worshippers as they prostrate themselves solemnly before Allah, I am reminded of an essay I once read, long ago. It examined the difference between Islam and Christianity by looking at the respective body gestures assumed in prayer. The author, whose name is lost in the mists of time, compared and contrasted the two religions as 'Servants and Soldiers of Allah' versus 'Brothers and Sisters of Christ' – as subordinates of a supreme general versus potential equals of a supreme lover. This article also explored the reserve which Christians, and the Western World in general, feel towards Islam, since Islam draws its identity, purpose and comfort from a complete submission that is alien to our fervent quest for individual freedom.

But does the Koran with detailed rules on the rightful way of living not aim to lift human nature to the rank of the angels who can do no wrong? The Bible seems more generic in its moral guidance and values the prodigal son – he who erred and sinned and then returned to the right path of his own free will – above those who never put a foot wrong. Ultimately, however, both paths aim for the same goal, even though they set out in opposite directions; for all religious endeavour is concerned with the self-improvement that is described so concisely by the Zoroastrian creed: 'To think good thoughts, to speak good words, and to do good deeds.' Hinduism, Judaism and Buddha's eightfold path are more variations on this theme ... so why should one of them be exclusively right?

On this journey around the world, I have come to see all religions more clearly as venerable paths that ascend the same divine mountain on separate routes. We all strive to reach the summit in our different ways, and eventually the Universal Spirit will be revealed to us, once we – flickering reflections of its light on the waters of the world – leave this mortal coil behind and return to the All, the divine Oneness that knows, values and welcomes our different paths in its compassionate embrace.

Leaflets available at the gate of the mosque explain Islam beautifully. The late emergence of this religion from the hot, shifting sands of Arabia appears as a profound work of socio-spiritual art, a divine impulse that "unified, guided, inspired and civilized the warring desert tribes and purified their hearts". Every aspect appears so well suited to the arid lands and their people, and the resulting culture is so at one with the prevailing conditions and imparts such beauty to harsh desert regions – one just has to observe and experience it to appreciate its greatness.

Our next visit takes us to the famous Topkapi Palace. It is closed on Tuesdays, but opens its doors exclusively to tours of our cruise line, owing to successful negotiations by the local tour operator.

And that is why we find these usually overcrowded courtyards peaceful and bare, filled with nothing but early primulas and scents of spring.

In the first courtyard we pass the church called Hagia Ireni, a little sister to the 'Holy Sophie'. In the second courtyard, a fountain by the wall served the sinister purpose of cleaning swords after executions. The chopping block is still nearby. The third courtyard, a palace garden, is bordered by the sultan's splendidly baroque reception rooms and the portico from which state functions were directed and state funerals departed. Behind the adjacent wall are immense storage and kitchen quarters that could feed many thousands every day. And the innermost area of the palace is the *harem*, the private living area of the sultan that was out of bounds to all but the members of his family.

There are two libraries, containing collections of old books and scriptures. Another wing close by harbours relics for the gullible: a bristly strand from the Prophet's beard, the staff of Moses, the turban of Joseph, a saucepan from the household of Abraham ...

And then there is the treasury, where things of truly breathtaking value are kept safe behind thick plate-glass. Because there are no crowds, we are able to walk right up and admire objects that illustrate the cliché of the riches of the Orient: finely crafted swords, daggers and aigrettes, adorned with gemstones and pearls of unbelievable size; a gold-plated cradle and decorated thrones, one of them inlaid with many thousands of pearls. Also flasks, dessert cups and writing boxes carved from solid rock crystal and encrusted with emeralds and rubies set in gold.

We are amazed by jade vessels inlaid with delicate ornaments of gold, by precious rings and brooches, and the Topkapi Diamond of over eighty carat, set in a coruscating ornament. Unfortunately it is not permitted to take pictures of these treasures, and the guards keep a watchful eye. But stunningly beautiful though they are, I notice that jewels and diamonds (supposedly a girl's best friends) do not appeal to me on a personal level. I am content to leave them to sultans and their wives, with not a hint of the sour grapes.

Now it is time to visit the undisputed highlight of Istanbul: the Hagia Sophia. Built as a Byzantine church and dedicated to Holy Wisdom in female form, it was later converted to a mosque by the invaders of the Ottoman Empire. Our guide explains that the Muslims' careful conservation of Christian churches and artworks had nothing to do with tolerance and everything with the belief that the worst of bad luck would befall anyone who destroyed places and objects of religious worship. And so the beautiful mosaic of Virgin and Child survives, throning high above the mihrab. In the triangular spaces where great arches join, Christian images of angels were covered with rosettes bearing inscriptions, according to the Islamic ban on the representation of human features, and yet their faces remain intact.

But one of these angel faces has been restored to full view. It looks down on the crowds, thronging the vast space, and betrays no more interest than a little grey tabby cat that found its way in without a ticket. Now it is grooming its coat delicately, right beside the imam's prayer niche in the cordoned-off area. Undisturbed by the milling multitudes and their flashing cameras, this cat seems completely at ease in its privileged place.

I leave our guide's history lecture and make my way to the gallery. There are no stairs to climb, because a paved slope spirals upwards, designed to accommodate travelling chaises of ladies and dignitaries of a long-gone age. From the balustrade at the back I view the magnificent interior space that was built as "the world's largest". Its soaring arches are decorated in muted colours, circles of light are formed by the little windows of the immense cupola above and the big chandeliers below, and calligraphy plaques are inscribed with the names of Allah, Mohammed and the four Caliphs. Centuries of worship and political importance permeate the atmosphere and are reflected by these walls. Looking down on the special floor tiles that mark the *omphalos,* the navel of the Byzantine Empire, I see the very spot where its emperors were once crowned.

But the *Deesis* mosaic, of which a fragment remains, is the most impressive sight. Mary and John the Baptist are flanking Christ, who is portrayed as the teacher of mankind. In his prime, a grown man with a short beard and abundant golden hair like the mane of a lion, He carries a substantial book: the record of His Father's Revelation. His right hand is raised to the level of the heart in the gesture of teaching that is traditionally used in icons. At the same time, it conveys a blessing. But most captivating is the face of Christ. Light and dark areas are modelled with incredibly delicate skin tones, square mosaic tiles joined and blended together to create a softness that could only have been achieved by a true master of this art. It seems to me that the subtle way in which beard grows from cheek in delicate strands surpasses all that has normally been accomplished in this technique.

Yet all of this is revealed to me by later study. What strikes me at once is the beauty of face and expression, and also the peculiar aspect of the eyes, for they are not equal in size and the one on the right is definitely slightly distorted. There is something odd about its shape and spacing, a not-quite-rightness that makes it hard to look away. Compelled to fix my gaze on them, I look at these eyes that are in their turn looking at me with the intent mildness associated with His nature. Whereas the eye on the left is looking at me with seriousness and realism, the right eye gazes into my soul with a dream-like inwardness, as if seen through a wave of liquid crystal that moves the lines of its shape. This slight imbalance gives life to the whole face and imparts depth to an expression I shall not easily tire to look upon.

We may understand Islam's (and Luther's) ban on images seeking to illustrate a faith that by its very nature has no need for such representation, may recognize the historic progress inherent in the injunction "thou shalt not worship images" – and still appreciate this mosaic picture as a greatly enriching gift to all who contemplate it. As a work of art it speaks, like the greatest and best, of a challenging path and a higher truth; of life beyond death in His image.

I return repeatedly to view the mosaic from different angles. Who was the artist able to find this vision in his soul, and to express it with such towering skill? – Now a visit to the gift shop becomes an urgent necessity, for I cannot leave without at least a postcard-sized version of this masterpiece.

Our last destination is the Grand Bazaar, where we have an hour to look around independently. And although our guide warned us about the aggressive nature of vendors, I wander about quite unmolested. There is nothing I want to add to my luggage, but I admire the stalls selling colourful lamps, pottery, carpets and slippers, and snap scores of shots.

An eager young shopkeeper notices my interest in the picturesque Arabic world maps and other nice designs his father's shop specializes in. Particularly intriguing is a delicately coloured drawing of cross-sections and site plans that show famous mosques and are decorated with beautiful calligraphy. It would be a great visual aid if I were ever to teach pupils about Islam again, but that is a long shot in the dark. In the end, my resolve not to spend any more money on things, however lovely, holds firm – much to the loudly proclaimed dismay of the charming vendor.

Outside a jewellery shop, an elderly cat sits on a mat with its paws tucked under. Beside it, small bowls of food and water indicate that this is indeed its customary spot. The cat is in a meditative mood. Like its cousin inside the Hagia Sophia, it ignores the crowds, although legions of feet march past. Sometimes people even head straight towards it if they wish to peer at the jeweller's display above, but the cat does not twitch a whisker. These Turkish cats certainly seem to be of sterner stuff than the ones I know!

On our way back to the port I notice how tidy this part of the city looks. There is no rubbish anywhere, not even under a road overpass. Our excellent coach, the clean state of the public toilets, the beautiful flowerbeds in the squares – all speak of the country's aim for a high standard. Our guide's speeches are permeated with fierce pride in the fine Turkish achievements throughout history, and now he remarks with bitterness that if *the Greeks* had accomplished this, *everyone* would know and be awestruck. Apparently, the prevailing sentiment among Turks is that their impressive cultural contributions are not receiving the recognition they justly deserve – particularly from the Western World, of which Turkey would like to be a respected partner.

At the end of the tour I follow my custom, recently evolved, and take a pic of our driver-and-guide team. These people are at least as important in conveying a good impression of their country as the typical or famous sights they show us, and I find that I want to remember their faces and names. Regarding my language studies, I now learn that the Turkish word for lion is *aslan*. Hmm ... might have guessed that one!

After nearly seven hours of walking we are back on board. I lie down at once and sleep deeply until after dinnertime. A quick supper at the Orangery is followed by a walk around the top deck to admire the twinkling lights of Istanbul's skyline at night. The Blue Mosque, the Hagia Sophia and the Topkapi Palace are floodlit, and now I recognize each one and can picture what they look like inside.

But suddenly a large cloud of black, billowing smoke begins to rise from a building on the hillside, and then sirens are heard, wailing in the distance. It looks serious and makes me wonder what happened.

Day 91 ~ Wednesday, 4th April 2012 ~ sunrise: 6.43am ~ sunset: 7.39pm ~ sea state: calm ~ wind: 1, light ~ weather: sunny ~ temperature: 14°C

Trouble in Istanbul

Three bombs have been set off in the city since yesterday! We should have had another half day in Istanbul, but the captain announces that all tours are cancelled for security reasons. We shall be leaving immediately. He explains that although there is no direct threat to the ship, he cannot risk putting passengers, staff and crew in danger on their shore excursions.

To me, this announcement comes as a relief. A restful day at sea is most welcome to process the impressions of yesterday. Tomorrow we shall arrive in Athens and – unless the Greeks should be rioting too – there will be more to see, to learn and to write about. Four shore days in a row are too intense for my taste, but other passengers are disappointed and tempers flare when another cruise ship docks at our berth just after Aurora left it. As the mood amongst the passengers becomes decidedly mutinous, the captain is compelled to explain the steps of his decision-making process yet again.

But will it make a difference? On this journey I have come to realize how attached people are to any theory they formed themselves, and how unwilling to listen to reasoned argument if it is not in line with their own view. But isn't it right to make a point of leaving any port, city or country where bombs are employed instead of due political process? Cruise liners do have a certain clout through the volume of business they bring to the places they visit, and they should use it to make a statement of protest against terror wherever they can. As we learnt from our guide in Egypt, withdrawal of tourism is an effective way of encouraging a less violent approach to political issues.

The morning haze is dense, visibility is reduced and the air is chilly. The tour I booked for this morning was 'A Cruise on the Bosporus'. No doubt it would have been very cold on the water in an open boat, and the shoreline would have been shrouded in mist. I am happy with the refund for the cancelled excursion and settle down in the Crow's Nest to fill several pages of my black notebook with impressions of Istanbul, pausing once in a while to look out at the misty Sea of Marmara.

Because of the changed itinerary, we shall now be traversing the Dardanelles in broad daylight and this ought to be some consolation. Up on deck, the wind twirls my hair skywards and attempts to steal my shawl, but by now the sunshine is warm and pleasant.

Cargo ships creep by at intervals and seagulls circle our bow as we are passing between Asia and Europe. I try to picture the scene as it must have been in ancient times when Egyptian, Phoenician and Greek ships crowded this narrow stretch of sea; when the immense Persian army marched up and prepared to cross over, unaware of how few would return, and none of them victorious …

In the afternoon I check my emails in the Cyb@study and am very glad to find Helena's enthusiastic response, confirming that she will pick me up in Southampton, and inviting me to stay on at her house.

Relieved by the good news, I head to the gym for a 'Stretch & Relax' session. At my unexpected reappearance in his domain, Jovan pinches himself as if seeing a ghost. I have not been exercising at all since the days before Egypt! There had been no time for anything other than shore excursions, intense writing sessions and extended periods of rest, but I hope to get back into the rhythm of daily exercise sessions in the coming days at sea.

Day 92 ~ Thursday, 5th April 2012 ~ sunrise: 7.07am ~ sunset: 7.55pm ~ wind: SW 2 ~ weather: cloudy ~ temperature: 15°C ~ distance travelled since Istanbul: 359 nautical miles ~ in total: 31,814 nautical miles

Athens

I shall finally meet the Acropolis in person! The last time I was in Athens, over twenty years ago, the Parthenon was surrounded by scaffolding and swathed in what looked like tarpaulin from a distance, and in my youthful insouciance I decided to give it a miss under the circumstances ... Not so this time, though there is still a fair bit of scaffolding around, and most likely will be for years to come.

Our tour takes us from the port of Piraeus into the city to other venerable sites of interest. In passing, we get to see the Old Olympic Stadium, Constitution Square, the Tomb of the Unknown Warrior, the Presidential Palace, Heinrich Schliemann's House, the University Library ... Important places, to be sure, and yet no more than obstacles on the way to the only monument I wish to see.

Finally we arrive at a car park above the city and walk up the hill among Athena's trees, wild olives with silvery leaves and tiny black fruit. At the stile we are each given a ticket to enter the precinct. Our group assembles to listen to the guide's history lesson, but I – having delivered similar lessons to my pupils not so long ago – keep going upwards through the Propylaea, thrilled at the first contact of my feet with marble steps that were trodden by Pericles and Phidias themselves. Rough column fragments along the way beg to be touched, but prominent signs and grimly bored-looking staff ensure that we keep our hands off. I shall have to find a less conspicuous place for a personal greeting.

And then I see it at last: the great Parthenon, sanctuary of the virgin goddess Athena who had sprung from her father Zeus's head as personified wisdom – wisdom once again in female form. My first impression is that the great columns are much chunkier than they appear in photographs taken at a distance. Their weight and volume has a presence that is not conveyed by any picture I have ever seen. My impulse is to run up and put my arms around such a pillar, as far as they would go, but this would be foolish in the extreme, for it would get me into big, fat, Greek trouble with the guards. And so a mental hug is all I can do, wondering at the same time if the gold-coloured columns would feel as warm to the touch as the limestone blocks of the pyramids did.

From the fantastic and highly recommended book 'The Secret Lives of Buildings' I learnt much about the disasters that befell the Acropolis and led to its present, ruined state. Lord Byron already made the point that the temple ought to be allowed to crumble and follow its natural process of decay – but this view is clearly not shared by the teams of restoration experts working here to preserve what remains. Like plastic surgeons armed with high-tech procedures they operate on the ruins of the Parthenon's body, repairing and remodelling its vital parts with care.

After circling the temples slowly while taking in their surefooted beauty and splendour, I become interested in the element of modern technology that is now interwoven with the ancient stone. A dense filigree of scaffolding around the western pediment gives access to the heights, while subtly stone-coloured cranes do their best not to distract from the main view. Similarly tinted huts are crouching low, trying to blend in with a yard full of fragmented stone blocks that are assembled here, awaiting their moment.

Clearly, this work will continue for years if not decades, and coexistence of the old and the new is a necessity now. Our own age may no longer be able to *create* a Parthenon, but it is better qualified than any other to keep it alive.

In the gym session this afternoon there appears a girl who is tall, willowy, brunette and not quite twenty yet. Seeing her gives me the strange sensation of looking at my youthful self, and I experience what the writer Fay Weldon described so poignantly when she observed that there is nothing more glorious than to be a young girl, and nothing worse than to have been one. This takes me by surprise, for I do not feel envious of younger women. Covertly I study her loveliness and her unselfconscious joy at inhabiting a perfect body. It makes me more aware of the changes effected on mine by the passing of time, and it occurs to me that the chief pain of ageing must be our body's betrayal of an identity that feels itself ageless. Only the marble beauty of Greek temples and statues shines on through old age and decay, and moves us to admiration even in ruins.

Then I return my attention to the stretching exercises, for I am aiming to learn this sequence by heart so that I may carry it out by myself, once I am off this ship and far from Jovan's motivating influence.

He makes me smile as I wonder if there is another man anywhere who can command a group of women to "spread your legs" and "open your groins" with such endearing innocence.

Day 93 ~ Friday, 6th April 2012 ~ sunrise: 7.20am ~ sunset: 8.28pm ~ sea state: calm ~ wind: N 2, light breeze ~ weather: overcast ~ temperature: 14°C ~ time zone: GMT+2

Talking about Tuna

Recent blasts of air conditioning brought on another cold. My nose is blocked and the head feels awful. After a quick breakfast upstairs I go to the Medina to find Bob and Norah because we have not seen each other since Istanbul. Poor Norah – her cold is even worse than mine! We agree to meet up for lunch and I withdraw to write about Athens.

Given our severely phlegm-clogged headspaces, the meal at lunchtime is unexpectedly enjoyable. Old Bob is in a good mood and contributes much to the conversation. The situation is hilarious. Norah's and my ears are so muffled by our colds that our hearing matches Bob's deafness. Not one of us can readily understand what the others are saying, and because of this shared handicap we laugh a lot.

The ship is now traversing the Ionian Sea, southeast of Italy. The sea is calm again after a spell of liveliness last night, but there is mist over the water and little visibility.

In the afternoon, as we had arranged earlier, Norah and I visit the steamroom together. The hot vapour really is a blessed relief! And then, as we are wallowing in the dry heat of the sauna for good measure, she tells me about her adventurous solo excursion to a Turkish bath in Istanbul.

Later I have another meeting with Jovan, this time about the nutrition aspect of his Body Composition Analysis plan, and it turns out that he has never heard of my favourite comic *Calvin & Hobbes*. The subject came up when we were talking about the nutritional value of tuna (as all fans know, this is the favourite food of Hobbes the Tiger) and I am pleased to be able to recommend Bill Watterson's fantastic contribution to the treasury of human genius once again.

Day 94 ~ Saturday, 7th April 2012 ~ sunrise: 7.00am ~ sunset: 8.10pm ~ sea state: slight ~ wind: W 2, light breeze ~ weather: cloudy ~ temperature: 16°C

Nice Surprises

It is still very quiet in the Orangery when I am having breakfast there early this morning, sitting at my favourite corner table and looking out at the sea. How I shall miss this view! Suddenly, a light rustling at my back announces a presence. It is Sandie, she has come to sing 'Happy Birthday' to me. Standing behind my chair, having signalled that I must not turn around, she sings softly as I continue to look across the waves, smiling at this nice surprise. It is not my birthday yet; that will be in Lisbon, but Sandie has other commitments on the day. So she has decided to treat this day as the one and, before leaving for her work at the spa, invites me to a special dinner tonight in celebration.

At ten o'clock, another 'Aurora Uncovered' event gives me the chance to ask our new first officer for the port-to-port distances we clocked up since Bali. He is ready to oblige and requests my cabin number to have the list delivered later, but a passenger, overhearing his question, remarks loudly, "I didn't know *that* was going on too!"

His comment is inappropriate and offensive, and the guy clearly no gentleman, but I have become so used to the lack of class and good manners among the cruising public that, thanks to Gandhi, I can let it pass without taking any notice. So does the officer. – There is indeed a satisfying measure of strength in non-retaliation, if one manages to resist that first, contrary impulse.

(*Cruiser's tip: Sexual relations with members of the crew are strictly forbidden and ought to be taboo for the passenger. They do happen, but, if caught, the unfortunate employee will be dismissed with a black mark on their record. Be aware that the ship's plain-clothes security are keeping a watchful eye by day and by night, and if you are not inside your cabin, chances are that your moves are being monitored by one surveillance camera or another.)

As I am looking around the display tables, one of the Indian waiters engages me in conversation. He demonstrates how to fold some of the easier napkin sculptures and asks where I am from. Talking about Switzerland leads to a mention of my son who lives there, which in turn prompts the question of his age, followed by the astonished exclamation: "That is not possible, madam! ... You hardly look older yourself!"

I counter this outrageous flattery with the statement that I shall be forty-nine in a few days, at which he gasps in disbelief and confides in a lowered voice, "But I have seen you by the pool, madam ... in your swimsuit!" He continues to shake his head in gratifying bewilderment.

Gym and spa sessions have done their bit, it seems, and I walk away from this exchange with an inward smile. Before I came on this cruise, I felt that I was getting tired, not to mention old, and it has been good to hear such differing opinions from other people – both male and female, younger and older. When I report this little conversation to Sandie, her face lights up in instant understanding. "Back at home, I too used to feel I was getting old," she says, "but on this ship so many people have made me feel good about myself that I feel young once more." – Surely large numbers of middle-aged women would take up cruising if they knew!

Rajiv from the team of Reception Angels is manning Aurora's merchandise stall and we talk a bit about the world cruise experience. He has a radiant smile that makes his eyes light up to an unusual degree. They beam pure sunshine and make me wonder how two patches of dark physical matter, such as these black irises, can project so much light. I greatly appreciate and admire these friendly young Indians on staff and crew. Always helpful and pleasant, they are dignified as well, and possess a natural tact and a courtesy which many of the cruise passengers sadly lack.

At half-past eight, elegantly dressed up for a formal evening and my birthday dinner, I wait for Sandie in Raffles bar. She is not there yet, but Erin, Paul and friends welcome me into their circle. We chat and laugh for a while and I tell them the fairy joke. As expected, the women laugh delightedly while the men look faintly guilty. Then Sandie pops out of a 'Crew only' door and we head to the Café Bordeaux for dinner. The table is decorated with balloons and – surprise, surprise – Manuel and Jovan are there too, smartly suited, and a friend of Sandie's from the spa. We have a lovely evening, and I am grateful to Sandie for having arranged a setting in which one may chat and laugh with these pleasant young men without being suspected of hitting on them. What a good, thoughtful friend she is, and how fortunate I am to have met her!

I return to my homely cabin-hut at midnight, trailing pink balloons and smiling happily.

Day 95 ~ Easter Sunday, 8*th* April 2012 ~ sunrise: 7.41am ~ sunset: 8.51pm ~ sea state: slight ~ wind: 1, light airs ~ weather: cloudy ~ temperature: 14°C

Before & After

It is still dark outside when I have breakfast at the Orangery. Manuel and Sandie, getting ready for work, come to join me at my table. I just have to give her a big, grateful bear hug in memory of last night's birthday dinner, and all the while a pink-tinted sunrise slowly brightens the sky in preparation for another beautiful day.

In the gym session, Jovan makes us work hard to the usual rap music that grates on my ears, not to mention my nerves, but then he suddenly switches to 'What a Wonderful World' by Louis Armstrong as he instructs us to squeeze our abdominals. I am surprised by this complete change of style and wonder at it; and the song, so fitting for this cruise, will remain in my mind for the rest of the day.

A final massage with Manuel completes the morning. Knowing that this is the last time I shall have such a treat, I enjoy it more consciously than ever. The agreeable heat of the lava stones, pressed against palms of hands and soles of feet, is wonderful. Everyone should have such opportunities of total relaxation and wellbeing once in a while, I think – hardworking teachers most of all.

Upon return to my cabin, the requested list of port-to-port distances is in my mailbox, dispatched by the first officer as promised. It is accompanied by a polite handwritten note of a professionalism that reflects extremely well on the bridge. It also conveys the reassuring impression that such a request from a passenger is not seen as a nuisance.

I collect two 'special occasions' portraits at the ship's photo desk. One was taken at the beginning of the cruise, on Martha's birthday, and the other one just last week. It is remarkable how different I look in the most recent picture: happier, brighter and younger. This cruise has indeed had the relaxing and revitalising effect I hoped for, and there is visible proof in these 'before and after' pictures.

I meet Norah and Bob for a final shared lunch on this Easter Sunday, for they shall be flying home from Lisbon. Oliver is serving, and again I am fascinated by his kind face that shows such saintly serenity. One could lose oneself in observation, for this quality is so very rare.

Knowing that the cruise is coming to an end puts a damper on our mood, and I sense that Norah is preoccupied with the impending task of making her frail husband as comfortable as possible on the long journey home. Being a fulltime carer for a man in his nineties, whose various handicaps can make him cantankerous, is not a job many women would want, nor could carry off with such grace. I am awed by Norah's commitment. But despite it all, we enjoy a pleasant meal and agree to meet again at dinner, to say goodbye.

Towards evening, the PA announces the Rock of Gibraltar. Sandie and I meet by chance and go up on deck to take a few pictures; but the wind is strong, the air is hazy and the light much too glaring for photographs. I also notice that in this strange mood of finality I cannot muster the enthusiasm for sightseeing any longer – or maybe I just don't care enough about this piece of rock.

Back in my homely hut I write a note of thanks to the first officer and ask him, via Reception, to add his signature to the double page of autographs by staff and crew in my journal. It means that I shall have to let go of my precious notebook for a while, but Rajiv of the Smiling Eyes assures me that it should not take long before it is returned.

Day 96 ~ Monday, 9th April 2012 ~ sunrise: 7.08am ~ sunset: 8.07pm ~ wind: 1 ~ weather: sunny ~ temperature: 20°C ~ distance travelled since Athens: 1,796 nautical miles ~ in total: 33,610 nautical miles

Lisbon

I awake early and hover on the fringe of sleep for some time. I am in no hurry to get up, for there is much to think about. Outside my cabin door, three balloons are tied to my letter box. A card from the cruise line with a (printed) signature by the captain acknowledges my birthday with best wishes.

So this is the day …! I entered this world when the sun stood high, and Leo was rising as I embarked upon my life's journey that is about to complete seven times seven yearly cycles. The past has a definite shape, but the future is a blank. I cannot begin to imagine what the coming years will bring – where and how I will live. Such uncertainty at this point in life could be scary, but the freedom that comes with it is exhilarating. What shall be, shall be! There can be no doubt about that.

From the top deck I watch the sun rise. Cascades of a piano concerto, possibly Schubert, can be heard below. The moon, no longer at its fullest, hangs in the clear blue sky above our stern and remains untouched by those lovely tints of rose, peach and gold that now begin to spread along the eastern horizon, heralding an exceptionally beautiful day.

As our ship glides up the Tagus River, the coastline catches the morning light and turns golden. What must it have been like for those sailors, who set out with Magellan to circumnavigate the world and returned as sole survivors, to see the sun rise over their homeland after a journey whose months of dreadful hardship and hunger added up to years? Did they *ever* go to sea again? … It had taken their ship three months to cross the uncharted Pacific – the time of our *entire* journey around the world! Dwindling supplies of drinking water turned foul, food ran out and, sickening with scurvy and spitting teeth, they had no clue *if* or *when* they would see land once more. How they must have longed for home!

In view of today's 'River Cruise' tour I take a travel sickness tablet for once, worried about having my birthday spoilt by waves of nausea. It turns out to be a misguided precaution, for this tablet makes me so sleepy that Lisbon's charms are lost on me. All I want is to return to my cabin and lie down – a great shame on such a lovely day!

Our river cruise sails past the Seafarer's Monument which commemorates Henry the Navigator, that Portuguese prince who initiated the Age of Discovery, and also past the Castle of Belem from which courageous caravels once set out to explore and map the globe.

On land, cobbled streets in appealing patterns of black and white invite us to stroll around the inner city of Lisbon in the sunshine, but I am unable to function in this drugged stupor. No postcards, no souvenirs – I just want to return to bed as soon as possible.

At last the tour is over and we return to the ship. The security officer at the checkpoint smiles warmly, shakes my hand and wishes me many happy returns of the day. Then a phone message from Reception informs me that my journal is signed and ready for collection, and Rajiv adds his best wishes for my birthday. – How do they even know about it? Does their computer screen tell them? I certainly didn't!

I spend the afternoon in bed, trying to sleep my way out of this chemically induced stupor of misery, but rouse myself when Sandie comes round to collect the clothes and shoes I am passing on. We end up in the Crow's Nest bar, chatting over mocktails, and slowly I begin to feel better.

At the Medina restaurant, lovely birthday cards are propped against my glass, written by Martha and the other dinner companions, but the team of waiters is quite unaware of my birthday. No balloons, no happy song …

Once the meal is over, Bruce has a quiet word with them about this oversight. All are extremely apologetic, say that nobody told them, and that they will make up for it tomorrow. The team of waiters and the headwaiter squeeze my hand with their best wishes, and it is plain to see how sorry they are. But isn't it strange that security and reception staff should know about birthdays unprompted, while staff at the restaurant need to be informed by family members or travel companions?

Where does this leave the single traveller? Surely we cannot be expected to point out our own birthdays?

I return to my cabin and to bed directly, saddened by a day that was hampered by so many unnecessary obstacles. And yet I decide to think nothing of it. Superstition certainly comes more easily with favourable portents!

(*Solo traveller's tip: Although your birthday is logged firmly in the computer system, make sure that you or someone else drops a hint in the right place as the day approaches.)

Day 97 ~ Tuesday, 10*th* April 2012 ~ sunrise: 7.08am ~ sunset: 8.13pm ~ sea state: rough ~ wind: 6-8, gale ~ weather: cloudy ~ temperature: 15°C ~ time zone: GMT+1

Seasick Again

The day begins with breakfast in Sandie's pleasant company. Manuel joins us and I promise to show him the print of the Acropolis I bought as a souvenir. (Sandie had told him about this print because he is so interested in historic places, and her report made him keen to see it.)

The Greek print is admired not just by Manuel, but by everyone on the spa team when I arrive for another session with Sandie. She tints and enhances my lashes and eyebrows with delicate care. Never before did they look so good – and they never will again, either.

Then I visit the gym for the very last time, and just for a brief chat with Britta and Jovan. No time for exercise now!

There is a lot of packing to tackle, and the sea is predicted to be rough again in the Bay of Biscay, whose waters we shall enter tomorrow. On top of this, the insides of my thighs are aching rather badly from Jovan's earlier "military exercise". He laughs merrily and pronounces it "right on target". Britta is happy to take some no longer needed items off my hands, such as high-factor sun lotion and mosquito repellent spray, because she is staying on for the following cruise. (Sorting through my belongings earlier, I weeded out anything I shall not need in Britain, excepting only Hawaiian tropical wear, favourite flip-flops, and of course The Dress.)

It is time to return a few borrowed books to the library, collect my passport from Reception, and attend the personal immigration interview. The British official chats in a relaxed, informal way not encountered in similar situations abroad. Bless the Brits! Although they like to complain, bureaucracy and administrative formalities seem a lot less threatening in their hands.

Meanwhile, our empty suitcases have been released from storage and are delivered to the cabins. This means that the dreaded process of clearing my dear, homely hut must now begin. I start by removing all posters, cards and maps, and the bare cabin walls, impersonal once more, sharply enhance those depressing feelings of finality.

After lunch the ship begins to rock and pitch unpleasantly, for we are once again sailing the restless waters of the Bay of Biscay. I realize that I shall not be able to continue packing under these circumstances and lie down amidst open cases and heaps of clothes. Intermittently, as important tasks come to mind, I drag myself to my feet to carry them out, only to collapse again into that horizontal state which alone makes the ship's movements bearable. But although I have taken a tablet and am wearing acupressure wristbands, my lunch suddenly announces that we must part company. Then I lie listlessly in the dark and know that the Bay of Biscay is most definitely my least favourite stretch of water.

In the evening I make an effort, put on glamorous evening wear one last time and join the Captain's Farewell Party in the Crow's Nest. He delivers a lovely final speech and gives us some interesting statistics of our voyage:

The total distance we travelled is 65,505 kilometres, about one fifth of the way to the moon. On her way around the globe, Aurora was propelled by 13,930 metric tons of fuel, at a sum total of 9.9 million US dollars. We visited thirty-eight ports in twenty-five countries on five continents and traversed three oceans and two canals. 3,831 passengers of twenty-seven nationalities spent time onboard on various legs of the journey. Passports had been stamped twenty-nine times, and face-to-face immigration interviews were undergone on five occasions (US, Australia, India, Israel and the UK). And then the captain ends with a song about our world cruise from his point of view, based loosely on the lyrics of 'My Way' and accompanied on the piano by a member of the Kool Blue trio:

OUR WAY

And now the end is near …
And so we face the final North Atlantic depression.
My friends (and you are friends), I'll say it clear
(Though it may fade at the end as it does on the PA)
I'll state my case, as I'm the Cap-tain.
My 1743 gazelles, we've lived a 98 nights

(Or part thereof) that's been full.
We've travelled five continents and three oceans
But more, much more than this –
You've not had to cook or cleanse.
Challenges, we've had a few; but then again, too few to mention.
I did what I had to do, and saw it through
Without getting arrested or losing you.
I planned each charted course;
Each careful step along the ocean highways,
But more, much more than this,
We didn't get boarded by pirates or targeted by terrorists.
Yes, there were times, I'm sure you knew,
When I got tired and a little stressed with the local boys in blue.
But through it all, when there was doubt,
I smoked an extra cigarette and made decisions as I saw fit.
I faced it all and stood tall;
And then lay down in a darkened room to sort my head out.
We've visited many foreign lands, we've laughed and sunbathed.
We've had our fill;
Our share of mosques, temples and storms of sand.
And now, as leaks subside, it's time to reflect
On the experience of a lifetime, as we return to our homeland.
To think we did all that,
And may I say – not in a shy way – no, oh no, not us
We are a hardy lot and don't let taxi drivers
Or harbour masters get in our way.
For what is a cruise, what have we got,
If not adventure, wonderful experiences, exotic locations –
Then it has naught.
To experience these things, one must truly feel
Honoured, privileged, enriched, and a better person.
And now the record shows, we toured the world –
And did it our way!

Sitting with Martha, I join the others in delighted laughter, even though I am not feeling at all well and have to keep my eyes fixed on the horizon as the ship heaves and sinks on the ocean's swell. After a compassionate glance at my greenish complexion, Martha advises that I should skip dinner and return to bed. It is certainly what I wish most, but I feel that in doing so I shall be letting Bruce down, who kindly made sure that our table would be decorated with balloons, and all our lovely waiters poised to sing 'Happy Birthday' tonight. But Martha assures me that she will explain and pass on my apologies, so I follow her advice. Upon reaching my cabin's bathroom, I am *very* glad that I did! ... Then, surrounded by the upheaval of unfinished packing, I go to bed, and almost instantly to sleep.

Day 98 ~ Wednesday, 11th April 2012 ~ sunrise: 6.50am ~ sunset: 7.59pm ~ sea state: less rough ~ wind: 6-5, strong breeze ~ weather: overcast ~ temperature: 12°C

The End of the Journey

The ship's motion lessened during the night and I feel much better when I awake at five o'clock. No longer sleepy, I write thank-you cards to my new friends on the staff, to our table waiters and the captain. Then the entire enormous harvest of photographs is copied to a DVD for safe storage.

On the way to breakfast, I become conscious of a dull pain in the lumbar region which intensifies over the next few minutes. – Great! This will help the slow packing process no end, I'm sure! But what could have brought it on? I have not had any back pain for a long time. Had I been sleeping in an unfavourable position, or is it the unacknowledged worry about my uncertain future that is drawing attention to itself? Quite likely it is a combination of both.

A final appointment with Sandie for one of her wonderful facials is my very last chance to relax and enjoy some serious pampering. Then I head to the gym to say goodbye to Britta and Jovan. They are so affectionate and so kind, it makes me tearful as I turn to leave for good. Should I ever visit another gym in the future, that place will have a hard time living up to the high standards of professional comportment, paired with the personal amiability encountered here.

I bring my thank-you card for the captain to Reception, and then there is no more putting it off: Suitcases and bags have to be filled and the cabin must be emptied. But my lumbar back pain has by now assumed an intensity that forces me to move with the pace and grace of an octogenarian. Bending is agony, and so the process of packing takes several hours. Fortunately the sea is calmer, and conditions are expected to improve further upon entering the English Channel.

So here I am at the end of this momentous journey: seasick, pale and in pain. Not quite as I had pictured it! Moreover, this final day is like being suspended in limbo, because one is no longer connected to life aboard, but not yet in touch with life ashore … It paralyses the spirit, and the mood is vaguely depressed.

At four o'clock my luggage is ready to be collected and lines the corridor in a neat row. I go up to the top deck for the last time, sit in the mild sunshine and breathe the sea air, filled with an aching sadness at leaving it all behind: the beautiful ship, the friendly crew and staff, my new friends, this easy lifestyle, the exciting dawn arrivals in unfamiliar places that are waiting to be explored. I wish I could continue travelling in this way, maybe to South America, to the Arctic and the Far East – but now there is a future to be plotted, a course to be charted and money to be earned, alas!

On impulse I decide to blow a few extra pounds on checking emails. Decidedly worth it, for Helena confirmed that she will be at the terminal to pick me up, and – great surprise – my son has mailed a lovely birthday message that lifts my mood considerably.

(*Cruiser's tip: If at all possible, deal with essential online business before the final day of your cruise. Everyone else will be wanting the internet to use up time remaining on pre-purchased blocks of minutes, to contact friends and family, to check travel details and confirm arrangements, and simultaneously the ship's own demand on the internet will be intense.)

The final meal with my dinner companions ends in a round of fond farewells and best wishes for our respective futures. Then we all shake hands with our lovely team of waiters and hand over their well-earned tips in little envelopes.

As I am leaving the restaurant, Oliver waves to me from the far corner, his saintly face wreathed in an angelic smile. He is setting the tables and I make a detour to say goodbye to him too. With a kiss on the cheek he expresses his hope to see me soon on another cruise. I reply that by the time this happens he will likely have been made restaurant manager, and this thought makes him laugh.

Since there remains nothing else for me to do, I attend the evening's entertainment at the Curzon theatre. The show by a comedian, an impersonator and a musician is enjoyable, and I notice with relief that the volume of sound has been reduced considerably.

Afterwards I sit with Erin, Paul and friends in Raffles bar, where we have a final drink and a chat. Unfortunately, Paul is upset at the insulting manner in which a problem he raised was dealt with by the staff. Everyone agrees that the managers do not appear adequately trained in dealing with complaints in a professional manner, for they usually upset unhappy clients further with inept handling.

(*Cruiser's tip: At the end of your cruise you may be asked to fill in a questionnaire, rating your experience and listing your praises and complaints. These are evaluated at the highest level and often have a direct impact on any member of crew and staff who failed to please. But "the very best thing you can do for a crew member is to write a glowing review, mentioning them specifically on your card of comments," points out a former cruise worker on Reddit. "Their superior's superiors take note of that.")

Close to midnight I return to my cabin and find the little red light on my phone flashing frantically with a message from Sandie, saying that she and Manuel would like to meet up with me for farewell mocktails. Oh dear, it is rather too late now! A few minutes later, Manuel calls from the spa where he is still "sorting numbers" and says that he has been trying repeatedly to reach me. I tell him with regret that I have to call it a day, but propose that we could meet at breakfast to say goodbye. And although my backache is pure agony by now, the mood is much lighter.

Day 99 ~ Tuesday, 12th April 2012 ~ weather: sunny ~ temperature: 10°C ~ distance travelled since Lisbon: 889 nautical miles ~ in total: 35,294 nautical miles

Southampton

Sleep had been frequently interrupted by stabs of back pain and faint clattering noises from the corridor, as if an empty champagne bottle were rolling around in its silver bucket. At six o'clock the familiar revving of the ship's engines signals that we arrived at our final destination – the starting point. How long ago the beginning of this journey seems!

A hot shower, a quick stowing of items in my hand luggage, and then I am ready, bidding a quiet farewell to my dear cabin-hut, now bare and strange and set to receive new passengers.

Up on deck, the air carries the familiar scents of an English spring, and Southampton lies in the faint light of a sunrise obscured by a dense cover of clouds. I feel no excitement at being back home, only a numb distance tinged with sadness. I cannot imagine what the coming days may bring. Taking one step at a time, a path will surely unfold; but today each step is painful, for my lumbar backache intensified to the point where I can barely move. Still, I am early enough to get my favourite table at the Orangery and set about eating enough to make lunch unnecessary.

Marcus, the waiter who helped in his modest way to brighten my dinnertimes, is on duty and stops by for a last, friendly chat. Oh, it is utterly awful, having to say goodbye! We wish each other all the best and I should like to give him a hug, but do not want to embarrass him. Other people have no such scruples, and it is touching to see old British couples taking leave of young members of the Indian serving staff as if they were their own children.

The restaurant fills up rapidly. I defend my table and its empty chairs, telling couple after hopeful couple that I am about to be joined by friends. But Sandie and Manuel do not appear, so I have to relinquish the saved places eventually. Sitting with unfamiliar people until eight o'clock, I wonder what circumstances might have delayed my friends. It is not possible to phone members of staff in their quarters, and the pain in my back prevents me from going to look for them. There must be a good reason for their absence, but cannot imagine what it might be and resign myself to hearing the explanation by email at some future date.

(I really should have been able to work it out, being right in the midst of the problem! All passengers are having breakfast around the same time, the place is overcrowded, and that is why the members of staff are not allowed to take breakfast here on this final day. Since it has been their first cruise as well, Sandie and Manuel did not know about this rule beforehand.)

Moving very slowly, I go to the top deck and look down on an army of suitcases, deployed on the Terrace Deck next to the empty pool and waiting to be stacked into cages of metal mesh. A crane lowers the cage to the quay, from whence it is moved to the terminal and emptied of its contents. There are rumoured to be around ten thousand items of luggage in all, and the captain jokes that we shall be going ashore "with the speed of a thousand suitcases". Nice one! … The disembarkkation process begins shortly after nine o'clock, with the first set of passengers being called to the gangway.

(*Cruiser's tip: If the time allotted for your disembarkation does not allow you to reach your next destination comfortably and in time, speak to the purser's desk at once to obtain a more suitable slot. Do not miss your call, and do not assume that you can just join another group.)

Yesterday, all received a card whose colour corresponds to a particular time for disembarkation. Never a favourite colour, my orange card means that I shall be called around half-past nine. Meanwhile I pass the time in the Crow's Nest, jotting down final thoughts in my journal.

(*Cruiser's tip: At the end of the cruise you will receive a detailed account statement and your bill is automatically settled via your credit card. Cash accounts need to be covered in person at the purser's desk on the last full day of the cruise. As long as you have not settled your balance, you will not be allowed to disembark.)

Before long, all holders of orange cards are called. It is time to leave! I make my way to the Atrium for the very last time, trying not to dwell on the fact. Rajiv mans the reception desk this morning. There is less sunshine beaming from his eyes as he wishes me all the best and hopes to see me on another cruise someday soon.

I join the long queue that is moving slowly towards the exit. There, the orange card is collected with my personal cruise card, scanned one last time to register final departure. One of the security officers I enjoyed friendly chats with is on duty at another desk and waves to me across the aisle … and then, leaving the ship, I look up from the gangway at Aurora's towering side, just as I did when boarding her for the first time, ninety-nine days ago.

If a fairy gave me the chance, would I want to set out on another voyage like this one right now? ... I certainly would!

An escalator floats me down into the terminal and I survey long rows of luggage, neatly set out in the vast hall. All items are arranged in deck order, so I head for 'C Deck' to begin my search. It soon becomes clear that manoeuvring a trolley through narrow aisles, full of people in Cairo-traffic mode, would be difficult even without a crippling backache, and, seeing no sign of my belongings, I feel overwhelmed.

Of course, the sensible thing to do would be to stand back and wait until people have collected their luggage, but there is a compelling sense of urgency, propelled by large signs with warnings that someone else might feel tempted to leave with our suitcases.

Eventually I discover my items of luggage in various locations and even manage to heave them onto the trolley, though my backache declares that I shall not be forgiven for this rashness anytime soon ... We pass the customs officials unmolested and spill out of the terminal into the arms of family and friends. Helena is here, happy and excited to see me, and I feel the same – as well as intensely grateful that she made the long journey to pick me up.

Then we drive along motorways, roads and country lanes to her home. The gorgeous English countryside is just preparing to burst forth in its annual symphony of birdsong, bluebells, hawthorn and apple blossom, tender greens and sweet scents, and the familiar scenery is oddly comforting and soothing – like balm for an aching heart.

~ ~ ~

CONCLUSIONS

To live on a cruise ship for three months and a week turned out to be every bit as easy and pleasant as expected. That cosy little cabin quickly became my home. It never felt like a prison, but always like a comfortable and comforting place to retreat to. A window to provide daylight and a glimpse of the world outside would have been nice, but was the easiest sacrifice to make with an eye on the budget.

The main objective of this trip, namely to see the world and cross its major oceans, was accomplished in a most pleasant way. The oceans, usually calm, were impressive in their immense size. On the few occasions when seas were rough, I felt confident that the ship would ride out the storm safely, expertly handled by the captain, his officers and the crew. Two bouts of seasickness were limited to the Bay of Biscay and patiently endured.

Whenever people realized that I was travelling solo, they responded with "You are very brave!" – I did not share this view, for a cruise is surely the safest and easiest way to travel and makes no demands on one's courage. The cruise line takes every possible precaution to minimize all risks so that passengers may enjoy themselves without a care. And the wholly avoidable accident of a Costa cruise liner while we were at sea only enhanced the impression that we were in good hands with P&O.

This world cruise has been a very pleasant way to travel all by myself, and I enjoyed the sense of freedom its safety granted. Of course, avoiding solo shore excursions enhanced personal safety in places where one is unfamiliar with the culture and the customs, the spoken language and the written word, and where a woman alone is usually the target of unwelcome attention. Yet one may find a measure of freedom on organized tours too, as I discovered; mainly by skipping the local guide's history lecture, or by forgoing dessert after lunch and using that extra half hour to ramble independently. Indeed, there may not be another way for women to travel solo this safely, and I would encourage them to make the most of it.

As a single woman on a cruise ship, one is the object of much speculation, curiosity and covert observation. It is naturally assumed that one must be in search of a mate, and the fact that one could be more interested in seeing the world does not readily occur to anyone. I met this irritating situation by calmly doing my own thing, cultivating a friendly but detached attitude and giving the regular coffee mornings for solo travellers a wide berth. Feeling reasonably certain that the soulmate I should like to find is not to be encountered on a cruise, I never expected to meet him there. But I was delighted to find new friends, at home in distant countries, yet nearer in mind.

That I am prone to car sickness presented a recurring problem on coach outings and was the only difficulty I had to deal with. I found that some fellow passengers were not prepared to accept my problem at face value, preferring to suspect me of dishonourable motives instead. But, learning from this unpleasant experience, I have since obtained a letter from my doctor for future use.

My earlier road trip with long rambles in the Scottish Highlands had been particularly suited to my solitary nature and temperament. By contrast, the cruise's intensely sociable setting was a challenge, and one that I was prepared to meet. I had hardly a thing in common with most other passengers, and though I did my best to conceal this, some of the arising unpleasantness was probably inevitable. Yet I soon figured out how to balance my need for solitude with participation in social events and found those people whose company was the most congenial. Many of them turned out to be younger and worked at the gym and the spa.

I gained first impressions of far-flung places around the globe in rapid succession, all of them interesting and mentally enriching. Cambodia touched me particularly with its fragile hope of a better future, and its lovely children. Visiting the more liberal part of the Arab world was the most eye-opening experience and left me wondering why we remain so unaware of the many positive things that are accomplished in this part of the world.

To hear about the intense demands of pilotage in the shipping lane of the Great Barrier Reef from the local pilot himself, and about piracy in Somalia from a commander of the Royal Navy were unexpected highlights. Also, to learn how the waste that is produced on a cruise ship is dealt with responsibly was reassuring, for the impact litter is having on any environment had made a deep impression. Worldwide, waste management is an area in which much urgent work needs to be done.

I did a few illustrations and found that drawing was as satisfying as I remembered. These little pictures enhanced the first half of my written journal, but then the balance of sea days and shore days shifted and left insufficient time for this pleasant activity. By contrast, the need to process in writing what I had seen and thought, felt and done, heard and learnt each day increased throughout the trip, and my notebook became a means to remain connected to a purpose, and an anchor in troubled waters.

General fitness levels, already much improved on my road trip earlier, increased further during the cruise. Free use of the gym under the expert guidance of an admirable gym team made it easy to see for myself how quickly regular exercise shows results. Additionally, the massage and spa sessions were a real treat, and after the cruise I was in better shape than I had been for a long time: more relaxed, happier, fitter and slimmer.

This journey around the world brought me in contact with friendly, kind and helpful people in every country and it has been reassuring to see how widespread goodness is. Every day, everywhere, almost everyone tries to do their best and takes pride in their role, their work and their surroundings. And as it evolved in the course of three months, this picture impressed me with its contrast to the image of the world as portrayed in the media. "What is the world coming to!" has not been a sentiment I felt on my travels. It remains reserved for the reading of newspapers, the watching of news. Is it right then that children should deduce the world must be a terrible place? Should the media not focus the beam of their attention on everyday goodness too? Yet it may be regarded as fortunate that mainly bad things are considered newsworthy. For, as long as goodness and kindness are still the rule, they will not seem sensational, and that is surely a good thing.

With this long cruise I finally fulfilled my childhood dream of circumnavigating the world; sought out and embraced a new measure of freedom, and followed a newly discovered urge to write about my own world-viewing, in the hope that others too may read and appreciate it.

Before We Say Goodbye ...

If you enjoyed this travel journal and would like to read more of a similar nature, check out my first volume of solo travel descriptions. *Reports from the Road ~ Solo around Britain* charts the highs and lows of a two-month road trip, prior to this cruise. This slim volume is a personal diary of happiness and freedom that revolves around yet more travel incidents and insights.

My Solo Travel Reports are available on Amazon, either as eBooks for Kindle or in a paperback format that is printed on demand.

If you liked these tales from the seas, I would be pleased to hear from you. Drop me a line at fabwolf@hotmail.com and tell me your thoughts, for writing is a lonely job and kind feedback is much appreciated.

Just as important to us self-published writers is a favourable review on Amazon. You will understand that it means a lot, so thank you very much for taking the time to describe your reading experience to other potential readers.

Finally, I wish you happy and exciting days as you set out on your own journeys. Solo or not – may you too have fair winds and a following sea!

~ ~ ~

Made in the USA
Las Vegas, NV
27 February 2022